T0255587

Lecture Notes in Computer Science 13895

Founding Editors

Gerhard Goos
Juris Hartmanis

Editorial Board Members

Elisa Bertino, *Purdue University, West Lafayette, IN, USA*
Wen Gao, *Peking University, Beijing, China*
Bernhard Steffen◉, *TU Dortmund University, Dortmund, Germany*
Moti Yung◉, *Columbia University, New York, NY, USA*

The series Lecture Notes in Computer Science (LNCS), including its subseries Lecture Notes in Artificial Intelligence (LNAI) and Lecture Notes in Bioinformatics (LNBI), has established itself as a medium for the publication of new developments in computer science and information technology research, teaching, and education.

LNCS enjoys close cooperation with the computer science R & D community, the series counts many renowned academics among its volume editors and paper authors, and collaborates with prestigious societies. Its mission is to serve this international community by providing an invaluable service, mainly focused on the publication of conference and workshop proceedings and postproceedings. LNCS commenced publication in 1973.

Felix Günther · Julia Hesse
Editors

Security
Standardisation
Research

8th International Conference, SSR 2023
Lyon, France, April 22–23, 2023
Proceedings

 Springer

Editors
Felix Günther (iD)
ETH Zurich
Zurich, Switzerland

Julia Hesse (iD)
IBM Research Europe - Zurich
Rüschlikon, Switzerland

ISSN 0302-9743   ISSN 1611-3349 (electronic)
Lecture Notes in Computer Science
ISBN 978-3-031-30730-0   ISBN 978-3-031-30731-7 (eBook)
https://doi.org/10.1007/978-3-031-30731-7

© The Editor(s) (if applicable) and The Author(s), under exclusive license
to Springer Nature Switzerland AG 2023
This work is subject to copyright. All rights are reserved by the Publisher, whether the whole or part of
the material is concerned, specifically the rights of translation, reprinting, reuse of illustrations, recitation,
broadcasting, reproduction on microfilms or in any other physical way, and transmission or information
storage and retrieval, electronic adaptation, computer software, or by similar or dissimilar methodology now
known or hereafter developed.
The use of general descriptive names, registered names, trademarks, service marks, etc. in this publication
does not imply, even in the absence of a specific statement, that such names are exempt from the relevant
protective laws and regulations and therefore free for general use.
The publisher, the authors, and the editors are safe to assume that the advice and information in this book
are believed to be true and accurate at the date of publication. Neither the publisher nor the authors or the
editors give a warranty, expressed or implied, with respect to the material contained herein or for any errors
or omissions that may have been made. The publisher remains neutral with regard to jurisdictional claims in
published maps and institutional affiliations.

This Springer imprint is published by the registered company Springer Nature Switzerland AG
The registered company address is: Gewerbestrasse 11, 6330 Cham, Switzerland

Preface

The 8th Conference on Security Standardisation Research (SSR 2023) was held in Lyon, France, on April 22–23, 2023, co-located with and as an affiliated event of the Eurocrypt 2023 conference. The goal of this conference was to bring together the academic, standardization, and industry communities to discuss the many research challenges arising in existing and newly developed security standards. The topics at the conference broadly covered cryptographic techniques, network security, identity management, security processes, standardization procedures, and more.

We received 10 submissions to SSR 2023 via the EasyChair system, each of which was reviewed by at least three Program Committee members in a double-blind review; submissions co-authored by Program Committee members received five reviews. After an active discussion phase, 6 papers were accepted for publication.

Following ideas from prior iterations of the conference, we this year again explicitly solicited submissions beyond regular research papers. For one, we invited papers that provide a systematization of knowledge (SoK) of areas related to security standardization. For another, we encouraged the submission of vision papers relating to security standardization, with an emphasis on sparking discussions on work in progress or concrete ideas for work that has yet to begin. We are delighted to see those diverse ideas reflected in the final program, which is made up of four research papers, one SoK paper, and one vision paper.

We were pleased to have three invited speakers contributing their expertise and perspectives across academia, industry, and the standardization community to the SSR 2023 program:

– Nadia Heninger (University of California, San Diego),
– Juraj Somorovsky (Paderborn University), and
– Christopher Wood (Cloudflare Research).

We want to thank everyone who contributed to the success of SSR 2023. Foremost, we thank all authors for submitting their work to the conference, and the speakers at the conference for contributing their share to the interesting program. We are indebted to the Program Committee which, collectively, did a great job in the interactive discussion, through thorough reviews, and in particular for their help and guidance in shepherding—it was a pleasure to work with you. For the local arrangements, our great thanks go to Alain Passelègue, responsible for the Eurocrypt 2023 affiliated events, and the other General Co-chairs of Eurocrypt 2023, Damien Stehlé and Benjamin Wesolowski. Finally, we thank all attendees of SSR 2023.

April 2023

Felix Günther
Julia Hesse

Organization

General and Program Committee Chairs

Felix Günther   ETH Zurich, Switzerland
Julia Hesse   IBM Research Europe – Zurich, Switzerland

Steering Committee

Liqun Chen   University of Surrey, UK
Shin'ichiro Matsuo   Georgetown University, USA
Thyla van der Merwe   Google, Switzerland
Chris Mitchell   Royal Holloway, University of London, UK
Bart Preneel   Katholieke Universiteit Leuven, Belgium

Program Committee

Nina Bindel   SandboxAQ, USA
Joppe Bos   NXP Semiconductors, Belgium
Sofía Celi   Brave, Portugal
Gareth T. Davies   Bergische Universität Wuppertal, Germany
Jean Paul Degabriele   Cryptography Research Center in TII, UAE
Benjamin Dowling   University of Sheffield, UK
Marc Fischlin   TU Darmstadt, Germany
Scott Fluhrer   Cisco Systems
Britta Hale   Naval Postgraduate School, USA
Christian Janson   TU Darmstadt, Germany
Saqib A. Kakvi   Royal Holloway, University of London, UK
John Kelsey   NIST, USA
Markulf Kohlweiss   University of Edinburgh and IOHK, UK
Thalia Laing   HP Inc., USA
Giorgia Azzurra Marson   NEC, Germany
Shin'ichiro Matsuo   Georgetown University, USA
Catherine Meadows   Naval Research Laboratory, USA
Maryam Mehrnezhad   Royal Holloway, University of London, UK
Chris Mitchell   Royal Holloway, University of London, UK
Elisabeth Oswald   University of Klagenfurt, Austria

Kenneth Paterson   ETH Zurich, Switzerland
Christopher Patton   Cloudflare, USA
Bertram Poettering   IBM Research Europe – Zurich, Switzerland
Kazue Sako   Waseda University, Japan
Stanislav Smyshlyaev   CryptoPro, Russia
Christoph Striecks   AIT Austrian Institute of Technology, Austria
Thyla van der Merwe   Google, Switzerland
Mathy Vanhoef   Katholieke Universiteit Leuven, Belgium
Gaven J. Watson   Meta, USA
Christopher Wood   Cloudflare, USA
Kazuki Yoneyama   Ibaraki University, Japan

Contents

Quantum-Resistant MACsec and IPsec for Virtual Private Networks

Stefan-Lukas Gazdag[4]($\boxtimes$), Sophia Grundner-Culemann[1]($\boxtimes$), Tobias Heider[4],
Daniel Herzinger[4], Felix Schärtl[2]($\boxtimes$), Joo Yeon Cho[3], Tobias Guggemos[1],
and Daniel Loebenberger[2]($\boxtimes$)

[1] Ludwig-Maximilians-Universität, Munich, Germany
{grundner-culemann,guggemos}@nm.ifi.lmu.de
[2] Fraunhofer AISEC, Weiden in der Oberpfalz, Germany
{felix.schaertl,daniel.loebenberger}@aisec.fraunhofer.de
[3] ADVA Optical Networking, Munich, Germany
[4] genua GmbH, Kirchheim near Munich, Germany
{stefan-lukas_gazdag,daniel_herzinger}@genua.de, me@tobhe.de

Abstract. Despite considerable progress in theoretical post-quantum cryptography we have yet to see significant advances in its practical adoption. The necessary protocol modifications need to be identified, implemented and tested; good solutions need to be standardized and finally adopted in the real world.

This work executes the first steps needed to standardize quantum-proof Virtual Private Networks (VPNs) on Layers 2 and 3 of the OSI model employing the MACsec/MKA and IPsec/IKEv2 protocols, respectively. We identify requirements and assemble a list of ideal features, discuss difficulties and possible solutions, point out our standardization efforts, and provide the results of some sample implementations for both layers.

Keywords: Post-quantum cryptography · VPN · IPsec · MACsec

1 Introduction

On business trips, employees often need a secure remote connection to their company's network. Virtual Private Networks (VPNs) are the go-to solution: They allow users to extend a private network across a public, untrusted network like the Internet. "Virtual" means that the participants are not physically in the same connected private network. Instead, multiple private networks are connected over a wide area network to emulate a single private network: The communication should be as secure as if all members were physically connected to the same private network. There are different methods to establish VPNs for

© The Author(s), under exclusive license to Springer Nature Switzerland AG 2023
F. Günther and J. Hesse (Eds.): SSR 2023, LNCS 13895, pp. 1–21, 2023.
https://doi.org/10.1007/978-3-031-30731-7_1

different communication layers as specified by the OSI model, e.g., the MACsec protocol on layer 2 and the IPsec protocol on layer 3.

All VPN methods rely on cryptography to ensure security of the connection. However, the asymmetric cryptographic primitives that are primarily used today will be broken once quantum computers become powerful enough to run Shor's algorithm [45]. This algorithm efficiently solves the integer factorization problem and the discrete logarithm problem, the two cornerstones of all currently prevalent asymmetric cryptographic algorithms.

Even though it is hard to tell if or when cryptographic relevant quantum computers can be built [55], countermeasures have to be taken in time: Messages that are encrypted now may be intercepted today and broken many years from now by tools that are not even invented yet. This is known as the "Store now, decrypt later"-strategy. And even if quantum computers should not become powerful enough for many decades: The mere threat has revealed the vulnerability of the current IT-security systems.

The threat to symmetric cryptography (which is also used in VPNs) is mitigated in a relatively easy way, since many protocols use a variant of AES or an equivalent block cipher and other symmetric primitives: The key size or output length should be increased to at least 192 bits or, if possible, 256 bits to withstand attacks that use the Grover algorithm [56]. But even though larger keys make implementations slower and one might also face some pitfalls, the adaptations are comparatively easy and still practicable in most VPN use-cases (as far as we know nowadays).

This is why we focus on the key exchange mechanisms that use asymmetric cryptography to establish symmetric keys between unacquainted parties.

1.1   Contribution

We identify requirements and list the features of an ideal solution for quantum-proof[1] VPNs on both layer 2 and 3. We analyze MACsec and its key agreement protocol MKA defined in IEEE 802.1X [30] and IEEE 802.1AE [29] in a post-quantum setting. For MACsec on layer 2, there are two approaches to agreeing on a shared key. For both, we explain what changes need to be made to keep MACsec safe from a quantum-based attack.

On layer 3, we examine the structure of IPsec with the key-agreement protocol IKEv2 [32]. We discuss obstacles and possible solution approaches that can be combined to address the various challenges. Our efforts are aligned with activities at the IETF, which have already resulted in corresponding RFCs and drafts [47,53,54].

We implemented and evaluated post-quantum extensions for both, MACsec on layer 2 and IPsec on layer 3. We plan a further evaluation of a combined system in an extended version of this work.

---

[1] We use quantum "-proof" / "-safe" / "-resistant" (and, where this is not ungrammatical, "post-quantum") interchangeably.

The paper is structured as follows: We outline related work in Sect. 2 and provide background on MACsec, IPsec and post-quantum cryptography in Sect. 3. In Sect. 4, we identify the core requirements and assemble a wish list for an ideal solution, and we point out difficulties. We discuss realistic solution approaches in Sect. 5 and propose, test, and evaluate specific setups in Sect. 6. Section 7 concludes this paper.

2   Related Work

In this chapter, we focus on network protocols other than IPsec and MACsec that have integrated post-quantum cryptography in some form; we discuss some related work regarding IPsec in Sect. 5 in the list of possible approaches. Previous work on post-quantum MACsec only considers the symmetric case [18].

TLS. The TLS protocol is one of the most widely used security protocols. Therefore, a quantum-safe version is important and there are many papers, IETF Internet-Drafts and practical tests on this topic. So far, the Internet-Drafts for quantum-safe versions of both TLS 1.2 [13] and TLS 1.3 [48] make comparatively minor changes to the protocol. They feature drop-in replacements for key exchange methods, for example. A paper from the year 2020 proposes authentication using Key Encapsulation Mechanisms (KEMs) instead of signatures ("KEMTLS" [44]), arguing that KEMs are faster and have smaller keys.

Efforts are also ongoing for hybrid quantum-safe TLS, so far without standardization or practical results. Testing of quantum-safe TLS started in 2016[2], when Google integrated an experimental version in the Chrome browser. There, they had a small portion of the connections between the desktop Chrome and Google servers use the post-quantum key exchange algorithm NewHope [5] in addition to the usual elliptic-curve-based one. In 2019, Cloudflare deployed a quantum-safe version of TLS 1.3[3], using Google Chrome on the client side and Cloudflare servers on the server side. The chosen methods were the lattice-based HRSS and the isogeny-based SIKE. An X25519 key-exchange was added to each so that the key exchange would be hybrid. Cloudflare also tested KEMTLS [15,40]. Lastly, Amazon integrated the three quantum-safe algorithms CRYSTALS-Kyber, BIKE and SIKE in their AWS Key Management Service[4], following a current Internet-Draft that describes a hybrid key exchange in TLS 1.3 [48]. However, not all algorithms that NIST recommends or considers fallback options are viable: Classic McEliece cannot be used according to the current Internet-Drafts, since they specify that the public key must not be larger than 65,535 bytes; even the smallest possible McEliece public key has 262,120 bytes [10], thus exceeding the limit by far.

---

[2] https://security.googleblog.com/2016/07/experimenting-with-post-quantum.html.

[3] https://blog.cloudflare.com/the-tls-post-quantum-experiment/.

[4] https://aws.amazon.com/blogs/security/post-quantum-tls-now-supported-in-aws-kms/.

SSH. There have been case studies on how to integrate post-quantum cryptography in the Secure Shell Protocol (SSH), which is used for remote login across a public network [20]. An IETF Internet-Draft for quantum-safe SSH [31] was re-newed in November 2022 (current expiration date: May 2023). A simple way to make SSH quantum-safe is to include a cryptographic primitive that is small enough for the protocol even in its current form. A possible candidate is NTRU Prime, which was an alternative candidate in the NIST standardization process in Round 3 [11]. Even though NTRU Prime was not included in Round 4, NIST deems the security comparable to that of the standardized KEM CRYSTALS-Kyber [2]. This kind of mechanism can already be found as a standard feature in the SSH implementations TinySSH[5] and OpenSSH[6].

Lower Layers. For security protocols operated at a lower layer than TLS or SSH, post-quantum key exchanges have not been studied much because symmetric-key encryption using pre-shared keys is more commonly used. Cisco has proposed using 256-bit pre-shared keys in symmetric-key cryptography to provide quantum-resistant encryption for the MACsec protocol in their switches [18]. While working on this paper, another publication emerged regarding post-quantum IPsec [42]. Their work also considers solutions that use Quantum Key Distribution; our work focuses on non-quantum-based solutions and provides a more detailed analysis for them. Their requirements analysis comes to very similar conclusions as ours and corroborates our results.

So far, there has not been much attention on fully implementing and standardizing post-quantum versions of MACsec/MKA or IPsec/IKEv2. This work fills this gap and adds an overview of the shared requirements and challenges for quantum-proof key exchange protocols.

3 Background

In this chapter we briefly introduce some technical details of the two aforementioned VPN-protocols MACsec and IPsec, and provide a short overview of the state of the art in post-quantum cryptography.

Both IPsec and MACsec feature a key establishment sub-protocol (MKA and IKEv2, respectively) where the communication partners establish so-called "associations" and arrive at a shared symmetric key to encrypt the respective payloads of the layer. Unacquainted parties (who have not pre-shared a suitable key) need to use asymmetric cryptography for this and are thus susceptible to quantum-based attacks.

3.1 MACsec (Layer 2)

MACsec is an IEEE standard protocol [29] which protects a layer 2-connection over an open channel against an eavesdropper. A MACsec frame consists of an

---

[5] https://tinyssh.org/.
[6] https://www.openssh.com/.

Ethernet frame that is enhanced with a Security Tag (SecTAG) and an Integrity Check Value (ICV). The SecTAG specifies the protocol that is used (e.g., IPv6), the cipher suites that the sender can offer, and the packet number for replay protection. The payload can be encrypted, but this is optional: There is also a packet-authentication-only mode, in which only the integrity of a transmitted packet is verified.

The standard MACsec sub-protocol for key establishment is called MACsec Key Agreement (MKA) and is defined in IEEE 802.1X-2010 [30]. It produces a so-called Connectivity Association (CA), which specifies the Connectivity Association Key (CAK). Each payload of an Ethernet frame is encrypted with a Secure Association Key (SAK), which is derived from a CAK.

Key Distribution Using EAP. There are two ways to establish a CAK: One is to configure it from a pre-shared key (which only works for acquainted parties). The other is to connect the parties using one of the Extended Authentication Protocol (EAP) methods, e.g. EAP-TLS, in order to agree on an asymmetric primitive to encapsulate the symmetric key material, i.e. a Master Session Key from which the CAK is derived. The possession of a CAK is a prerequisite for the MACsec membership, and all potential members hold the same CAK. When EAP is used for authentication, it involves a supplicant (client device), authenticator (switch), and authentication server. According to the MKA standard, any EAP method is allowed as long as it supports mutual authentication and a minimum key length. This is also referred to as a hierarchical key exchange, because the CAK is a root key for many key derivations.

Ephemeral Key Exchange. Aside from this standard protocol, the industry has also widely adopted a version that executes an ephemeral key exchange, because even though MKA is efficient and suitable for LANs, it risks severe breaches in entire networks when the CAK is disclosed. With ephemeral keys, each session key is derived independently of the previous session keys. Thus, the disclosure of the current session key does not compromise any data encrypted in the past, achieving forward secrecy. To use ephemeral keys, an Initiator and a Responder can perform an Authenticated Key Exchange (AKE) protocol.

3.2   IPsec (Layer 3)

Internet Protocol Security (IPsec) is a protocol suite for securing communication over potentially insecure IP networks, such as the Internet [33]. Two security protocols go along with IPsec: The Authentication Header (AH) [34], which provides data integrity and sender authentication, and the Encapsulating Security Payload (ESP) [35], which provides confidentiality, data integrity, and data origin authentication. Both use symmetric cryptography to achieve those goals; unacquainted parties therefore need a key exchange protocol using asymmetric cryptography to agree on a shared secret, which is then used as the key in the symmetric procedure. There are several ways to establish a shared key, but

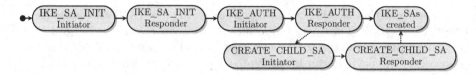

Fig. 1. IKEv2's state machine: First, Initiator and Responder exchange the IKE_SA_INIT-handshake and agree on a shared key; then they authenticate each other (the IKE_AUTH messages are encrypted under the shared key); optionally, they create one or more CHILD_SA to communicate further.

Internet Key Exchange Version 2 (IKEv2) [33] is what is most commonly used today.

IKEv2 Handshake. The goal of the so-called IKEv2 handshake is to establish Security Associations (SAs): data structures that contain all the necessary information to send data securely through a VPN tunnel. There are two different SA types: The IKE SA, which specifies the connection for the handshake messages and meta-information, and the Child SA, which specifies the connection for sending the payload data. This distinction allows VPN-gateways to establish a meta-channel (as specified by the IKE SA) and then use this to create multiple separate payload tunnels (as specified by the Child SAs). Each Child SA must be re-keyed after a certain number of packets have been encrypted with the corresponding key. The IKE SA will also be re-keyed according to its lifetime policy.

Two communication partners, Initiator I and Responder R, connect via IKEv2 as follows: In a first message exchange (called IKE_SA_INIT), I and R perform a Diffie-Hellman (DH)-key-exchange, agree on cryptographic parameters and exchange a nonce along with other metadata. The DH-key, together with the nonces, is used to derive the so-called SKEYSEED, from which in turn all keys for this IKE SA are derived. These include one key each for authentication, encryption and decryption, for generating the AUTH payload, and for the derivation of further key material for the Child SAs.

After the IKE_SA_INIT exchange, I and R create an IKE SA. All further messages between them are encrypted, starting with I's IKE_AUTH message to R. The IKE_AUTH exchange ensures the authenticity and integrity of their communication. After this second exchange, the IKEv2 handshake is complete and I and R can create a CHILD_SA. If this fails, it can later be done with a CREATE_CHILD_SA exchange, which also serves for creating new Child SAs and to rekey IKE SAs and Child SAs. Figure 1 shows the state machine of the IKEv2-handshake with a CREATE_CHILD_SA exchange.

The security of IKEv2 has been analyzed repeatedly using various formal analysis tools, including Scyther [19], Spin Modeling, ProVerif, and Tamarin [39]. Thus, the protocol's security is well-analyzed by both, formal proofs and expert reviews in practice.

3.3 Post-quantum Cryptography

Virtually all research in modern post-quantum cryptography is conducted in the orbit of the standardization efforts of the US-American National Institute of Standards and Technolog (NIST). These were started in December 2016 and aim at selecting several algorithms for post-quantum encryption, signatures, and key exchanges[7] starting with the actual standardization by 2024.

In 2022, NIST concluded the first three selection rounds by announcing four mechanisms that will be standardized [3]. These are the key encapsulation mechanism CRYSTALS-Kyber [7] and the three signature schemes CRYSTALS-Dilithium [36], Falcon [25], and SPHINCS+ [9]. The selection was augmented by four KEM candidates for the standardization Round 4 of the process: BIKE [6], Classic McEliece [10], HQC [38] and SIKE [23]. SIKE was later broken by a devastating attack [14]; specific parameters for SPHINCS+ were also successfully attacked [43]. Including the Round 3 candidate Rainbow [12], the number of NIST candidates that were (partly) broken in the year 2022 was therefore three. Of course, other schemes were also broken earlier, such as GeMSS in 2020 [50,51].

These attacks reinforce previous concerns on how much the proposed post-quantum algorithms can be trusted yet. Many of the candidates and the underlying primitives have not been around long enough to have gained full confidence in their security. The most conservative choice, in our opinion, is using Classic McEliece, which is based on work by Robert McEliece dating back to the late 1970th [37]. Since the huge public keys of this scheme limit its practical use (they amount to several MB), it is also a good worst-case example for the integration of quantum-safe cryptography into protocols and implementations. In case no other primitives hold, network protocols should be prepared to handle this scheme.

4 Requirements for Quantum-Safe VPNs

Scenarios where key material or authentication certificates can be pre-shared pose rather minor challenges against quantum computers, because the corresponding key-sizes and protocols can be adapted relatively easily, see for example [22]. We therefore consider a use-case where the communicating entities are unacquainted, have no opportunity to pre-share key material and want to communicate in a quantum-safe manner over a common public internet link. The communication should be private with respect to layer 2 and layer 3, which we secure with the MACsec and IPsec protocol, respectively.

Especially for key agreement, we are looking for practical solutions that will be deployed by the industry and are secure for the foreseeable future. Compared to state-of-the-art VPNs, a quantum-proof VPN therefore needs to

---

[7] https://csrc.nist.gov/News/2016/Public-Key-Post-Quantum-Cryptographic-Algorithms.

1) be as usable (i.e., as reliable and not significantly slower) *(otherwise, changes will not be accepted and adopted by the industry, making all efforts futile)*,
2) maintain at least the security level against classical computers *(otherwise, the changes are not an improvement over the current state of the art)*, and
3) be easier to adapt to future threats and findings *(because if the solution is, for example, designed too closely around specific primitives or schemes which are later broken, the system is very difficult to fix)*.

In contrast, post-quantum cryptography – compared to classical state-of-the-art cryptography – enjoys more confidence in its security against quantum computers, but has

a) slower algorithms,
b) rather large (often: much larger) key sizes, and
c) has been studied much less extensively, thus enjoying less confidence in its overall security (which, in turn, is an incentive to choose rather conservative parameters that imply even larger keys and even slower computations).

We propose the following, six-item wish list for a close-to-ideal solution (in no particular order):

Hybrid approach. To ensure that security is not reduced compared to the current standard (which could for example happen if only post-quantum algorithms are used in a protocol, and they all prove to be insecure), a hybrid approach using both classical and post-quantum cryptography should be chosen. This way, if the post-quantum elements fail, the classical elements still provide a basic level of security, and vice versa. A hybrid approach is also useful when it allows the users to agree on various post-quantum keys so that less trust has to be put in each individual one.

Managing large keys. Since the most trusted quantum-proof primitives and parameters sets tend to imply much bigger key sizes than the classical ones, it is important to design key exchange protocols that can handle them.

Minimal design. Bigger and/or more messages make the protocol process slower, less reliable, and thus more prone to attacks. Therefore, a minimal design supports usability and security. It is complemented in the implementation decisions by choosing shorter and fewer keys and primitives or schemes with fast cryptographic operations. Fast operations are important because some values need to be computed during key exchange, but longer wait-times between messages make Denial-of-Service- or Man-in-the-Middle-attacks easier. Also, critical processes like re-keying are slower. Hence, algorithms with fast operations are preferable.

Crypto-agility. This is the property of a modular cryptographic architecture where broken algorithms can be replaced fairly easily. Classical cryptography is so deeply integrated in the current network architecture that enhancing or replacing it with post-quantum alternatives is often very difficult. To mitigate the damage from future breakthroughs in cryptanalysis, new systems should be designed more replacement-friendly from the get-go.

Cipher suites. If all cryptographic mechanisms can be chosen completely freely, the key agreement processes may become hard to implement, ill-performant and thus impractical.

The selection of a few, well implemented cipher suites can be a middle ground to unite hybrid, crypto-agile solutions and usability.

Fast initial connection. The (first) key exchange and authentication should be completed quickly to avoid time-outs or real-time attacks like Denial-of-Service (DoS) or Man-in-the-Middle-attacks (MitM). An example for quantum-proof keys inviting DoS-attacks would be an attacker sending large payloads, pretending that they are Classic McEliece key fragments, thus forcing the communication partner to process megabytes of data in vain.

Some of those items contradict each other, for example: Managing large keys is a task at odds with the wish for a minimal and slender design, as is a hybrid solution that implies the handling of several keys. In the same way, a fast initial connection aims at protecting from real-time attacks but are probably often easier achieved with key material that is less trusted for the long term. Crypto-agility is also a difficult goal: The requirements stipulated by ecosystems like the Internet as the biggest IP network are often quite strict. Agile solutions also tend to be complex – e. g., when multiple consecutive cryptographic schemes are used for a single key establishment to have more exchangeable modules –, which makes them more error-prone and thus, less secure.

5   Post-quantum VPNs on Two Layers

Creating quantum-proof VPNs on layer 2 or layer 3 requires solutions for quantum-resistant MKA or IKEv2, respectively. There are various possibilities for each:

5.1   Post-quantum MKA

A post-quantum key exchange and signature scheme should be conservatively secure as well as sufficiently fast so that they should not be a bottleneck of layer 2 performance. In particular, an end-to-end MACsec for WAN is more challenging because MACsec packets should travel through multiple networking switches and routers. Hence, a network- and device-agnostic protocol is required. The public-key size is another important point of consideration for the MACsec protocol since a maximum payload size of an Ethernet frame is only 1500 bytes and exceeding a payload size may cause unexpected security weaknesses and performance degradation. We consider two approaches to quantum-proof MKA: One for the standard, hierarchical protocol and one for the ephemeral key exchange.

$$\begin{array}{ll}
\underline{Initiator(I)} & \underline{Responder(R)} \\
pk_I, sk_I \leftarrow PQKGEN() & pk_R, sk_R \leftarrow PQKGEN() \\
& \xleftrightarrow{\ Start\ } \\
r_I, k_I \leftarrow rand() & r_R, k_J \leftarrow rand() \\
X_I = \{pk_I, PQSIGN_{sk_I}(pk_I, r_I)\} & X_R = \{pk_R, PQSIGN_{sk_R}(pk_R, r_R)\} \\
& \xrightarrow{X_I, r_I} \\
& \xleftarrow{X_R, r_R} \\
Verify\ X_R & Verify\ X_I \\
Y_I = PQENC_{pk_R}(k_I) & Y_R = PQENC_{pk_I}(k_R) \\
& \xleftrightarrow{Y_I, Y_R} \\
k_R = PQDEC_{sk_I}(Y_R) & k_I = PQDEC_{sk_R}(Y_I) \\
K = k_I\|k_R\|r_I\|r_R & K = k_I\|k_R\|r_I\|r_R \\
M_I = MAC_{k_I}(K) & M_R = MAC_{k_R}(K) \\
& \xleftrightarrow{M_I, M_R} \\
Verify\ M_R & Verify\ M_I \\
Accept\ /\ Reject\ K & Accept\ /\ Reject\ K
\end{array}$$

Fig. 2. An ephemeral authenticated key exchange protocol using quantum-proof cryptographic primitives: The generation of a quantum-proof asymmetric key pair (PQK-GEN) and the signing operation, encryption, decryption operations using the quantum-proof keys (PQSIGN, PQENC, PQDEC) ensure that the key exchange is quantum-proof overall.

Hierarchical Key Distribution via EAP. Since the security of key hierarchy stems from a master session key, which is derived from the EAP method, it suffices to use post-quantum cryptosuites for EAP, in particular, for a key exchange and a certificate-based authentication where the use of a quantum-resistant encryption suite is mandated. If the EAP packet size exceeds the EAP Maximum Transfer Unit (MTU) of the link (1500 B for Ethernet), most EAP methods may encounter difficulties due to the large size of public keys of post-quantum cryptographic schemes. The EAP-TLS method supports fragmentation and reassembly. We therefore propose an EAP-TLS-PQ method mandated to use post-quantum cipher suites which support the certificate-based mutual authentication and a key derivation. The main difference to a normal EAP-TLS is to use a PQ key exchange and a PQ certificate exchange between an authentication server and a supplicant. This approach allows a hybrid exchange, managing large keys and the use of various cryptographic primitives. The downside is that the protocol is redundant and may cause performance degradation. Also the parameters of cryptographic primitives should be agreed beforehand.

Ephemeral Key Exchange via AKE. In the ephemeral case, the parties perform an AKE protocol, which can simply be used with quantum-proof cryptographic primitives instead of classical cryptography; a hybrid key is achieved by combining a post-quantum authenticated key exchange with classical cryptographic schemes. For instance, a McEliece KEM with a Falcon signature can be combined with the Diffie-Hellman key exchange protocol and an RSA signature. By using a hybrid AKE scheme, the derived keys will remain secure as long as at least one of the component schemes is secure. It's important to note that post-quantum cryptographic protocols should be added on top of the standard protocol to maintain the established security of each run, rather than combining the two exchanges in one run (which would require a separate security analysis). NIST revised their recommendation for key-derivation methods in key-establishment schemes to permit the use of a hybrid key establishment construction in the FIPS 140 validation of cryptographic modules [8]. A high-level description of the quantum-proof version of the protocol is depicted in Fig. 2; see also our previous publication [16,17]. The keys to sign, encrypt and decrypt the shared-key parts are generated to be quantum-proof, thereby quantum-proofing the entire protocol run.

Discussion. Both solutions allow a hybrid key exchange and can be shaped to rely on cipher suites. Also, the protocol is not designed around a specific flavor of cryptography and thus crypto-agile. Even large keys can be managed with EAP-TLS-PQ, as demonstrated in our test (see Sect. 6).

5.2   Post-quantum IKEv2

For IPsec, there are two main obstacles for integrating post-quantum cryptography with IKEv2: The practical restrictions on packet size (→ MTUs and Fragmentation on layer 3) and the theoretical restrictions from addressing large payloads (→ size field of the payload header).

Maximum Transfer Unit and Fragmentation. Theoretically, an IP packet can have a length of up to $64\,kB = 65656\,B$. However, only a total packet length of $576\,B$ for IPv4 and $1280\,B$ for IPv6 is reliably accepted [46]; in practice, a slightly higher limit of $\sim 1500\,B$ (the MTU) usually still work well for both. Usually, large payloads can be fragmented, that means: A big message is split into several IP packets, the fragments. However, some network devices – especially some NAT boxes – do not let IP-fragments through, often dropping them silently (even in non-UDP settings), thus preventing message exchange. To circumvent this and other problems, fragmentation is often avoided on the IP layer and handled on a higher layer instead. As any connection settings – including fragmentation – can only be negotiated after a connection is established successfully, fragmentation cannot be used in the IKE's initial exchanges. This can only be avoided if the exchanges are on top of a connection-oriented protocol such as TCP.

At the same time, most post-quantum keys easily exceed the MTU limits, especially those with conservative parameter sets. Thus, they do not fit into

a single IP packet or IKEv2 packet, respectively, even before adding the necessary meta-information (like header data) or combining them with classical Diffie-Hellman keys (for a hybrid solution). In fact, even classical Diffie-
Hellman values alone could outgrow the limits given by the MTU, should
their size need to increase in the future.

The problem of large data sizes occurs not only in the initial key exchange:
Another example is the IKE_AUTH exchange, which may exceed the MTU
and cause fragmentation issues. IKEv2 also provides a fragmentation mechanism for layer 3 [46], but does not allow it for the first message exchange, and
even if it did, this would be an undesired property (as pointed out in Sect. 4):
The first handshake should be fast, so that the first packet in either direction
finds its destination even on an unreliable, lossy network. However, the IKE
fragmentation mechanism may be agreed on during the IKE_SA_INIT. Fragmentation is then only used for *encrypted* payloads after the IKE_SA_INIT.
The user data in the IKE_SA_INIT exchange cannot be encrypted because
no key exchange has taken place yet.

The size field of the payload header is only 16 bits long, hence only 64 kB of
payload data can be addressed. If all KEMs in the NIST competition should
be integrable, including the McEliece cryptosystem, 64 kB is not enough.
Classic McEliece public keys take up to 1 MB and more for high-security
parameter sets, exceeding the 64 kB limit by far.

We now discuss five approaches for integrating post-quantum cryptography with
IKEv2, which can be combined freely. Stated in *italics* are the wish list items at
which the corresponding proposal aims or that are at odds with the proposal.
Items that are not named can still be compatible with the proposed approach,
but are not explicitly enhanced by it. In Sect. 6.2, we describe and discuss the
concrete combinations we chose and tested.

IKE_INTERMEDIATE with Multiple Key Exchanges
Aims at: Hybrid approach, Managing large keys, Crypto-agility, Cipher suites
At odds with: Minimal design, fast initial connection

This approach combines two IETF proposals that were specifically designed
to facilitate a quantum-proof IKEv2 version. The first, RFC 9242 [47], introduces an additional message exchange (called *IKE_INTERMEDIATE*) after
the IKE_SA_INIT messages and before IKE_AUTH, in which post-quantum
keys can be exchanged.

The second is a draft [54] that uses IKE_INTERMEDIATE-exchanges to
facilitate up to seven key exchanges, in addition to the key exchange that
takes place in the IKE_SA_INIT. Different cryptographic schemes may be
used (one per IKE_INTERMEDIATE roundtrip), which is useful if one does
not want to trust a single, newly introduced post-quantum scheme or primitive, but would, for example, like to combine a lattice-based scheme with
a code-based one. After each IKE_INTERMEDIATE exchange, the SKEY-
SEED (first calculated after IKE_SA_INIT) has to be recalculated. Also, each

exchange contributes some input to IKE_AUTH, because all exchanges need to be authenticated.

The IKE_INTERMEDIATE-messages (which carry the big post-quantum keys) can be fragmented if this is agreed on in the IKE_SA_INIT messages. This approach allows a hybrid exchange: The INIT-messages can still use a Diffie-Hellman key exchange and with the multiple exchanges, various methods can be combined. The INIT-messages are exchanged fast; however, the complete run (including authentication) of the initial exchange adds latency and contains between 6 and 18 messages instead of 4, see also our previous publication on this matter in [27].

A formal analysis conducted by us in [26] using the automated prover Tamarin [52] showed that extending the basic IKEv2 protocol with IKE_INTERMEDIATE yields the same security properties against a quantum attacker as the basic protocol has against a classical attacker.

Large Key Payload
Aims at: Hybrid approach, Managing large keys, Crypto-agility, Cipher suites

This IETF draft [53] allows the distribution of large key material over several payloads. This is possible because the IKEv2 message header (in contrast to the payload header) has a large enough size field (namely of 32 bit), which allows sending up to 4 MB of data via IKE fragmentation. The 64 kB payload could also be exceeded if large or multiple certificates are used in the IKE_AUTH exchange: Quantum-safe certificates are often much larger than classical certificates, especially when they employ hybrid mechanisms, and can, like keys, be split across multiple payloads. If more than one certificate is sent, an empty certificate payload is inserted between each certificate to indicate that a new one starts. While this solution makes big keys at least viable in IKEv2, fragmentation is far from ideal: A small cryptoscheme may only take up two to four IP fragments; a conservative Classic McEliece key of around 1 MB, however, requires 16 payloads, resulting in 781 fragments in the IPv6 setting (with a 1280 B MTU), or even 1736 in IPv4 (with a 576 B MTU). If one of these fragments is lost, all fragments have to be resent until a loss-free exchange occurs. In lossy networks, the connection might therefore be hard to establish.

Small quantum-proof keys in IKE_SA_INIT
Aims at: Hybrid approach, Minimal design, Fast initial connection

A simple way to make IKEv2 quantum-proof is to include a small cryptographic scheme like NTRU Prime [11] in the IKE_SA_INIT. This mechanism is already a standard function for IKEv2 in the implementation of OpenIKED[8] and has been implemented for SSH, as explained in Sect. 2. This facilitates a

---

[8] https://www.openbsd.org/openiked/.

fast initial key exchange and mitigates DoS- or MitM-attacks against the key exchange.

But while NTRU Prime fits well in the IKE_SA_INIT (thus avoiding the MTU issue), produces minimal overhead of only a few milliseconds and has a fast and well-written code base, there are also a few post-quantum alternatives (all lattice-based): CRYSTALS-Kyber512 [7] and Ntruhps2048509 [28] to just name a few. It is, however, unlikely that there will be many alternatives in the future that meet these specific size requirements.

TCP-based IKEv2
Aims at: Managing large keys

IKEv2 is normally based on UDP. RFC 9329 [41] describes IKEv2 over TCP, intended as a fallback option if IKE cannot be negotiated over UDP (as network middleboxes sometimes block IKE negotiation). This RFC could be used to make the connection more reliable for PQ key exchanges with large keys that rely on fragmentation.

For most PQ algorithms, the UDP-based solution is more performant than the TCP-based solution; but for high-security domains, this drawback of using TCP may be worthwhile in exchange for using more trusted cryptography.

Quantum-proof-key exchange in CHILD_SA
Aims at: Hybrid approach, Managing large keys, Crypto-agility, Fast initial connection

Quantum-proof keys can also be negotiated after the initial SA establishment by negotiating them in a CHILD_SA. This way, the communication is better protected because the initial exchange happens fast, and at the same time, it allows the exchange of bigger, more trusted keys for long-term-protection. On the downside, the initial key exchange is not protected against a real-time or long-term attacker that can break the less trusted cryptography used in the first exchange.

6   Implementation and Performance Results

6.1   MACsec (Layer 2)

MACsec and MKA allow only a few cryptographic primitives for key derivation and encryption. A secure connection is quickly established and operated with small overhead. Consequently, there is no need to install a full cryptographic library that includes quantum-resistant algorithms, and instead, post-quantum cryptographic primitives can be individually implemented and integrated into the MACsec software. However, there are several requirements for secure implementation in software. For instance, an implemented protocol should run in

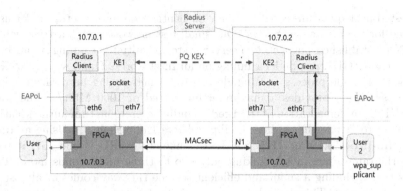

Fig. 3. A test platform for post-quantum MACsec key agreement

constant time to avoid side-channel attacks. In particular, MACsec is sometimes operated on embedded platforms which may have limited computing power and memory resources. We therefore implemented the new version using a low level programming language and aimed at optimal resource use. An overall structure of the test platform is shown in Fig. 3. We set up a direct MACsec connection between two sets of ADVA FSP 150 ProVMe [1], each of which is composed of an FPGA and a Linux host using DPDK. Actual data communication occurs through an in-band channel established by DPDK KNI (Kernel NIC Interface) [21]. We tested a post-quantum key exchange using Classic McEliece, NTRU, CRYSTALS-Kyber and SABER, together with classical Diffie-Hellman key exchange, on the application running in the host. For a user authentication, we tested CRYSTALS-Dilithium and Falcon through the client port, which interacts with a Radius server. ASIC-based MACsec adds an average latency of 1–3 μs and an overhead of 32 bytes in a point-to-point direct link. To assess the performance impact of the key exchange protocol, we conducted a software-based AES-GCM-256 MACsec evaluation and found that while the latency is higher compared to ASIC-based MACsec, the throughput is comparable. We measured the throughput and average latency with various packet sizes. For 64 B packets, the MACsec performance was around 2300 Mbps and 34 μs for throughput and latency respectively. For 1420 B packets, the throughput and latency were approximately 9000 Mbps and 149 μs, respectively. Our test results showed that the post-quantum key primitives did not significantly impact MACsec performance.

6.2   IPsec (Layer 3)

In our experiments for IKEv2 in the IPsec context, we used an X25519 Diffie-Hellman key exchange to be done as the classical part, but also tested other classical options with sometimes slightly higher run-times (very few ms). We have not tested post-quantum certificates for authentication in our setup, but this is planned for the future, see Sect. 7. Our small test network uses hardware where a VPN is established between two server systems (initiator running on an Intel Xeon with 3.2 GHz, responder running on an Intel Core 2 Quad with 2.66 GHz, each with a single process on a single core). All networking hardware (including the switches) provides a maximum line speed of 1000 Mbit/s. The standard IKEv2 implementation of the iked including a pre-quantum authentication runs in 18 to 20 ms when using an elliptic-curve Diffie-Hellman. Using a **small quantum-proof key in IKE_SA_INIT**, namely NTRU Prime 761, it took about the same time, mostly taking only two to three milliseconds more. This means that including a small and efficient scheme this way comes at almost no overhead and cost. This could be a good basis for whatever other post-quantum solution may be used additionally.

For testing **IKE_INTERMEDIATE with Multiple Key Exchanges**, we used a combination of classical Diffie-Hellman with lattice-based schemes like CRYSTALS-Kyber 1024 or FrodoKEM 640 [4] that are too big for the IKE_SA_INIT messages (with about 1.5 kB and 9.6 kB for the public keys of the named parameters sets). In these cases, it mostly took less than 25 ms for key establishment. Also, here the time for the cryptographic operations are only a few ms, but times can easily increase for the schemes with bigger parameter sets. Problems arise in slow or lossy networks, when each additional round and the packets sent mean longer or even failed key establishment. We consider a maximum of two rounds of IKE_INTERMEDIATE to be practical on actual IP networks like the internet.

As a worst-case example regarding runtime, we tested the isogeny-based SIKE. It is comparatively slow, especially for the largest parameter set. By now, SIKE is considered insecure [14], so our results are academically interesting but not practically relevant until a similar scheme is proposed.

We also tested the UDP-based variant for **large keys**, starting with a classical key exchange, followed by FrodoKEM with the smallest parameter set using the IKE_INTERMEDIATE. Our first solutions used Classic McEliece with a 1 MB and even a 1.3 MB public key (as of the respective parameter sets mceliece6960119 and mceliece8192128) following directly. We also tested the **quantum-proof key exchange when creating the CHILD_SA**. Therefore, the exchange with FrodoKEM was done before the IKE_AUTH, the Classic McEliece exchange was only done after authentication.

The results show that the solution is acceptable for well-functioning networks, but is susceptible to increasing network losses, making it impractical for use cases with high packet losses (see Fig. 4). These test results are consistent with the theoretical analysis of the fragmentation problem in Sect. 5. For the biggest McEliece parameter set, the full IKEv2 procedure took about 2.5 s on average without packet loss. We expect that establishing a connection this way would take significantly more time over a lossy network. Over a somewhat reliable IP network, however, a exchange of big keys (especially if it is TCP-based) could be worthwhile for high-security connections.

(a) Distribution of the handshake duration on a 100Mbit line.   (b) Distribution of the handshake duration on a 1Mbit line.

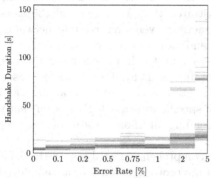
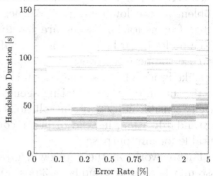

Fig. 4. The distribution of the handshake duration for a key exchange attempt using a 1 MB Classic McEliece key. A stable latency around 100 ms was simulated for 100 runs per test configuration. The worse the network conditions get, the more handshake attempts fail, reducing the actual number of measurable results. Measurements are depicted by color in their total number of occurrence, going from light blue to red. (Color figure online)

7   Conclusion and Future Work

In this work we investigated how post-quantum VPN protocols on layer 2 and layer 3 can remain as usable, secure and as adaptable as their classical versions. To do so, we assembled a list of requirements for post-quantum VPNs and implemented proof-of-concept variants of MACsec/MKA and IPsec/IKEv2, respectively. Parallel to the implementation efforts, we engaged in standardization efforts at the IETF, which resulted in some individual internet drafts and RFCs addressing the interoperability requirements needed for any large-scale network protocol.

We found that such protocols should ideally be hybrid, crypto-agile and able to manage big key material while maintaining fast initial connection establishment and slender protocol design.

The MACsec protocol can be adapted relatively easily by either employing a quantum-proof version of EAP-TLS in the key agreement, or by adding a quantum-safe AKE to the classical one, since the capabilities of fragmentation and re-assembly of fragments can be handled in a satisfactory manner. Our experiments show that well-working implementations can be realized on layer 2 using even the most conservative (and thus most practically challenging) post-quantum scheme, the McEliece cryptosystem.

IPsec can also be enhanced by an intermediate exchange in the first handshake, which makes using many cryptographic primitives in parallel very easy, but increases complexity and latency. It can also be tweaked to support larger payloads (for big keys), include a small quantum-safe key (for minimal postquantum security) or feature additional key-exchanges after the initial one. To support fragmentation issues in high-stakes cases (that require large keys), TCP-based IKEv2 might also be used in the future. This, however, is clearly a big problem at the lower layer 3. We demonstrated that McEliece and the associated fragmentation issues are hardly practical even over reliable networks, which bodes ill for lossy networks. Smaller and more performant schemes hardly increase the network overhead in our experiments (such as rather conservative ones like FrodoKEM), so they should be suitable for many, if not most, use cases.

We therefore urge regulating agencies to take practicability into account and specify sensible subsets of the solutions (for specific use-cases) that are currently in standardization, instead of just recommending all-in-one protocol extensions suitable for any purpose.

Future work on the topic will give a comprehensive analysis of the joint system, where layer 2 and layer 3 post-quantum protocol extensions are employed together. To better understand the fragmentation problem on layer 3, an IPsec over TCP-based implementation is planned. Also, post-quantum certificates for authentication shall be examined.

Hopefully, the standardization efforts at IETF that have already resulted in a few post-quantum RFCs and Internet-Drafts will continue and either specify the proposed protocol extensions in even more detail or provide more modern solutions in the future [24,47,49,53,54]. This could be a good starting point for further discussions on this topic.

Acknowledgements. This research was co-funded by the Federal Ministry of Education and Research of Germany under the QuaSiModO project (Grant agreement No 16KIS1051). We thank Robin Lösch for his support and the anonymous reviewers for their valuable comments.

References

1. ADVA Optical Networking: FSP 150 ProVMe Series. https://www.adva.com/en/products/packet-edge-and-aggregation/edge-computing/fsp-150-provme-series
2. Alagic, G., et al.: Status report on the third round of the NIST post-quantum cryptography standardization process. Technical report, National Institute of Standards and Technology, Gaithersburg, MD (2022). https://doi.org/10.6028/NIST.IR.8413
3. Alagic, G., et al.: Status report on the third round of the NIST post-quantum cryptography standardization process (2022). https://doi.org/10.6028/NIST.IR.8413-upd1. https://tsapps.nist.gov/publication/get_pdf.cfm?pub_id=935591
4. Alkim, E., et al.: FrodoKEM learning with errors key encapsulation algorithm specifications and supporting documentation. NIST Submissions (2019)
5. Alkim, E., Ducas, L., Pöppelmann, T., Schwabe, P.: Post-quantum key exchange: a new hope. In: Proceedings of the 25th USENIX Conference on Security Symposium, SEC 2016, pp. 327–343. USENIX Association (2016)
6. Aragon, N., et al.: BIKE. Submission to the NIST Post-Quantum Cryptography Standardization (2017)
7. Avanzi, R., et al.: CRYSTALS-Kyber. Submission to the NIST Post-Quantum Cryptography Standardization (2017)

8. Barker, E., Chen, L., Davis, R.: Recommendation for Key-Derivation Methods in Key-Establishment Schemes. NIST Special Publication 800-56C Revision 2 (2020). https://csrc.nist.gov/publications/detail/sp/800-56c/rev-2/final
9. Bernstein, D., Hülsing, A., Kölbl, S., Niederhagen, R., Rijneveld, J., Schwabe, P.: The SPHINCS+ Signature Framework, pp. 2129–2146 (2019). https://doi.org/10.1145/3319535.3363229
10. Bernstein, D.J., et al.: Classic McEliece: conservative code-based cryptography. Submission to the NIST Post-Quantum Cryptography Standardization (2017)
11. Bernstein, D.J., Lange, T., Chuengsatiansu, C., van Vredendaal, C.: NTRU Prime. NIST Submissions (2017)
12. Beullens, W.: Breaking rainbow takes a weekend on a laptop. Cryptology ePrint Archive, Report 2019/482 (2022). https://eprint.iacr.org/2019/482
13. Campagna, M., Crockett, E.: Hybrid Post-Quantum Key Encapsulation Methods (PQ KEM) for Transport Layer Security 1.2 (TLS). Internet-Draft draft-campagna-tls-bike-sike-hybrid-07, Internet Engineering Task Force (2021). https://datatracker.ietf.org/doc/html/draft-campagna-tls-bike-sike-hybrid-07. Work in Progress
14. Castryck, W., Decru, T.: An efficient key recovery attack on SIDH (preliminary version). Cryptology ePrint Archive, Paper 2022/975 (2022). https://eprint.iacr.org/2022/975
15. Celi, S., et al.: Implementing and measuring KEMTLS. In: Longa, P., Ràfols, C. (eds.) LATINCRYPT 2021. LNCS, vol. 12912, pp. 88–107. Springer, Cham (2021). https://doi.org/10.1007/978-3-030-88238-9_5
16. Cho, J.Y., Sergeev, A.: Post-quantum MACsec key agreement for ethernet networks. In: Proceedings of the 15th International Conference on Availability, Reliability and Security, ARES 2020. Association for Computing Machinery, New York (2020). https://doi.org/10.1145/3407023.3409220
17. Cho, J.Y., Sergeev, A.: TLV-to-MUC express: post-quantum MACsec in VXLAN. In: Asplund, M., Nadjm-Tehrani, S. (eds.) NordSec 2020. LNCS, vol. 12556, pp. 127–141. Springer, Cham (2021). https://doi.org/10.1007/978-3-030-70852-8_8
18. Cisco: Configuring Post-Quantum MACsec in Cisco Switches (2020). https://www.cisco.com/c/dam/en_us/about/doing_business/trust-center/docs/configuring-post-quantum-macsec-in-cisco-switches.pdf
19. Cremers, C.: Key exchange in IPsec revisited: formal analysis of IKEv1 and IKEv2. In: Atluri, V., Diaz, C. (eds.) ESORICS 2011. LNCS, vol. 6879, pp. 315–334. Springer, Heidelberg (2011). https://doi.org/10.1007/978-3-642-23822-2_18
20. Crockett, E., Paquin, C., Stebila, D.: Prototyping post-quantum and hybrid key exchange and authentication in TLS and SSH. Cryptology ePrint Archive, Report 2019/858 (2019). https://eprint.iacr.org/2019/858
21. DPDK documentation: Kernel NIC Interface. https://doc.dpdk.org
22. Eronen, P., Tschofenig, H.: Pre-shared Key Ciphersuites for Transport Layer Security (TLS). RFC 4279, RFC Editor (2005). http://www.rfc-editor.org/rfc/rfc4279.txt
23. Feo, L.D., Jao, D., Plût, J.: Towards quantum-resistant cryptosystems from supersingular elliptic curve isogenies. J. Math. Cryptol. 8(3), 209–247 (2014). https://doi.org/10.1515/jmc-2012-0015
24. Fluhrer, S., Kampanakis, P., McGrew, D., Smyslov, V.: Mixing Preshared Keys in IKEv2 for Post-quantum Security (2020). https://draft-ietf-ipsecme-qr-ikev2-11
25. Fouque, P.A., Hoffstein, J., Kirchner, P., et al.: Falcon: Fast-Fourier Lattice-Based Compact Signatures over NTRU. NIST Submissions (2020)

26. Gazdag, S.L., Grundner-Culemann, S., Guggemos, T., Heider, T., Loebenberger, D.: A formal analysis of IKEv2's post-quantum extension. In: Annual Computer Security Applications Conference, ACSAC, pp. 91–105. Association for Computing Machinery, New York (2021). https://doi.org/10.1145/3485832.3485885

27. Herzinger, D., Gazdag, S.L., Loebenberger, D.: Real-world quantum-resistant IPsec. In: 2021 14th International Conference on Security of Information and Networks (SIN), vol. 1, pp. 1–8 (2021). https://doi.org/10.1109/SIN54109.2021.9699255

28. Hoffstein, J., Pipher, J., Silverman, J.H.: NTRU: a ring-based public key cryptosystem. In: Buhler, J.P. (ed.) ANTS 1998. LNCS, vol. 1423, pp. 267–288. Springer, Heidelberg (1998). https://doi.org/10.1007/BFb0054868

29. IEEE: Local and metropolitan area networks-Media Access Control (MAC) Security. 802.1AE: MAC Security (MACsec). https://1.ieee802.org/security/802-1ae/

30. IEEE: Local and metropolitan area networks-Port-Based Network Access Control. IEEE Std 802.1X-2010 (Revision of IE EE Std 802.1X-2004), pp. 1–205 (2010)

31. Kampanakis, P., Stebila, D., Hansen, T.: Post-quantum Hybrid Key Exchange in SSH. Internet-Draft draft-kampanakis-curdle-ssh-pq-ke-00, Internet Engineering Task Force (2022). https://www.ietf.org/id/draft-kampanakis-curdle-ssh-pq-ke-00.html. Work in Progress

32. Kaufman, C.: Internet Key Exchange Protocol Version 2 (IKEv2). RFC 4306 (2005). https://datatracker.ietf.org/doc/html/rfc4306

33. Kaufman, C., Hoffman, P., Nir, Y., Eronen, P., Kivinen, T.: Internet Key Exchange Protocol Version 2 (IKEv2). RFC 7296 (2014). https://doi.org/10.17487/RFC7296. https://datatracker.ietf.org/doc/html/rfc7296.txt

34. Kent, S.: IP Authentication Header. RFC 4302 (2005). https://doi.org/10.17487/RFC4302. https://www.rfc-editor.org/info/rfc4302

35. Kent, S.: IP Encapsulating Security Payload (ESP). RFC 4303 (2005). https://doi.org/10.17487/RFC4303. https://www.rfc-editor.org/info/rfc4303

36. Lyubashevsky, V., et al.: CRYSTALS-Dilithium. Submission to the NIST Post-Quantum Cryptography Standardization (2017)

37. McEliece, R.: A public-key cryptosystem based on algebraic coding theory. Coding Thv **4244**, 114–116 (1978)

38. Melchor, C.A., et al.: Hamming quasi-cyclic (HQC). Submission to the NIST Post-Quantum Cryptography Standardization (2017)

39. Ninet, T.: Formal verification of the Internet Key Exchange (IKEv2) security protocol. Theses, Université Rennes 1 (2020). https://tel.archives-ouvertes.fr/tel-02882167

40. Paquin, C., Stebila, D., Tamvada, G.: Benchmarking post-quantum cryptography in TLS. In: Ding, J., Tillich, J.-P. (eds.) PQCrypto 2020. LNCS, vol. 12100, pp. 72–91. Springer, Cham (2020). https://doi.org/10.1007/978-3-030-44223-1_5

41. Pauly, T., Smyslov, V.: TCP Encapsulation of Internet Key Exchange Protocol (IKE) and IPsec Packets. RFC 9329 (2022). https://doi.org/10.17487/RFC9329. https://www.rfc-editor.org/info/rfc9329

42. Pazienza, A., Lella, E., Noviello, P., Vitulano, F.: Analysis of network-level key exchange protocols in the post-quantum era. In: 2022 IEEE 15th Workshop on Low Temperature Electronics (WOLTE), pp. 1–4 (2022). https://doi.org/10.1109/WOLTE55422.2022.9882818

43. Perlner, R., Kelsey, J., Cooper, D.: Breaking category five SPHINCS+ with SHA-256. Cryptology ePrint Archive, Paper 2022/1061 (2022). https://eprint.iacr.org/2022/1061

44. Schwabe, P., Stebila, D., Wiggers, T.: Post-quantum TLS without handshake signatures, pp. 1461–1480. Association for Computing Machinery, New York (2020). https://doi.org/10.1145/3372297.3423350
45. Shor, P.: Polynomial-time algorithms for prime factorization and discrete logarithms on a quantum computer. SIAM Rev. **41**(2), 303–332 (1999). https://doi.org/10.1137/S0036144598347011
46. Smyslov, V.: Internet Key Exchange Protocol Version 2 (IKEv2) Message Fragmentation. RFC 7383, Internet Engineering Task Force (2014). https://doi.org/10.17487/RFC7383. https://datatracker.ietf.org/doc/html/rfc7383.txt
47. Smyslov, V.: Intermediate Exchange in the Internet Key Exchange Protocol Version 2 (IKEv2). RFC 9242, Internet Engineering Task Force (2022). https://doi.org/10.17487/RFC9242. https://www.rfc-editor.org/info/rfc9242
48. Stebila, D., Fluhrer, S., Gueron, S.: Hybrid key exchange in TLS 1.3. Internet-Draft draft-ietf-tls-hybrid-design-01, Internet Engineering Task Force (2020). https://datatracker.ietf.org/doc/html/draft-ietf-tls-hybrid-design. Work in Progress
49. Stebila, D., Fluhrer, S., Gueron, S.: Hybrid key exchange in TLS 1.3. Internet-Draft draft-ietf-tls-hybrid-design-04, Internet Engineering Task Force (2022). https://datatracker.ietf.org/doc/html/draft-ietf-tls-hybrid-design-04. Work in Progress
50. Tao, C., Petzoldt, A., Ding, J.: Improved Key Recovery of the HFEv- Signature Scheme. Cryptology ePrint Archive, Paper 2020/1424 (2020). https://eprint.iacr.org/2020/1424
51. Tao, C., Petzoldt, A., Ding, J.: Efficient key recovery for all HFE signature variants. In: Malkin, T., Peikert, C. (eds.) CRYPTO 2021. LNCS, vol. 12825, pp. 70–93. Springer, Cham (2021). https://doi.org/10.1007/978-3-030-84242-0_4
52. Team, T.T.: Tamarin-Prover Manual (2016). https://tamarin-prover.github.io/manual/tex/tamarin-manual.pdf
53. Tjhai, C., Heider, T., Smyslov, V.: Beyond 64KB Limit of IKEv2 Payloads. Internet-Draft draft-tjhai-ikev2-beyond-64k-limit-03, Internet Engineering Task Force (2022). https://datatracker.ietf.org/doc/html/draft-tjhai-ikev2-beyond-64k-limit-03. Work in Progress
54. Tjhai, C., et al.: Multiple Key Exchanges in IKEv2. Internet-Draft draft-ietf-ipsecme-ikev2-multiple-ke-06, Internet Engineering Task Force (2022). https://datatracker.ietf.org/doc/html/draft-ietf-ipsecme-ikev2-multiple-ke-06. Work in Progress
55. Wilhelm, F., et al.: Status of quantum computer development (2020). https://www.bsi.bund.de/SharedDocs/Downloads/DE/BSI/Publikationen/Studien/Quantencomputer/P283_QC_Studie-V_1_2.pdf
56. Zalka, C.: Grover's quantum searching algorithm is optimal. Phys. Rev. A **60**, 2746–2751 (1999). https://doi.org/10.1103/PhysRevA.60.2746

Post-quantum Security for the Extended Access Control Protocol

Marc Fischlin[1] , Jonas von der Heyden[2]([✉]) , Marian Margraf[3],
Frank Morgner[4], Andreas Wallner[5], and Holger Bock[5]

[1] Technische Universität Darmstadt, Darmstadt, Germany
[2] Bergische Universität Wuppertal, Wuppertal, Germany
jvdh@uni-wuppertal.de
[3] Fraunhofer AISEC, Berlin, Germany
[4] Bundesdruckerei GmbH, Berlin, Germany
[5] Infineon Technologies, Graz, Austria

Abstract. The *Extended Access Control* (EAC) protocol for authenticated key agreement is mainly used to secure connections between machine-readable travel documents (MRTDs) and inspection terminals, but it can also be adopted as a universal solution for attribute-based access control with smart cards. The security of EAC is currently based on the Diffie-Hellman problem, which may not be hard when considering quantum computers.

In this work we present PQ-EAC, a quantum-resistant version of the EAC protocol. We show how to achieve post-quantum confidentiality and authentication without sacrificing real-world usability on smart cards. To ease adoption, we present two main versions of PQ-EAC: One that uses signatures for authentication and one where authentication is facilitated using long-term KEM keys. Both versions can be adapted to achieve forward secrecy and to reduce round complexity. To ensure backwards-compatibility, PQ-EAC can be implemented using only Application Protocol Data Units (APDUs) specified for EAC in standard BSI TR-03110. Merely the protocol messages needed to achieve forward secrecy require an additional APDU not specified in TR-03110. We prove security of all versions in the real-or-random model of Bellare and Rogaway.

To show real-world practicality of PQ-EAC we have implemented a version using signatures on an ARM SC300 security controller, which is typically deployed in MRTDs. We also implemented PQ-EAC on a VISOCORE® terminal for border control. We then conducted several experiments to evaluate the performance of PQ-EAC executed between chip and terminal under various real-world conditions. Our results strongly suggest that PQ-EAC is efficient enough for use in border control.

Keywords: Access Control · Machine Readable Travel Documents · Post-Quantum Cryptography · Smart Cards

© The Author(s), under exclusive license to Springer Nature Switzerland AG 2023
F. Günther and J. Hesse (Eds.): SSR 2023, LNCS 13895, pp. 22–52, 2023.
https://doi.org/10.1007/978-3-031-30731-7_2

1 Introduction

EAC Protocol. The Extended Access Control(EAC) protocol for authenticated key agreement was proposed by the *German Federal Office for Information Security* (BSI) for German ePassports in 2005 and is defined in the technical guideline TR-03110 [17]. EAC is meant to provide authenticated key establishment between a terminal and a smart card. ICAO Doc 9303 [31], a standard for electronic machine-readable travel documents (eMRTDs) such as ePassports, mandates authentication via EAC before a terminal may request sensitive data such as fingerprints from the chip in an eMRTD. The security of EAC rests on assumptions about the hardness of computing discrete logarithms. Due to the results of Shor [56], these assumptions are now considered to be false when taking into account quantum computers. In this work we present PQ-EAC, a new version of the EAC protocol that achieves security against attacks from quantum computers by substituting Diffie-Hellman key exchange with post-quantum Key Encapsulation Mechanisms (KEMs).

Post-quantum Cryptography. In 1994, Peter Shor presented a quantum algorithm that solves integer factorization and discrete logarithms—two problems for which no efficient algorithm on classical computers is known—in polynomial time [56]. Shor's work thereby falsified the foundational assumption of public-key cryptography that factorization and discrete logarithms are hard problems. While only a quantum computer of sufficient size could break public-key cryptography as used in modern internet infrastructure, recent developments show that such a machine is a realistic scenario [4]. Michele Mosca estimates a 1/7 chance of a quantum computer breaking RSA-2048 by 2026 and a 1/2 chance of this break occurring by 2031 [46].

Fortunately, there are alternatives to cryptography based on factorization or discrete logarithms. As proposed by Bernstein [11] we say that a cryptographic construction is *'post-quantum secure'* when it is assumed to be appropriately secure against quantum adversaries. For performance reasons, one of the most promising approaches to post-quantum cryptography is *lattice-based* cryptography. In regards to post-quantum digital signatures, hash-based signatures are an interesting alternative to classical constructions. They have been known since the 1970s [39,44] and provide provable security under the weak assumption that one-way functions exist. They require careful state management and might therefore not be suitable for all use cases. However, due to the confidence in their security, they could serve as a useful building block for *cryptographic agility* in smart cards: In the case that the post-quantum algorithms deployed on a smart card turn out to be insecure, they could be replaced with an update whose integrity is secured by a hash-based signature.

NIST Competition. To alleviate the threat of quantum computers against cryptography, the US National Institute of Standards and Technology (NIST) initiated a post-quantum cryptography (PQC) competition in 2017. In 2022, NIST announced that they will standardize the lattice-based Key Encapsulation Mechanism (KEM) Kyber [54], two lattice-based signature schemes (Dilithium [41],

Falcon [50]) and the hash-based signature scheme SPHINCS+ [29] as quantum-resistant cryptographic mechanisms [2]. In addition, the hash-based signature schemes LMS [43] and XMSS [28] havealready been recommended in NIST SP 800-208 [47].

Hybrid Protocols. Many of these conjecturally *post-quantum secure* schemes have not yet been adequately studied in terms of their security. This concerns not only cryptanalytic attacks using classical computers, but also side-channel and error attacks and the exploitation of implementation errors. Therefore,it is prudent to use hybrid protocols, i.e., a combination of classical and quantum-resistant primitives; see also, for example, the recommendations of the German Federal Office for Information Security [18].

Quantum-Resistant Versions of EAC. Even though a quantum computer powerful enough to break modern cryptography might be more than a decade away, in the context of identity documents urgent action is required. This is because identity documents typically have a validity period of ten years and technical changes require lengthy regulatory approval. Therefore, the development of a new quantum-resistant version of the EAC protocol, ideally using hybrid schemes that combine post-quantum and classical algorithms, is imperative. This should be accompanied by a software implementation of this new protocol for contactless smart cards (in eMRTDs) as well as inspection terminals, in order to create a blueprint for the standardization of the new EAC protocol with ICAO. In this paper, we showcase several versions of a quantum-resistant EAC protocol with varying security properties and trade-offs.

1.1   Outline

We start out with a discussion of ePassports in Sect. 2 and exhibit the original EAC protocol in Sect. 3. In Sect. 4 we subsequently propose several modifications to EAC, which will replace the Diffie-Hellman-style key exchange with *Key Encapsulation Mechanisms* (KEMs). Afterwards, we discuss our implementation and give performance benchmarks in Sect. 5.

To distinguish between the EAC protocol as defined by BSI [17] and our proposal for post-quantum EAC, we call the former *classic EAC* or *EAC classic* and the latter *PQ-EAC*. We continue to write EAC when referring to the protocol as such. EAC is usually conducted between two parties: One the one side we have an eMRTD which might be an identity card, a passport or similar, in the following called 'chip'. On the other side we have a chip reader, which could be an inspection terminal at border control, a device to authenticate identity cards for e-government services, or similar, in the following called 'terminal'. The terms MRTD and eMRTD are used in this document as a generic reference to all types of Machine Readable Travel Documents in, respectively, optical character reading and electronically enabled forms. Examples of MRTDs are ePassports, laissez-passer, identity cards, seafarer cards and refugee travel documents.

We use the notion of *forward secrecy* as given in Boyd and Gellert [15]: An authenticated key exchange (AKE) protocol provides forward secrecy (resp. is *forward-secure*) if compromise of long-term secrets does not lead to compromise of session keys of previously completed sessions.

1.2 Related Work on Post-quantum Cryptography for MRTDs

Post-quantum Cryptography. NIST recently announced [2] that as an outcome of the competition they will recommend and standardize the lattice-based KEM Kyber [54] and the lattice-based signature scheme Dilithium [41] as quantum-resistant schemes. Accordingly, we instantiate the KEMs and signature schemes in our PQ-EAC implementation with Kyber and Dilithium. As we will detail in Sect. 5, both schemes are efficient enough for use in ressource-constrained environments such as smart cards typically deployed in MRTDs.

Simultaneously, there have been multiple works concerned with making Diffie-Hellman-based protocols quantum-resistant: Schwabe et al. [55] present post-quantum versions of TLS, including a version with mutual authentication. Hülsing et al. [30] show how to achieve post-quantum security for the handshake protocol of the WireGuard VPN. Brendel et al. [16] attempt to give a post-quantum alternative to Signal's X3DH handshake using split KEMs. Finally, Angel et al. [3] introduce a post-quantum variant of the Noise framework. Unlike PQ-EAC, the protocols mentioned above cannot serve as drop-in replacements for EAC as standardized in TR-03110. However, our work and the mentioned protocols share the basic idea of replacing a Diffie-Hellman key exchange with KEMs to achieve post-quantum security.

PAKE. In BSI standard TR-03110 [17], the Password Authenticated Connection Establishment (PACE) protocol – a variant of *Password-Authenticated Key Exchange* (PAKE) – is used to set up the initial communication between MRTD chip and terminal reader. Since the security of PACE is based on hardness assumptions about discrete logarithms, it needs to be modified to become quantum-resistant. Fortunately, there have been a number of attempts to devise post-quantum PAKE, for example by Katz and Vaikuntanathan [36] and Katz and Groce [26]. Moreover, there has been a recent proposal for PAKE based on group actions by Abdalla et al. [1]. However, since the only known quantum-resistant instantiation of group actions is based on CSIDH [21], this construction would not be efficient enough for use in smart cards.

PKI. Regarding public-key infrastructure (PKI), there has been work by Bindel et al. [13] towards hybrid PKI (meaning PKI that combines classical and post-quantum constructions). Additionally there are proposals by Pradel and Mitchell [49] as well as Vogt and Funke [57] specifically in regards to post-quantum PKI for MRTDs.

ePassports. Recent publications in regards to ePassports have been concerned with the security of Basic Access Control (BAC) [5,10,23], the security of PACE [9,10] and the security of classic EAC [22].

However, besides a requirement overview [45] for post-quantum resistance in the area of MRTDs, to the best of our knowledge there have not been any publications regarding the post-quantum security of the EAC protocol.

2   ePassports

History. Extended Access Control (EAC) was devised as a mechanism to protect biometric data stored in machine-readable travel documents (MRTDs). The International Civil Aviation Organization (ICAO), a specialized agency of the United Nations, introduced standards for electronic MRTDs and specifically ePassports in 2006 in Volume 2 of the sixth edition of ICAO Doc 9303 [31]. Since then, more than 140 countries have adopted ePassports, with 90 countries enrolled in the ICAO Public Key Directory (PKD).

ICAO mandates in Doc 9303 [31] the execution of EAC before terminals may read sensitive data from MRTDs. The technical specification of EAC for EU passports has been devised by the Brussels Interoperability Group (BIG) and is published by the German Federal Office for Information Security (BSI) in their technical report TR-03110 [17].

EAC as defined in this specification includes two authentication mechanisms, Chip Authentication (CA) and Terminal Authentication (TA): CA authenticates the chip and TA prevents the reading of biometric data from unauthorized terminals. While EAC originated in the context of travel documents, it is also utilized in different contexts: For example, version 2 of EAC authenticates transactions performed by the German identity card, such as proof of identity or e-government. While we focus on the passport context in this work, most of our results apply more generally.

PACE and BAC. To establish connection, chip and terminal first generate a high-entropy shared key through *Password Authenticated Connection Establishment* (PACE), an asymmetric key exchange procedure based on a shared (possibly low-entropy) password. In the context of ePassports, the password is either the machine-readable zone (MRZ) or the card access number (CAN). Some document types (for example the German identity card) also support a secret user PIN. As such, the terminal authenticates itself to the chip by proving that the holder has entered a pin or put the document on the terminal reader. PACE creates an end-to-end encrypted communication channel and allows terminals to read less sensitive data groups such as name, nationality and other information. EAC is usually executed over the PACE-secured communication channel.

Alternatively, MRTDs issued before 2018, may use *Basic Access Control* (BAC) instead of PACE to establish a shared key from the MRTD's MRZ. Due to several shortcomings in the BAC protocol [5,23,40], it is however recommended (and even mandated for ePassports issued after 2017) to use PACE instead of BAC [10].

Public-Key Infrastructure. In order for chip and terminal to be able to mutually authenticate each other, each document issuing country has established a

PKI, which consists of the following entities (among others): a Country Signing Certificate Authority (CSCA) and a Country Verifying Certificate Authority (CVCA), Document Signer certificates, Document Verifier certificates and certificate revocation lists (CRLs). Document Signer certificates and key-pairs are issued by the CSCA to the entity that is manufacturing the MRTDs. The private key is then used to sign a list of hashes of the data groups of the MRTD. The signature, hashes and the respective Document Signer certificate are then stored in the SO_D and can be used by the MRTD to authenticate itself to a terminal.

Similarly, the CVCA issues manufacturers of terminals Document Verifier key-pairs and certificates, which can be used by a terminal to authenticate itself towards chips.

To enable international interoperability, all countries share their CSCA and CVCA public keys (via a master list), Document Signer certificates, Document Verifier certificates and CRLs in the ICAOPKD.

Passive Authentication. The terminal uses a protocol called *Passive Authentication* to authenticate the data that is stored on the chip. Passive Authentication involves the following steps:

- The terminal reads the *Document Security Object* (SO_D) from the chip and retrieves the corresponding Document Signer certificate, the CSCA certificate and the corresponding certificate revocation list. The SO_D holds hashes of all data groups and a signature over these hashes. Note that the chip's public key is also stored in one of these data groups.
- The terminal verifies the Document Signer certificate.
- The terminal then computes the hash values of all data groups it has access to and compares them to the hash values from the SO_D. Subsequently it verifies the signature over these hash values using the public key from the Document Signer certificate.

Passive Authentication does not protect against cloning attacks, where the SO_D (but not the secret key which is assumed to be secured against copying) is copied from one MRTD to another, but only verifies the integrity of the data groups on the chip. To prove that the chip is actually in possession of the corresponding secret key, EAC and Chip Authentication come into play.

3   Classic EAC Protocol

Overview. EAC works as follows: The terminal uses *Chip Authentication* (CA) to verify the authenticity of the chip. Vice versa, the chip can verify the inspection system's authorization to read sensitive biometric data such as fingerprints or iris data during *Terminal Authentication* (TA) [31]. In EAC version 1, which is included in ICAO's standard for ePassports, chip and terminal first execute CA and then TA. If EAC is not executed, the terminal is not allowed to read secondary biometric data. To assure more privacy for the MRTD holder, in (the otherwise identical) version 2 of EAC chip and terminal first perform TA and then CA, and the terminal is only allowed to read data groups once PACE, TA and CA have completed. EAC version 2 is, for example, used by the German identity card. In this work we aim for the stronger security properties of EAC version 2 but maintain compatibility with EAC version 1.

We say $x \leftarrow \{0,1\}^n$ to denote that a n-bit string x is sampled uniformly at random from $\{0,1\}^n$. With $x \leftarrow F(\ldots)$ we refer to a non-deterministic assignment for a function F, or, if F is a distribution, random assignment using this distribution. We denote the Diffie-Hellman (DH) key generation procedure with DH.KeyGen and the derivation of a shared DH key with $\mathsf{DH}(\cdot, \cdot)$.

Terminal Authentication. The goal of TA as shown in Fig. 1 is to prove to the chip that the inspection terminal is authorized to view sensitive data of the chip. In the context of passports, sensitive data means secondary biometric data such as fingerprints or iris data of the passport holder. To show that the terminal is in possession of a key-pair $(\mathsf{pk}_{\mathcal{T}}, \mathsf{sk}_{\mathcal{T}})$ that is validated by a Document Verifier certificate, the terminal initiates a challenge-response procedure.

Terminal Authentication	
Chip $\mathcal{C}$	**Terminal $\mathcal{T}$**
CVCA root certificate $\mathsf{cert}_{\mathsf{CVCA}}$	certificate $\mathsf{cert}_{\mathcal{T}}$ for $\mathsf{pk}_{\mathcal{T}}$
$\mathsf{pk}_{\mathsf{CVCA}}$	long-term key pair $(\mathsf{pk}_{\mathcal{T}}, \mathsf{sk}_{\mathcal{T}})$
	$\xleftarrow{\quad \mathsf{cert}_{\mathcal{T}} \quad}$
check $\mathsf{cert}_{\mathcal{T}}$ with $\mathsf{pk}_{\mathsf{CVCA}}$	
extract $\mathsf{pk}_{\mathcal{T}}$ from $\mathsf{cert}_{\mathcal{T}}$	$(\mathsf{pk}_{\mathcal{T}}^{\mathsf{e}}, \mathsf{sk}_{\mathcal{T}}^{\mathsf{e}}) \leftarrow \mathsf{DH.KeyGen}(1^n)$
	$\xleftarrow{\quad \mathsf{pk}_{\mathcal{T}}^{\mathsf{e}} \quad}$
$r_1 \leftarrow \{0,1\}^n$	
	$\xrightarrow{\quad \mathrm{ID}_{\mathcal{C}}, r_1 \quad}$
	$\sigma_1 \leftarrow \mathsf{Sig}(\mathsf{sk}_{\mathcal{T}}, \mathrm{ID}_{\mathcal{C}} \parallel r_1 \parallel \mathsf{pk}_{\mathcal{T}}^{\mathsf{e}})$
	$\xleftarrow{\quad \sigma_1 \quad}$
if $\mathsf{Vf}(\mathsf{pk}_{\mathcal{T}}, \mathrm{ID}_{\mathcal{C}} \parallel r_1 \parallel \mathsf{pk}_{\mathcal{T}}^{\mathsf{e}}, \sigma_1) \neq 1$	
then abort	
store $\mathsf{pk}_{\mathcal{T}}$ for CA	
store $\mathsf{pk}_{\mathcal{T}}^{\mathsf{e}}$ for CA	

Fig. 1. Terminal Authentication in the classic EAC protocol.

Firstly, the terminal generates an ephemeral Diffie-Hellman key pair $(\mathsf{pk}_{\mathcal{T}}^{\mathsf{e}}, \mathsf{sk}_{\mathcal{T}}^{\mathsf{e}})$ and sends $\mathsf{pk}_{\mathcal{T}}^{\mathsf{e}}$ to the chip. It also sends its certificate $\mathsf{cert}_{\mathcal{T}}$, which consists of the Document Verifier certificate and the validation of its public key $\mathsf{pk}_{\mathcal{T}}$ by the Document Verifier. Subsequently, the chip verifies the certificate and the terminal's public key $\mathsf{pk}_{\mathcal{T}}$.

To generate the challenge, the chip chooses uniformly at random a nonce r_1 and sends it to the terminal. In addition, it sends a pre-agreed value $\mathrm{ID}_{\mathcal{C}}$. If

PACE is used, ID_C is a suitable hash of the chip's public key from the PACE key agreement; this serves to bind EAC with the previous PACE execution. If BAC is used, it is the document number read from the MRZ.

Finally, the terminal proves possession of the secret key sk_T by generating a signature over r_1, ID_C and its ephemeral public key. The chip concludes the TA if it can successfully verify the signature using pk_T.

Chip Authentication. In CA (shown in Fig. 2), the chip C authenticates itself to the terminal T with its static DH public key pair (sk_C, pk_C) that is validated by the Document Signer. At the outset, the chip sends the terminal its Document Signer certificate, its SO_D and its static public key pk_C, all of which we will call $cert_C$ in Fig. 2.[1] Afterwards, the terminal sends the ephemeral public Diffie-Hellman key pk_T^e generated during the TA. As the chip already received pk_T^e during TA, one might wonder whether this message could be eliminated. Unfortunately, this is not possible due to the need to maintain compatibility with EAC version 1 where the TA is optional.

Chip Authentication	
Chip C	**Terminal** T
static DH key pair (sk_C, pk_C)	CSCA root certificate $cert_{CSCA}$
certificate $cert_C$ for pk_C	ephemeral key pair (pk_T^e, sk_T^e)
$r_2 \leftarrow \{0,1\}^n$	
$\xrightarrow{\quad cert_C, cert_{DS} \quad}$	
	check $cert_C$ with $cert_{CSCA}$
	extract pk_C from $cert_C$
$\xleftarrow{\quad pk_T^e \quad}$	
verify that pk_T^e matches pk_T^e from TA	$k = DH(sk_T^e, pk_C)$
$k = DH(sk_C, pk_T^e)$	
$k_{MAC} = KDF_{MAC}(k, r_2)$	
$k_{ENC} = KDF_{ENC}(k, r_2)$	
$t = MAC(k_{MAC}, pk_T^e)$	
$\xrightarrow{\quad r_2, t \quad}$	
	$k_{MAC} = KDF_{MAC}(k, r_2)$
	$k_{ENC} = KDF_{ENC}(k, r_2)$
	if $t \neq MAC(k_{MAC}, pk_T^e)$
	then abort
return k_{ENC}	**return** k_{ENC}

Fig. 2. Chip Authentication in the original EAC protocol.

---

[1] This is usually performed during Passive Authentication but to simplify the presentation, we show it as part of the CA.

To avoid non-repudiation—which is undesirable from a privacy standpoint— $\mathcal{C}$ does not produce a signature to authenticate itself. Instead, chip and terminal establish a shared key k via a DH key exchange using the chip's long-term DH key $pk_\mathcal{C}$ and the terminal's ephemeral DH key $pk_\mathcal{T}^e$. Afterwards, the chip generates a nonce r_2 uniformly at random and derives keys k_{MAC}, k_{ENC} from the shared key k and r_2. Finally, $\mathcal{C}$ sends r_2 and a Message Authentication Code (MAC) t over $pk_\mathcal{T}^e$ under the key k_{MAC} to $\mathcal{T}$. If t matches the MAC computed by $\mathcal{T}$, the Chip Authentication concludes successfully. k_{ENC} can be used to encrypt any further communication between terminal and chip after the completion of EAC.

Security Properties. The main goals of EAC are the authentication of chip and terminal to each other and the establishment of a shared secret key between chip and terminal. Dagdelen and Fischlin [22] have proven authenticated key-exchange (AKE) security for EAC in the random oracle model (ROM). However, there are also other security properties that the EAC protocol is supposed to provide: Firstly, the protocol should provide *forward secrecy*, meaning that past session keys are protected from being recovered, even if the long-term secrets of chip or terminal are compromised. While the classic EAC version only provides this for the terminal's long-term secret [22], we will present versions of PQ-EAC providing forward secrecy for the long-term keys of both chip and terminal in Sect. 4.

Secondly, since the chip represents a travel document, it is desirable for the chip to have plausible deniability of participation in EAC, meaning we do **not** want *non-repudiation*. Since signatures usually provide non-repudiation, in EAC the authenticity of the chip is established through a key-agreement.

4   Quantum-Resistant EAC Protocol Versions

4.1   Overview

This section is concerned with our efforts towards a quantum-resistant version of EAC (called PQ-EAC). EAC is subject to many, sometimes conflicting constraints. For example, to reduce waiting times for access control, it would be beneficial to use round-reduced EAC. However, for privacy reasons, it may not be desirable that the chip sends information about its public key to an unauthenticated terminal. Similarly, forward secrecy helps to protect earlier messages in the case that the private key of the chip is compromised but increases the number of cryptographic operations. An additional consideration is that some versions of PQ-EAC might be more suitable than others for maintaining backwards-compatibility with EAC classic.

We distinguish between solutions with the terminal signing the data (SigPQEAC, see Sect. 4.2) and an alternative where the terminal uses a long-term KEM for authentication (KemPQEAC, see Sect. 4.3). The common approach in both cases is to replace the Diffie-Hellman key agreement step in the CA by having the terminal send a secret key protected under the chip's long-term KEM key $pk_\mathcal{C}$. The KEM itself is assumed to be *post-quantum secure*.

For each of the two types we can consider a forward-secure variant where the chip, in addition to the long-term KEM key pk_C, also generates an ephemeral KEM key pk_C^e during protocol execution. The terminal then encapsulates another key k^e under pk_C^e. The long-term key is then used for authentication, especially of the ephemeral part. Both parties derive the session key from either the encapsulated key k (in the non-forward-secure version) resp. together with the encapsulated key k^e (in the forward-secure version with the ephemeral KEM). Another option we discuss below is to combine the TA and CA phases and save on the round-trip time by joining some data into single transmissions.

We thus have eight protocol variants via possible combinations: with and without terminal signatures, with and without forward security, and potentially combining messages. The combined versions allow for further simplifications, e.g., by letting the terminal only create a single signature instead of two signatures. We present the two fundamentally different versions, one with signatures for terminal authentication and one with KEMs for authentication, and discuss the other four sub versions for either one within. We discuss further options for the combined versions afterwards. We leave it to the discretion of the implementing bodies to weigh advantages and disadvantages of the various versions.

Assumptions. For all protocols we assume that the following holds:

- Passive Authentication binds the chip's data groups with its key-pair (pk_C, sk_C).
- The communication partners have agreed on ID_C. If PACE is used, it is a suitable hash of the chip's public key from the previous PACE execution; if BAC is used, it is the document number read from the machine-readable zone (MRZ).
- The protocol is instantiated with a post-quantum or hybrid *IND-CCA-secure* key encapsulation mechanism, a post-quantum or hybrid *EUF-CMA-secure* signature scheme, a key derivation function KDF with output length n and a dual pseudorandom key combiner KComb. See Appendix A for the respective definitions and security experiments of the mentioned primitives.
- The security parameter n is of appropriate size and all keys have been generated according to n.

We note that while chip and terminal send the EAC protocol messages in an encrypted channel that was established through BAC or PACE, PQ-EAC would still provide AKE security if all messages were sent in the open.

4.2 Authentication with Signatures

We start with the four variants in which the terminal uses a quantum-resistant signature scheme to authenticate. The protocol framework is given in Fig. 3 and describes the plain variant, as well as the forward-secure variant (with the optional ephemeral KEM steps written as []) and the combined version of TA and CA (with the dashed arrows indicating which protocol messages can be combined).

In the protocol we use all relevant exchanged data $(\mathsf{cert}_{\mathcal{T}}, \mathsf{cert}_{\mathcal{C}}, r_2, c, [\mathsf{pk}_{\mathcal{C}}^e, c^e])$ for authentication purposes, including the certificates and the nonce and ciphertexts sent by the terminal. Since these data coincide with the session identifier sid used in the security proof we conveniently write sid in the protocol, too. We note that the final value $\mathsf{k}_{\mathsf{CNF}}$ transmitted by the chip with the last protocol messagealso serves as an authentication tag for all values in sid $= (\mathsf{cert}_{\mathcal{T}}, \mathsf{cert}_{\mathcal{C}}, r_2, c, [\mathsf{pk}_{\mathcal{C}}^e, c^e])$. Instead of using a message authentication code we use a derived key under the KDF directly, inserting sid into the key derivation step instead, and taking advantage of the pseudorandomness of the KDF. This method has been suggested for example in [24] for key confirmation. In principle, one could also use $\mathsf{k}_{\mathsf{CNF}}$ in a message authentication code, applied to some public input.

Terminal Authentication. The terminal $\mathcal{T}$ initiates the TA protocol by sending the chip its certificate $\mathsf{cert}_{\mathcal{T}}$, which contains its public key $\mathsf{pk}_{\mathcal{T}}$, a signature over $\mathsf{pk}_{\mathcal{T}}$ and its Document Verifier certificate. The certificates can be validated by the chip with its CVCA certificate. If the verification of certificates was successful, the chip chooses a nonce r_1 uniformly at random and sends it to $\mathcal{T}$, along with $\mathsf{ID}_{\mathcal{C}}$. Subsequently, $\mathcal{T}$ signs r_1 and $\mathsf{ID}_{\mathcal{C}}$, and sends the signature to $\mathcal{C}$. The TA protocol completes successfully if the chip can verify the signature using $\mathsf{pk}_{\mathcal{T}}$. We note that for the authentication of the terminal only, the Terminal Authentication protocol may be run solely, without the subsequent Chip Authentication. The Chip Authentication requires the (valid) public key $\mathsf{pk}_{\mathcal{T}}$ obtained during Terminal Authentication.

Chip Authentication. While certificates are usually checked during Passive Authentication before EAC starts, here we move this part of the process into the CA to simplify the presentation. $\mathcal{C}$ sends its Document Signer certificate, its SO_D and its public key (all of which we will call $\mathsf{cert}_{\mathcal{C}}$) to $\mathcal{T}$. The terminal can then verify the certificate chain using the CSCA root certificate. In addition, $\mathcal{C}$ sends a n-bit number r_2, chosen uniformly at random.

In order to check that $\mathcal{C}$ is in possession of the secret key $\mathsf{sk}_{\mathcal{C}}$ pertaining to $\mathsf{pk}_{\mathcal{C}}$, the terminal uses $\mathsf{pk}_{\mathcal{C}}$ to encapsulate a shared key k in a ciphertext c. It then sends c to $\mathcal{C}$, along with a signature to prove integrity of the encapsulation. Next, $\mathcal{C}$ verifies the signature and decapsulates c to obtain k. k is then used along with the session id sid to derive a confirmation key $\mathsf{k}_{\mathsf{CNF}}$ and an encryption key $\mathsf{k}_{\mathsf{KEY}}$. The final value $\mathsf{k}_{\mathsf{CNF}}$ serves as an authentication tag for all values in sid.

Forward Secrecy. As is, the plain version of SigPQEAC provides forward secrecy for the case that only the terminal's long term keys are corrupted. However, an adversary would still be able to decrypt past communication after corrupting the chip. To achieve real forward secrecy, we propose several changes to the CA protocol, written as [ ].

In a nutshell, the chip generates an additional, ephemeral key-pair $(\mathsf{pk}_{\mathcal{C}}^e, \mathsf{sk}_{\mathcal{C}}^e)$ and sends the public key to $\mathcal{T}$. The terminal then uses $\mathsf{pk}_{\mathcal{C}}^e$ to encapsulate a second key k^e, and sends the encapsulation c^e back to $\mathcal{C}$, along with the encapsulation c of the first key and a signature over both encapsulations. Both keys, k and k^e, serve as input to derive k_{CNF} and k_{KEY}. This way, an attacker that compromises the chip after EAC and subsequent communication has terminated will not be able to recover the ephemeral key k^e of that session or other previous sessions, and therefore will not be able to generate the session key k_{KEY}.

One potential attack that is enabled by sending the ephemeral public key to $\mathcal{T}$, is that an active adversary could exchange pk_C^e by a different public key and bring himself in possession of k^e, which is half of the input required to generate k_{KEY}. However, since both keys k, k^e are combined using a dual pseudorandom key combiner, the adversary still only has negligible chance of guessing the correct session key.

Round-Reduced Combined Version. At the cost of sacrificing some privacy it is easy to improve efficiency of the protocol described above. In particular, we can combine two pairs of messages into one message each: Instead of exchanging a challenge and a signature during TA as well as during CA, the terminal can encapsulate a key, sign a concatenation of the session id sid and the encapsulation and send the signature and the encapsulation to the chip in one go. The resulting combined variant of PQ-EAC is shown with the dashed arrows indicating which protocol messages can be combined.

As shown in Sect. 5.1, saving two messages and the signature verification improves performance significantly. On the flip side, the combined version forces the chip to send its public key before the terminal has been authenticated. Even though the public key is usually considered public information, it is desirable to avoid sending it to unauthorized terminals to protect the MRTD holder's privacy as much as possible. This could be important in contexts where an execution of PACE does not already authorize the terminal to read data.

4.3 Authentication via Long-Term KEMs

Next we present in Fig. 4 the four variants in which the terminal avoids signatures, which are usually expensive, but uses a long-term key of a KEM to authenticate instead. To this end, the chip sends a key k_{TA} encapsulated under the terminal's long-term key. While the chip has to perform an additional key encapsulation to do so, this is less expensive than the signature verification it would have to perform normally. The key is used to derive a confirmation value k_{TCNF}, replacing the signature in terminal authentication, and a MAC key k_{TMAC} used instead of the second signature. A noteworthy feature of these versions is that now the certificate $cert_C$ can be sent encrypted in the CA step to hide the long-term identity of the card. The key k_{TENC} for this encryption is also generated in the TA phase with the help of the terminal's long-term KEM.

4.4 Instantiation with Hybrid Schemes

The push for quantum-resistant identity documents is subject to two opposed constraints: On the one hand, the demand to secure transactions from the threat posed by quantum computers and the long validity of MRTDs make it imperative

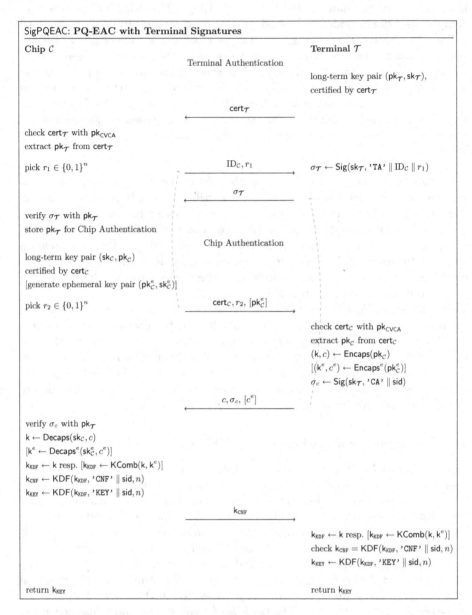

Fig. 3. PQ-EAC with terminal signatures, divided into TA and CA phase. Optional steps for achieving forward security are given in blue and brackets [ ]. In the combined version we can save a full round trip by combining protocol messages as indicated by the arrows. We note that each party sets the partner identity pid to be the distinguished name in the received certificate. The session identifier consists of all sent data, except for the authentication parts, $sid = (cert_{\mathcal{T}}, cert_{\mathcal{C}}, r_2, c, [pk_{\mathcal{C}}^e, c^e])$. (Color figure online)

KemPQEAC: PQ-EAC with Terminal Authentication through Long-Term KEM

Chip $\mathcal{C}$		Terminal $\mathcal{T}$
	Terminal Authentication	
		long-term key pair $(pk_{\mathcal{T}}, sk_{\mathcal{T}})$, certified by $cert_{\mathcal{T}}$
	$\xleftarrow{\quad cert_{\mathcal{T}} \quad}$	
check $cert_{\mathcal{T}}$ with pk_{CVCA}		
extract $pk_{\mathcal{T}}$ from $cert_{\mathcal{T}}$		
pick $r_1 \in \{0,1\}^n$		
$(k_{TA}, c_{TA}) \leftarrow \mathsf{Encaps}(pk_{\mathcal{T}})$	$\xrightarrow{\quad ID_{\mathcal{C}}, r_1, c_{TA} \quad}$	$k_{TA} \leftarrow \mathsf{Decaps}(sk_{\mathcal{T}}, c_{TA})$
$k_{TMAC} \leftarrow \mathsf{KDF}(k_{TA}, \text{'TMAC'} \| r_1)$		$k_{TMAC} \leftarrow \mathsf{KDF}(k_{TA}, \text{'TMAC'} \| r_1)$
$k_{TENC} \leftarrow \mathsf{KDF}(k_{TA}, \text{'TENC'} \| r_1)$		$k_{TENC} \leftarrow \mathsf{KDF}(k_{TA}, \text{'TENC'} \| r_1)$
$k_{TCNF} \leftarrow \mathsf{KDF}(k_{TA}, \text{'TCNF'} \| r_1)$		$k_{TCNF} \leftarrow \mathsf{KDF}(k_{TA}, \text{'TCNF'} \| r_1)$
	$\xleftarrow{\quad k_{TCNF} \quad}$	
verify k_{TCNF}		
store $pk_{\mathcal{T}}, k_{TENC}, k_{TMAC}$ for Chip Authentication		
	Chip Authentication	
long-term key pair $(sk_{\mathcal{C}}, pk_{\mathcal{C}})$		
certified by $cert_{\mathcal{C}}$		
[generate ephemeral key pair $(pk_{\mathcal{C}}^e, sk_{\mathcal{C}}^e)$]		
pick $r_2 \in \{0,1\}^n$		
$c_{CA} \leftarrow \mathsf{Enc}(k_{TENC}, cert_{\mathcal{C}} \| r_2 [\| pk_{\mathcal{C}}^e])$	$\xrightarrow{\quad c_{CA} \quad}$	$cert_{\mathcal{C}} \| r_2 [\| pk_{\mathcal{C}}^e] \leftarrow \mathsf{Dec}(k_{TENC}, c_{CA})$
		check $cert_{\mathcal{C}}$ with pk_{CVCA}
		extract $pk_{\mathcal{C}}$ from $cert_{\mathcal{C}}$
		$(k, c) \leftarrow \mathsf{Encaps}(pk_{\mathcal{C}})$
		$[(k^e, c^e) \leftarrow \mathsf{Encaps}^e(pk_{\mathcal{C}}^e)]$
		$\sigma_c \leftarrow \mathsf{MAC}(k_{TMAC}, \text{'CA'} \| sid)$
	$\xleftarrow{\quad c, \sigma_c, [c^e] \quad}$	
verify σ_c with k_{TMAC}		
$k \leftarrow \mathsf{Decaps}(sk_{\mathcal{C}}, c)$		
$[k^e \leftarrow \mathsf{Decaps}^e(sk_{\mathcal{C}}^e, c^e)]$		
$k_{KDF} \leftarrow k$ resp. $[k_{KDF} \leftarrow \mathsf{KComb}(k, k^e)]$		
$k_{CNF} \leftarrow \mathsf{KDF}(k_{KDF}, \text{'CNF'} \| sid, n)$		
$k_{KEY} \leftarrow \mathsf{KDF}(k_{KDF}, \text{'KEY'} \| sid, n)$	$\xrightarrow{\quad k_{CNF} \quad}$	
		$k_{KDF} \leftarrow k$ resp. $[k_{KDF} \leftarrow \mathsf{KComb}(k, k^e)]$
		check $k_{CNF} = \mathsf{KDF}(k_{KDF}, \text{'CNF'} \| sid, n)$
		$k_{KEY} \leftarrow \mathsf{KDF}(k_{KDF}, \text{'KEY'} \| sid, n)$
return k_{KEY}		return k_{KEY}

Fig. 4. PQ-EAC with terminal authentication through long-term KEMs, divided into TA and CA phase. Optional steps for achieving forward security are given in blue and brackets [ ]. In the combined version we can save a full round trip by combining protocol messages as indicated by the arrows. (Color figure online)

to take care of post-quantum security in the short term. On the other hand, one cannot be truly confident in the concrete security of post-quantum schemes yet: Parameter choices for post-quantum schemes might not yet be reliable [59] and evolving cryptanalysis could show them to be vulnerable even to classical attacks [20,42]. Hybrid schemes offer a way out: they combine two or more algorithms of the same kind such that the combined scheme provides security as long as one of the components provides security.

Of course, if the attacker is in possession of a quantum computer and the post-quantum scheme is flawed, security can only be restored by repair- or replacement of the post-quantum cryptographic scheme. However, in the case that the post-quantum scheme turns out to be insecure against classical attacks, but no quantum computer is available yet, hybrid schemes can thwart attacks by falling back on the security of the classical scheme. In Appendix B we present combiner schemes, which are a drop-in solution to achieve hybrid security. The PQ-EAC protocols defined above achieve hybrid security if they are instantiated with hybrid KEMs and signature schemes. Our implementation as described in Sect. 5 is using non-hybrid quantum-resistant schemes.

4.5 Security Proofs

A security proof for PQ-EAC in the real-or-random security model of Bellare and Rogaway [8] can be found in the full version of this paper. Below we provide a short sketch of the proof. The security properties to show are session matching and key secrecy. Session matching covers fundamental properties such as partnered sessions deriving the same key, pairwise uniqueness of partners, and correct identification of roles and partners. For all protocol versions (SigPQEAC and KemPQEAC, with or without forward secrecy, with or without round reduction) this property follows by protocol construction and the uniqueness of nonces. We note that all proofs take into account potential decryption errors of KEMs. Key secrecy ensures that only the intended partner shares the derived session key and that session keys are indistinguishable from random to the adversary, unless the adversary trivially knows the key. The proof for key secrecy for the variants of SigPQEAC is via game-hopping. Here, we only outline the main steps. We first exclude attacks in which a party accepts a different public key pk as identified in the issued certificate cert. By the unforgeability of the certificate scheme this cannot occur, except with negligible probability. But it follows that, if the chip accepts only the certified public key of the terminal, then the unforgeability of the terminal's signature scheme ensures that only the honest terminal is able to create the valid signature σ_c over the ciphertext c (and the ephemeral values pk_T^e and c^e in the forward-secure version). We can conclude that the encapsulated key k (resp. keys k and k^e) must have been created by an honest terminal, such that the IND-CCA security of the chip's long-term KEM guarantees that they are hidden from the adversary. The security of the key derivation function (together with the key combiner in the forward-secure version) ensure that the session key is indistinguishable from random for the adversary.

We note that in the analysis the final confirmation value sent by the chip is only required for the forward-secure case. Here the adversary may impersonate a chip and later learn the long-term secret key of the KEM. But the adversary would have to create a valid confirmation value *before* it later corrupts the chip's long-term secret. This once more is infeasible by the security of the chip's KEM.

The proof of the KEM-based variant KemPQEAC is very similar to the signature-based protocol. Only here we need to argue that only the honest terminal can create the valid MAC σ_c over the ciphertext(s). This can be shown via two extra steps in which we argue that only the terminal can decapsulate k_{TA} in terminal authentication (by the IND-CCA security of the terminal's long-term KEM) and that the derived keys from k_{TA} are random by the security of the key derivation function. The other steps are as in the proof of SigPQEAC.

We finally remark that our proofs show post-quantum security of the protocols. The proof steps consist of (straightline) reductions to the involved standard primitives like signature schemes, KEMs, or key derivation functions, and do not require idealized primitives such as random oracles. Hence, any successful quantum adversary against the key exchange protocol would thus yield a successful quantum adversary against the underlying primitive. Assuming that the primitives are all quantum-resistant, it follows that the overall protocol also withstands such attacks.

5 Implementation

To show the feasibility of PQ-EAC for border control systems and to evaluate the chip-side of the protocol proposals in resource-constrained environments, we implemented the combined version of SigPQEAC (without forward secrecy) on a chip similar to those deployed in ePassports and on a terminal of the type that is used for border control checks. The chip is integrated in a proof of concept post-quantum MRTD and runs an ePassport application compliant with ICAO standards. Our performance tests reveal that the post-quantum version of EAC is practical and only slightly slower than the classic version. We published the benchmarking tool that we used to measure the performance of SigPQEAC on a smart card[2]. Other components utilized for benchmarking such as the VISOCORE® terminal software, the ePassport application and our customized Dilithium and Kyber implementations are part of confidential proprietary software libraries and remain unpublished.

We designed the Application Protocol Data Unit (APDU) interface for reading files or initiating cryptographic operations on the chip to be compatible with the existing standards of ICAO, BSI, and ISO [17,31–33]. For this reason, our implementation uses more than the minimal number of messages possible. We proceed by stating the results of our runtime experiments with our implementation in 1sec:perf. Finally, we analyze the impact of data transmission rates on the performance of the protocol in Sect. 5.2. Since transmission speeds vary between platforms, and because incorrect placement of the MRTD can slow transmission

---

[2] https://github.com/frankmorgner/OpenSC-pqc-SSR2023.

rates significantly, this analysis will help to gauge the real-world performance of PQ-EAC more precisely.

5.1 Performance Evaluation

In our experimental setup we instantiated Combined PQ-EAC without forward secrecy with the post-quantum signature scheme Dilithium3 [41] and the post-quantum KEM Kyber1024 [14,54]. NIST's security level 3 (for the signature scheme) and 5 (for the KEM), respectively, were chosen to support the MRTD's long lifetime of typically ten years. AES256 and SHA256 were used as supporting cryptographic building blocks for the message authentication codes and key derivation functions. In our implementation we assume that the certificates are based on post-quantum signatures. For the sake of data minimization we stick to a single post-quantum signature and public key per certificate.

Chip Specification. A proof of concept post-quantum MRTD was implemented on a contactless security controller from Infineon Technologies based on an ARM SC300 architecture. The security controller comes with significantly increased RAM-size of 96 kBytes, which is more than double the amount of RAM compared to previous security controller chips in this application domain, to support memory-intensive lattice-based schemes such as Kyber and Dilithium.

Chip Software. We implemented Kyber and Dilithium in C according to specifications given in the NIST PQC competition round 3 submissions [41,54], taking into account the requirements posed by the hardware architecture of our security controller. In particular, memory requirements had to be carefully managed: Our implementation utilizes almost the full RAM capacity of 96 kBytes. However, not all memory optimization opportunities have been exploited by us: By assigning overlapping memory segments to public-key and symmetric cryptographic operations, it would be possible to reduce memory usage to ca. 60 kBytes. Other than memory optimizations, our versions stay close to the mostly unoptimized reference implementation. Since the focus of our work has been the creation of a functional proof of concept for PQ-EAC, most cryptographic building blocks have not been optimized for performance or hardened against side channel analysis (SCA) and fault attacks (FA). To improve the security of Kyber and Dilithium against SCA and FA the strategies described in Oder et al. [48], Saarinen [52], Ravi et al. [51], Bache et al. [6] or Heinz et al. [27] could be used.

Besides a hardware-based random number generator, no acceleration has been used in the project. The chip's ePassport application is running as native code on the hardware without an intermediate operating system. All state management (which needs to carefully consider hardware limitations around the volatile and non-volatile memory) is done in that application. For communication with the terminal we utilize a proprietary ISO/IEC 14443 communication library.

Terminal Implementation. For demonstration purposes, we modified terminal hard- and software of the type that is used by German border control with post-quantum algorithms. Specifically, we used a Bundesdruckerei VISOTEC® Expert 800[3] running the verification software VISOTEC® Inspect, which was extended by us with the same post-quantum schemes as the MRTD.

Benchmarking. We ran 1000 experiment executions with the test chip to benchmark the performance of the combined version of SigPQEAC. We measured the time it took to send and receive the card commands via the PC/SC API on the terminal's operating system. Thus, this duration includes the terminal's overhead of processing the data with the smart card reader's driver, its firmware, transceiving data via ISO 14443, and finally the processing by the test chip. For PQ-EAC, we reliably measured a total runtime of 1.28 s. The standard deviation for a single command-response pair was between 0.0001 and 0.0003 ms.

In a second experiment we used the same setup with a smart card emulation device (Hitex Tanto3 FPGA) instead of the MRTD. This device emulates all electrical properties of the MRTD's chip and allows control and inspection of the card's internal workflow. This way we were able to determine or manually control the connection parameters between reader and card. Specifically, we set the data rate to 848 kBit/s and controlled the frame size for sending 4089 bits of payload data. The emulated chip was constantly run with 100 MHz and didn't suffer any throttling due to, for example, bad coupling with the smart card reader (a common problem in practice).

The total time for performing all PQ-EAC operations on the emulated chip and the data transfer is 1.28 s. In Fig. 5 we can see that the execution time on the chip is heavily dominated by the cryptographic operations during signature validation and KEM decapsulation. As such, Kyber decapsulation takes 596 ms, Dilithium verification takes 86 ms, but choosing a nonce and reading cert$_C$ only take 0.01 ms each.

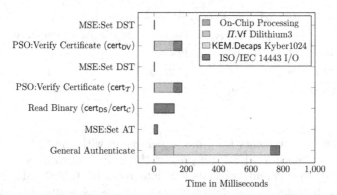

Fig. 5. Measurements of combined SigPQEAC with 848 kBit/s via ISO/IEC 14443 using an emulated chip.

---

[3] https://www.bundesdruckerei-gmbh.de/en/solutions/visocore.

The rest of the transaction time is caused by transferring the data back and forth between terminal and card. Again, most of this can be attributed to the large ciphertexts, public keys, and signatures of Dilithium and Kyber. For example, $cert_T$ contains a Dilithium signature (2701 bytes) and the terminal's Dilithium public key (1472 bytes) which add up to 97.6% of the overall size of the certificate. Transferring this data with a data rate R_b of 848 kBit/s takes roughly 50 ms including the ISO/IEC 14443 overhead.

Our analysis shows that the processing time on the chip is almost exclusively caused by the post-quantum algorithms. Further, we observe that in our proof of concept implementation each of encapsulation, decapsulation and key generation take around five times longer than verifying a signature. However, the literature suggests that a better optimized implementation on similar hardware speeds up the Kyber1024 encapsulation by an order of magnitude to half the execution time of the signature verification of Dilithium3 [34]. Such an improvement would most likely allow an overall execution time for PQ-EAC of one second or below.

5.2   Impact of the Data Transfer Rate

We observed that the post-quantum algorithms are causing most of the data that needs to be transceived between MRTD and chip. Using our experimental data we can confirm that the (extended) ISO/IEC 14443 I-Block framing is causing an overhead of roughly 26% of the transmitted protocol data[4]. Also, we observe that the constant overhead for encoding the data into command and response APDUs varies between 9 and 35 bytes. This observation allows to approximate the runtime of other variants of PQ-EAC in relation to data transfer rates.

Table 1. Estimation for the protocol variants for typical transmission rates. For details on PQ-EAC Combined at 848 kbit/s see Fig. 5.

Data Rate (R_b)	Estimated Runtime (in milliseconds)		
	SigPQEAC	Combined SigPQEAC	KemPQEAC
848 kbit/s	1406	1280	1569
424 kbit/s	1718	1530	1754
106 kbit/s	3586	3204	2865

Using the measurements from our experiments with the test chip and the estimated communication load, we present the estimated runtime for the protocols relative to different transmission data rates in Table 1. Mostly due to the fact that it transfers less data and uses one less signature verification, the combined version of SigPQEAC achieves the shortest runtime. The advantage of

---

[4] The ISO/IEC 14443 overhead is between 23% for very big APDUs and 72% for very small APDUs. Since most of the EAC protocols' runtime is spent on big commands, we stick to an approximation near that of bigger commands.

KemPQEAC under low data rates is due to the fact that no signatures, which are typically larger than ciphertexts or keys, need to be sent. The slow key encapsulation of the KEM in our proof-of-concept implementation, however, causes it to be the slowest protocol for higher data transfer rates. Given that benchmarks [34] show that KEM encapsulation is usually much faster than signature verification, runtime of PQ-EAC and especially of KemPQEAC should significantly benefit from further optimizations of the implementation.

Comparison with Classical EAC. An execution of classical EAC on MRTDs and terminals commonly in use today typically takes around 1.5 to 2 s. Noting that most deployed electronic passports and verification terminals are already supporting 848 kbit/s data rate, our proof-of-concept implementation for PQ-EAC with well below 2 s execution time supports the conclusion that eMRTDs can be migrated to quantum-resistant algorithms. Considering performance gains from hardware acceleration and general implementation improvements we assume that instantiations with hybrid schemes are also feasible.

6   Conclusions

In the preceding sections we have presented and implemented quantum-resistant versions of the EAC protocol. Our results show that post-quantum travel documents are practical. Moreover, our implementation of PQ-EAC can still be optimized. It can also easily be instantiated with alternative KEMs and signature schemes. Below, we document a few opportunities for future research.

Post-quantum PKI and PACE. In our protocols we assumed that the authenticity of the chip and terminal are secured by quantum-resistant certificates: A quantum-resistant PKI that will provide such certificates is a challenge to be addressed by future research. The transition towards a post-quantum PKI could potentially be conducted by means of intelligent composed algorithms as described in Byszio et al. [19]. Similarly, we assumed that the initial connection between chip and terminal is secured via PACE. As current versions of PACE are based on classical assumptions, there is need for a quantum-resistant construction that can secure the transmission of less sensitive data groups.

Cryptographic Agility. Another problem we leave for future research is cryptographic agility in MRTDs. In particular it is desirable to have an update mechanism that provides an authenticated update for MRTDs in the case that the deployed quantum-resistant algorithms need to be replaced. This would be the case when flaws in the used algorithms have been discovered. The challenge here is that we have a chicken-egg situation: Ultimately the authentication mechanism of the update would have to inspire more confidence than the post-quantum schemes we have instantiated EAC with. A potential candidate for such an authentication mechanism are hash-based signatures [28,43]: While they are less practical than lattice-based constructions, their security rests on weaker assumptions, namely on the one-wayness of certain hash functions.

Acknowledgements. This work was funded through the project PoQuID (WIPANO project 03TNK011A-C). WIPANO projects are financed by the German Federal Ministry for Economic Affairs and Energy and managed by Forschungszentrum Jülich. The authors thank all PoQuID project partners for the discussions and support.

A   Security Definitions

In this section we introduce the underlying primitives and their security notions for building the key exchange protocols as defined in, for example, [35].

A.1   Key Encapsulation

Definition 1 (Key Encapsulation Mechanism). *A key encapsulation mechanism* KEM = (KeyGen, Encaps, Decaps) *consists of three efficient algorithms where:*

Key Generation: *Algorithm* KeyGen *on input the security parameter 1^n (in unary) outputs a key pair,* (sk, pk) ← KeyGen(1^n). *We assume that 1^n is recoverable from either key.*

Encapsulation: *The encapsulation algorithm takes as input a public key* pk *and returns a ciphertext and a key,* (c, k) ← Encaps(pk). *We assume usually that the key is of bit length n.*

Decapsulation: *The decapsulation algorithm takes as input a secret key* sk *and a ciphertext c, and returns a key or an error symbol,* k ← Decaps(sk, c), *where* k *is either of size n or equals $\perp$. Usually decapsulation is deterministic.*

We require that decapsulation merely has a negligible error. That is, we denote by $\Pr\left[\boldsymbol{Exp}_{\mathsf{KEM}}^{decErr}(n) = 1\right]$ *the probability of an encryption error for* KEM = (KeyGen, Encaps, Decaps), *where* Decaps(sk, c) $\neq$ k *for* (sk, pk) ← KeyGen(n) *and* (c, k) ← Encaps(pk).

We next define CPA- and CCA-security for key encapsulation mechanism in one go:

Definition 2 (IND-CPA and IND-CCA security of KEM). *For a key encapsulation mechanism* KEM = (KeyGen, Encaps, Decaps) *and adversary $\mathcal{A}$ define experiment* $\boldsymbol{Exp}_{\mathsf{KEM},\mathcal{A}}^{IND\text{-}att}(n)$ *as in Fig. 6. We say that* KEM *is IND-att secure (for att = CPA or CCA) if for any efficient adversary $\mathcal{A}$ we have that*

$$\boldsymbol{Adv}_{\mathsf{KEM},\mathcal{A}}^{IND\text{-}att}(n) := \Pr\left[\boldsymbol{Exp}_{\mathsf{KEM},\mathcal{A}}^{IND\text{-}att}(n) = 1\right] - \frac{1}{2}$$

is negligible.

For our key exchange protocol KemPQEAC we also use a symmetric encryption scheme (for keys k from $\{0, 1\}^n$) where c ← Enc(k, m) creates a ciphertext, and m ← Dec(k, c) always recovers the encrypted message m. In the protocol this encryption step provides extra privacy for the chip by encrypting its identity. We do not discuss this privacy property formally here and thus neither the security notions for the encryption scheme.

Experiment $\mathbf{Exp}_{\mathsf{KEM},\mathcal{A}}^{\text{IND-att}}(n)$	Oracle $\mathcal{O}_{\mathsf{Decaps}}(c)$
1 : $(\mathsf{sk},\mathsf{pk}) \leftarrow \mathsf{KeyGen}(1^n)$	1 : if $c = c^*$ or att=CPA then
2 : $b \leftarrow \{0,1\}$	2 : return $\perp$
3 : $(k_0^*, c^*) \leftarrow \mathsf{Encaps}(\mathsf{pk})$	3 : else
4 : $k_1^* \leftarrow \{0,1\}^{|k_0^*|}$	4 : return $\mathsf{Decaps}(\mathsf{sk}, c)$
5 : $b^* \leftarrow \mathcal{A}^{\mathcal{O}_{\mathsf{Decaps}}(\cdot)}(\mathsf{pk}, k_b^*, c^*)$	
6 : return $[b = b^*]$	

Fig. 6. IND-CPA/IND-CCA security experiment for key encapsulation mechanism

A.2 Message Authentication, Signature Schemes, and Certificate Schemes

We define message authentication schemes, signature schemes, and certificate schemes with a single definition. All schemes serve the purpose of authenticating data. The only difference between the private-key message authentication codes (MACs) and the public-key signature and certificate schemes lies in the verification key vk: MACs use the key vk = sk to verify authenticity, whereas signatures and certificates are verified against the public key vk = pk. In the descriptions and security games we thus set vk accordingly, and the public key for MACs to be empty and for signatures and certificates equal to vk. We call the primitive abstractly an authentication scheme:

Definition 3 (Authenticaton Scheme). *An authentication scheme* $\mathcal{AS} =$ (AKGen, AAuth, AVf) *consists of three efficient algorithms such that:*

Key Generation: *Algorithm* AKGen *on input* 1^n *returns a key triple* (sk, pk, vk) $\leftarrow$ SKGen(1^n). *We assume that n is recoverable from either key.*
Authentication: *On input the secret key* sk *and a message* $m \in \{0,1\}^*$, *the authentication algorithm outputs an authenticator,* $\sigma \leftarrow$ AAuth(sk, m).
Verification: *On input a verification key* vk, *a message* m, *an authenticator* σ, *the verification algorithm outputs a decision bit,* $d \leftarrow$ AVf(vk, m, σ). *Usually,* AVf *is deterministic.*

We require that verification always succeeds. That is, it never happens that AVf(sk, m, σ) $= 0$ *for any* (sk, pk, vk) $\leftarrow$ SKGen(1^n), *any* $m \in \{0,1\}^*$, *and any* $\sigma \leftarrow$ AAuth(sk, m).

Unlike key encapsulation we define authentication schemes with perfect correctness since all known schemes in practice achieve this.

Definition 4 (EUF-CMA of Authentication Schemes). *For an authentication scheme* $\mathcal{AS} =$ (AKGen, AAuth, AVf) *and adversary* $\mathcal{A}$ *define experiment* $\mathbf{Exp}_{\mathcal{AS},\mathcal{A}}^{EUF\text{-}CMA}(n)$ *as in Fig. 7. We say that* $\mathcal{AS}$ *is EUF-CMA if for any efficient adversary* $\mathcal{A}$ *we have that* $\Pr\left[\mathbf{Exp}_{\mathcal{AS},\mathcal{A}}^{EUF\text{-}CMA}(n) = 1\right]$ *is negligible.*

Experiment $\mathbf{Exp}^{\text{EUF-CMA}}_{AS,\mathcal{A}}(n)$	Oracle $\mathcal{O}_{\text{AAuth}}(\text{sk}, m)$
1 : $(\text{sk}, \text{pk}, \text{vk}) \leftarrow \text{AKGen}(1^n)$	1 : $\mathcal{Q} \leftarrow \mathcal{Q} \cup \{m\}$
2 : $\mathcal{Q} \leftarrow \emptyset$	2 : $\sigma \leftarrow \text{AAuth}(\text{sk}, m)$
3 : $(m^*, \sigma^*) \leftarrow \mathcal{A}^{\mathcal{O}_{\text{AAuth}}(\text{sk}, \cdot)}(\text{pk})$	3 : **return** σ
4 : **return** $[\text{SVf}(\text{vk}, m^*, \sigma^*) \text{ and } m^* \notin \mathcal{Q}]$	

Fig. 7. EUF-CMA security experiment for authentication schemes

A signature scheme $\mathcal{S} = (\text{SKGen}, \text{Sig}, \text{SVf})$ is an authenticator scheme where $(\text{sk}, \text{pk}, \text{vk}) \leftarrow \text{AKGen}(1^n)$ for $(\text{sk}, \text{pk}) \leftarrow \text{SKGen}(1^n)$ and $\text{vk} \leftarrow \text{pk}$. A certificate scheme $\mathcal{C} = (\text{CKGen}, \text{CSign}, \text{CVf})$ is an authenticator scheme where $(\text{sk}, \text{pk}, \text{vk}) \leftarrow \text{AKGen}(1^n)$ for $(\text{sk}, \text{pk}) \leftarrow \text{CKGen}(1^n)$ and $\text{vk} \leftarrow \text{pk}$. A message authentication code $\mathcal{M} = (\text{MKGen}, \text{MAC}, \text{MVf})$ is an authenticator scheme where $(\text{sk}, \text{pk}, \text{vk}) \leftarrow \text{AKGen}(1^n)$ for $\text{sk} \leftarrow \text{MKGen}(1^n)$ and $\text{vk} \leftarrow \text{sk}$ and $\text{pk} \leftarrow \bot$. EUF-CMA security now follows from the general definition. We usually assume that the key generation algorithm simply generates a uniformly distributed key of n bits.

A.3 Key Derivation Functions

We assume that key derivation functions act as pseudorandom functions, as long as the keying material contains enough (min-)entropy. The latter is captured by considering arbitrary distributions $\mathcal{D}$ which take the seucurity parameter 1^n as input and output IKM with min-entropy $H_\infty(\text{IKM}) \geq n$. We call such distributions *non-trivial*. We follow here the presentation of Krawczyk [38].

Definition 5 (Key Derivation Function). *A key derivation function* KDF *takes as input keying material* IKM, *context information* ctxt, *and an integer* ℓ, *and outputs a string of length* ℓ. *We assume that the length of* IKM *determines the security parameter* n.

Security now requires that the key derivation function's output for IKM looks random, even if the adversary sees actual derived keys at other inputs (ctxt, ℓ):

Definition 6 (Pseudorandomness of Key Derivation Function). *For a key derivation function* KDF, *adversary* $\mathcal{A}$, *and distribution* $\mathcal{D}$ *define experiment* $\mathbf{Exp}^{PRF}_{\text{KDF},\mathcal{A},\mathcal{D}}(n)$ *as in Fig. 8. We say that* KDF *is pseudorandom if for any efficient adversary* $\mathcal{A}$ *and any non-trivial distribution (with min-entropy n), we have that*

$$\mathbf{Adv}^{PRF}_{\text{KDF},\mathcal{A},\mathcal{D}}(n) := \Pr\left[\mathbf{Exp}^{PRF}_{\text{KDF},\mathcal{A},\mathcal{D}}(n) = 1\right] - \frac{1}{2}$$

is negligible.

Experiment $\mathbf{Exp}^{PRF}_{KDF, \mathcal{A}, \mathcal{D}}(n)$

1: $\quad$ IKM $\leftarrow \mathcal{D}(1^n)$

2: $\quad \mathcal{Q} \leftarrow \emptyset$

3: $\quad b \leftarrow \{0,1\}$

4: $\quad b^* \leftarrow \mathcal{A}^{\mathcal{O}_{KDF}(IKM,\cdot,\cdot), \mathcal{O}_b(IKM,\cdot,\cdot)}(1^n)$

5: $\quad$ **return** $[b = b^*]$

Oracle $\mathcal{O}_{KDF}(IKM, ctxt, \ell)$

1: $\quad$ **if** $(ctxt, \ell) \in \mathcal{Q}$ **then**

2: $\quad\quad$ **return** $\bot$

3: $\quad \mathcal{Q} \leftarrow \mathcal{Q} \cup \{(ctxt, \ell)\}$

4: $\quad$ k $\leftarrow$ KDF(IKM, ctxt, ℓ)

5: $\quad$ **return** k

Oracle $\mathcal{O}_b(IKM, ctxt, \ell)$

1: $\quad$ **if** $(ctxt, \ell) \in \mathcal{Q}$ **then**

2: $\quad\quad$ **return** $\bot$

3: $\quad \mathcal{Q} \leftarrow \mathcal{Q} \cup \{(ctxt, \ell)\}$

4: $\quad$ $k_0 \leftarrow$ KDF(IKM, ctxt, ℓ)

5: $\quad$ $k_1 \leftarrow \{0,1\}^\ell$

6: $\quad$ **return** k_b

Fig. 8. Pseudorandomness experiment for Key Derivation Functions

A.4   Key Combiners

For the forward-secure version of the PQEAC protocols we use a static KEM and an ephemeral KEM to share keys k and k^e. In this case the parties need to derive a single key from the two keys. This has been discussed more broadly in the context of KEM combiners in [25] and for quantum adversaries in [12], but since we have already embedded the KEM mechanism in the key exchange protocol, we focus here on the pure key combining part. We note that we cannot immediately rely on the KEM combiner in [12], since it assumes faithfully created but potentially weak encapsulations, whereas in our setting the adversary may choose the encapsulations maliciously. While Bindel et al. [12] argue that such genuine encapsulations are sufficient to build hybrid authenticated key exchange protocols via Krawczyk's SIGMA compiler [37], the EAC protocol does not perfectly comply to the SIGMA standard.

Definition 7 (Key Combiner). *A key combiner* KComb *takes as input keying material* IKM_0, IKM_1, *both of length* n, *and outputs a string of length* n.

Security demands that KComb is a dual pseudorandom function, meaning that both KComb($IKM_0, \cdot$) and KComb($\cdot, IKM_1$) are pseudorandom functions. It follows that we can reasonably assume that HKDF resp. HMAC [7,38] or the TLS-based nested key derivation function in [53] is an appropriate instantiation for a key combiner.

Definition 8 (Dual Pseudorandomness of Key Combiner). *For a key combiner* KComb *and adversary* $\mathcal{A}$ *define experiment* $\mathbf{Exp}^{dPRF-\beta}_{KComb, \mathcal{A}}(n)$ *as in Fig. 9.*

We say that KComb is (dual) pseudorandom if for any efficient adversary $\mathcal{A}$ we have that

$$\boldsymbol{Adv}^{dPRF}_{\mathsf{KComb},\mathcal{A}}(n) := \max_{\beta \in \{0,1\}} \left\{ \Pr\left[\boldsymbol{Exp}^{dPRF-\beta}_{\mathsf{KComb},\mathcal{A}}(n) = 1\right] - \frac{1}{2} \right\}$$

is negligible.

Experiment $\mathbf{Exp}^{\mathrm{dPRF}-\beta}_{\mathsf{KComb},\mathcal{A}}(n)$	Oracle $\mathcal{O}_{b,\beta}(\mathsf{IKM}_0, \mathsf{IKM}_1, x)$
1 : $\mathsf{IKM}_0, \mathsf{IKM}_1 \leftarrow \{0,1\}^n$	1 : if $x \in \mathcal{Q}$ then return $\perp$
2 : $b \leftarrow \{0,1\}$	2 : $\mathcal{Q} \leftarrow \mathcal{Q} \cup \{x\}$
3 : $\mathcal{Q} \leftarrow \emptyset$	3 : if $\beta = 0$ then
4 : $b^* \leftarrow \mathcal{A}^{\mathcal{O}_{b,\beta}(\mathsf{IKM}_0,\mathsf{IKM}_1,\cdot)}(1^n)$	4 : $\mathsf{k}_0 \leftarrow \mathsf{KComb}(\mathsf{IKM}_0, x)$
5 : return $[b = b^*]$	5 : else
	6 : $\mathsf{k}_0 \leftarrow \mathsf{KComb}(x, \mathsf{IKM}_1)$
	7 : $\mathsf{k}_1 \leftarrow \{0,1\}^{|\mathsf{k}_0|}$
	8 : return k_b

Fig. 9. Dual pseudorandomness experiment for Key Combiners

B Hybrid Schemes

KEM Combiner. To achieve hybrid security, we make use of combiner schemes as proposed by Bindel et al. [12]. In the following, let $\mathsf{KEM}_1 = (\mathsf{KeyGen}_1, \mathsf{Encaps}_1, \mathsf{Decaps}_1)$ and $\mathsf{KEM}_2 = (\mathsf{KeyGen}_2, \mathsf{Encaps}_2, \mathsf{Decaps}_2)$ be two KEMs and let $\mathcal{C}[\mathsf{KEM}_1, \mathsf{KEM}_2] = (\mathsf{KeyGen}_\mathcal{C}, \mathsf{Encaps}_\mathcal{C}, \mathsf{Decaps}_\mathcal{C})$ be the hybrid KEM constructed by combiner mechanism $\mathcal{C}$ from KEM_1 and KEM_2. For all combiners, the key generation of the combined scheme will simply be the concatenation of the two scheme's keys as shown in Fig. 10.

A combiner is called **robust** if it combines two or more algorithms of the same kind such that the combined scheme provides security as long as one of the components provides security.

The XOR-Combiner. A naive method to combine two KEMs would be to take the XOR of their keys $k = k_1 \oplus k_2$ as shown in Fig. 11. As noticed by Giacon et al. [25] this results in a KEM that is IND-CPA, but not IND-CCA secure. Assuming that the challenger combines two IND-CCA secure KEMs by taking the XOR of their keys as described, then an adversary in the IND-CCA experiment can proceed as follows: Given a challenge (c_1^*, c_2^*), the adversary makes two decapsulation requests for (c_1^*, c_2) and (c_1, c_2^*) with randomly chosen ciphertexts $c_1 = c_2$. This information then allows the adversary to compute the decapsulation of the challenge ciphertext by taking the xor: $k = k_1^* \oplus k_2 \oplus k_1 \oplus k_2^* = k_1^* \oplus k_2^*$.

$$\underline{\mathcal{C}[\Sigma_1, \Sigma_2].\mathsf{KeyGen}(1^n)}$$

1 : $(\mathsf{pk}_1, \mathsf{sk}_1) \leftarrow \Sigma_1.\mathsf{KeyGen}(1^m)$

2 : $(\mathsf{pk}_2, \mathsf{sk}_2) \leftarrow \Sigma_2.\mathsf{KeyGen}(1^m)$

3 : $\mathsf{pk} = (\mathsf{pk}_1, \mathsf{pk}_2)$

4 : $\mathsf{sk} = (\mathsf{sk}_1, \mathsf{sk}_2)$

5 : **return** $(\mathsf{pk}, \mathsf{sk})$

Fig. 10. Key generation function $\mathcal{C}[\Sigma_1, \Sigma_2].\mathsf{KeyGen}(1^n)$. The security parameter m needs to be derived from n depending on the requirements of the combiner.

$\mathsf{Encaps}_{\mathrm{xor}}(\mathsf{pk}_1, \mathsf{pk}_2)$	$\mathsf{Decaps}_{\mathrm{xor}}((\mathsf{sk}_1, \mathsf{sk}_2), (c_1, c_2))$
1 : $(c_1, k_1) \leftarrow \mathsf{KEM}_1.\mathsf{Encaps}(\mathsf{pk}_1)$	1 : $k_1 \leftarrow \mathsf{KEM}_1.\mathsf{Decaps}(\mathsf{sk}_1, c_1)$
2 : $(c_2, k_2) \leftarrow \mathsf{KEM}_2.\mathsf{Encaps}(\mathsf{pk}_2)$	2 : $k_2 \leftarrow \mathsf{KEM}_2.\mathsf{Decaps}(\mathsf{sk}_2, c_2)$
3 : $k \leftarrow k_1 \oplus k_2$	3 : $k \leftarrow k_1 \oplus k_2$
4 : $c \leftarrow (c_1, c_2)$	4 : **return** k
5 : **return** (c, k)	

Fig. 11. KEM XOR[$\mathsf{KEM}_1, \mathsf{KEM}_2$] constructed by the naive XOR combiner (not IND-CCA secure).

The XOR-then-MAC Combiner. A better way to combine two KEMs is the XOR-then-MAC combiner as specified in Fig. 12. This approach prevents the mix-and-match attack. The construction requires a strongly robust MAC combiner $\mathcal{C}[\mathsf{MAC}_1, \mathsf{MAC}_2]$ that provides one-time unforgeability even if one of the keys are chosen adversarially. Such a MAC combiner can be instantiated based on the Carter-Wegman paradigm [58] using universal hash functions. The XOR-then-MAC combiner is shown by Bindel et al. [12] to be **robust**. One drawback of this construction is that the resulting key-length is only half of that of the underlying KEMs.

Signature Combiner. As with KEMs there are also combiners that provide hybrid security for signature schemes. One might be tempted to avoid the use of signature combiners and instead deploy hash-based signature schemes, which are well-known to provide post-quantum security based on very weak assumptions. Such kinds of schemes have been around since the 1980s, which means that the usual concerns over the maturity of post-quantum cryptography do not apply here. However, even when using hash-based signatures it might be wise to combine them with a classical scheme as a fallback. This is because hash-based signatures require careful state management that is often difficult to assure.

$\text{Encaps}_{\text{XtM}}(\text{pk}_1, \text{pk}_2)$

1 : $(c_1, k_{\text{KEM}_1} \| k_{\text{MAC}_1}) \leftarrow \text{KEM}_1.\text{Encaps}(\text{pk}_1)$

2 : $(c_2, k_{\text{KEM}_2} \| k_{\text{MAC}_2}) \leftarrow \text{KEM}_2.\text{Encaps}(\text{pk}_2)$

3 : $k_{\text{KEM}} \leftarrow k_{\text{KEM}_1} \oplus k_{\text{KEM}_2}$

4 : $k_{\text{MAC}} \leftarrow \mathcal{C}[\text{MAC}_1, \text{MAC}_2](k_{\text{MAC}_1}, k_{\text{MAC}_2})$

5 : $c \leftarrow (c_1, c_2)$

6 : $\tau \leftarrow \text{MAC}(k_{MAC}, c)$

7 : $\textbf{return } ((c, \tau), k_{\text{KEM}})$

$\text{Decaps}_{\text{XtM}}((\text{sk}_1, \text{sk}_2), (c_1, c_2), \tau)$

1 : $k'_{\text{KEM}_1} \| k'_{\text{MAC}_1} \leftarrow \text{KEM}_1.\text{Decaps}(\text{sk}_1, c_1)$

2 : $k'_{\text{KEM}_2} \| k'_{\text{MAC}_2} \leftarrow \text{KEM}_2.\text{Decaps}(\text{sk}_2, c_2)$

3 : $k'_{\text{KEM}} \leftarrow k'_{\text{KEM}_1} \oplus k'_{\text{KEM}_2}$

4 : $k'_{\text{MAC}} \leftarrow \mathcal{C}[\text{MAC}_1, \text{MAC}_2](k'_{\text{MAC}_1}, k'_{\text{MAC}_2})$

5 : $\textbf{if } \text{Vf}(k'_{\text{MAC}}, (c_1, c_2), \tau) = 0 : \textbf{return } \perp$

6 : $\textbf{return } k'_{\text{KEM}}$

Fig. 12. KEM $\text{XtM}[\text{KEM}_1, \text{KEM}_2]$ constructed by the XOR-then-MAC combiner.

Let $\Pi_1 = (\text{KeyGen}_1, \text{Sig}_1, \text{Vf}_1)$ and $\Pi_2 = (\text{KeyGen}_2, \text{Sig}_2, \text{Vf}_2)$ be two signature schemes. Then denote as $\mathcal{C}[\Pi_1, \Pi_2] = (\text{KeyGen}_{\mathcal{C}}, \text{Sig}_{\mathcal{C}}, \text{Vf}_{\mathcal{C}})$ the hybrid signature scheme constructed from Π_1 and Π_2 using combiner mechanism $\mathcal{C}$. For all combiners, the key generation of the combined scheme will simply be the concatenation of the two scheme's keys as shown in Fig. 10. A signature combiner is called **robust** if it combines two or more algorithms of the same kind such that the combined scheme provides security as long as one of its components provides security.

$\mathcal{C}_{\|}$ *Combiner.* This trivial combiner concatenates independent signatures from the two schemes side-by-side, as defined in Fig. 13. Even though very simple, the construction is shown to be robust by Bindel et al. [13].

$\text{Sig}_{\mathcal{C}_{\|}}(\text{sk}, m)$

1 : $\sigma_1 \leftarrow \Pi_1.\text{Sig}(\text{sk}_1, m)$

2 : $\sigma_2 \leftarrow \Pi_2.\text{Sig}(\text{sk}_2, m)$

3 : $\textbf{return } \sigma \leftarrow (\sigma_1, \sigma_2)$

$\text{Vf}_{\mathcal{C}_{\|}}(\text{pk}, \sigma)$

1 : $\textbf{return } \Pi_1.\text{Vf}(\text{pk}_1, m, \sigma_1) \wedge \Pi_2.\text{Vf}(\text{pk}_2, m, \sigma_2)$

Fig. 13. Hybrid signature scheme $\mathcal{C}_{\|}[\Pi_1, \Pi_2]$ constructed by concatenation.

$\mathcal{C}_{\text{str-nest}}$-*Combiner.* One problem with the $\mathcal{C}_{\|}$-Combiner is that due to downgrade attacks, separability of signatures is usually considered a liability in signature combiners. In downgrade attacks an adversary queries a signing oracle for a combined signature and later pretends to know only one of the schemes – this makes it possible for the adversary to *separate* a signature from a combined signature and pass it as a forgery. If downgrade attacks are to be expected – as it might be the case with an international protocol like EAC with multiple versions in concurrent use – it is recommended to use a $\mathcal{C}_{\text{str-nest}}$-Combiner. Here, the second signature scheme signs both the message and the signature from the first signature scheme, as defined in Fig. 14. Bindel et al. [13] show that the $\mathcal{C}_{\text{str-nest}}$-Combiner is robust and inseparable.

$\mathsf{Sig}_{\mathcal{C}_{\text{str-nest}}}(\mathsf{sk}, m)$

1 : $\sigma_1 \leftarrow \Pi_1.\mathsf{Sig}(\mathsf{sk}_1, m)$

2 : $\sigma_2 \leftarrow \Pi_2.\mathsf{Sig}(\mathsf{sk}_2, (m, \sigma_1))$

3 : $\mathbf{return}\ \sigma \leftarrow (\sigma_1, \sigma_2)$

$\mathsf{Vf}_{\mathcal{C}_{\text{str-nest}}}(\mathsf{pk}, \sigma)$

1 : $\mathbf{return}\ \Pi_1.\mathsf{Vf}(\mathsf{pk}_1, m, \sigma_1)$

$\wedge\ \Pi_2.\mathsf{Vf}(\mathsf{pk}_2, (m, \sigma_1), \sigma_2)$

Fig. 14. Hybrid signature scheme $\mathcal{C}_{\text{str-nest}}[\Pi_1, \Pi_2]$ constructed by nesting.

References

1. Abdalla, M., Eisenhofer, T., Kiltz, E., Kunzweiler, S., Riepel, D.: Password-authenticated key exchange from group actions. Cryptology ePrint Archive (2022). https://eprint.iacr.org/2022/770
2. Alagic, G., et al.: Status report on the third round of the NIST post-quantum cryptography standardization process, NIST IR 8413. Technical report, National Institute for Standards and Technology (NIST) (2022)
3. Angel, Y., Dowling, B., Hülsing, A., Schwabe, P., Weber, F.: Post quantum noise. In: Proceedings of the 2022 ACM SIGSAC Conference on Computer and Communications Security, CCS 2022, pp. 97–109. ACM (2022)
4. Arute, F., et al.: Quantum supremacy using a programmable superconducting processor. Nature **574**(7779), 505–510 (2019)
5. Avoine, G., Kalach, K., Quisquater, J.-J.: ePassport: securing international contacts with contactless chips. In: Tsudik, G. (ed.) FC 2008. LNCS, vol. 5143, pp. 141–155. Springer, Heidelberg (2008). https://doi.org/10.1007/978-3-540-85230-8_11
6. Bache, F., Paglialonga, C., Oder, T., Schneider, T., Güneysu, T.: High-speed masking for polynomial comparison in lattice-based KEMs. IACR Trans. Cryptogr. Hardw. Embed. Syst. **2020**(3), 483–507 (2020)
7. Bellare, M., Lysyanskaya, A.: Symmetric and dual PRFs from standard assumptions: A generic validation of an HMAC assumption. IACR Cryptology ePrint Archive, p. 1198 (2015). http://eprint.iacr.org/2015/1198
8. Bellare, M., Rogaway, P.: Random oracles are practical: a paradigm for designing efficient protocols. In: Proceedings of the 1st ACM Conference on Computer and Communications Security, CCS 1993, pp. 62–73. Association for Computing Machinery (1993)
9. Bender, J., Dagdelen, Ö., Fischlin, M., Kügler, D.: The PACE|AA protocol for machine readable travel documents, and its security. In: Keromytis, A.D. (ed.) FC 2012. LNCS, vol. 7397, pp. 344–358. Springer, Heidelberg (2012). https://doi.org/10.1007/978-3-642-32946-3_25
10. Bender, J., Fischlin, M., Kügler, D.: Security analysis of the PACE key-agreement protocol. In: Samarati, P., Yung, M., Martinelli, F., Ardagna, C.A. (eds.) ISC 2009. LNCS, vol. 5735, pp. 33–48. Springer, Heidelberg (2009). https://doi.org/10.1007/978-3-642-04474-8_3
11. Bernstein, D.J.: Introduction to post-quantum cryptography. In: Bernstein, D.J., Buchmann, J., Dahmen, E. (eds.) Post-Quantum Cryptography, pp. 1–14. Springer, Heidelberg (2009). https://doi.org/10.1007/978-3-540-88702-7_1
12. Bindel, N., Brendel, J., Fischlin, M., Goncalves, B., Stebila, D.: Hybrid key encapsulation mechanisms and authenticated key exchange. In: Ding, J., Steinwandt, R. (eds.) PQCrypto 2019. LNCS, vol. 11505, pp. 206–226. Springer, Cham (2019). https://doi.org/10.1007/978-3-030-25510-7_12

13. Bindel, N., Herath, U., McKague, M., Stebila, D.: Transitioning to a quantum-resistant public key infrastructure. In: Lange, T., Takagi, T. (eds.) PQCrypto 2017. LNCS, vol. 10346, pp. 384–405. Springer, Cham (2017). https://doi.org/10.1007/978-3-319-59879-6_22

14. Botros, L., Kannwischer, M.J., Schwabe, P.: Memory-efficient high-speed implementation of Kyber on Cortex-M4. In: Buchmann, J., Nitaj, A., Rachidi, T. (eds.) AFRICACRYPT 2019. LNCS, vol. 11627, pp. 209–228. Springer, Cham (2019). https://doi.org/10.1007/978-3-030-23696-0_11

15. Boyd, C., Gellert, K.: A modern view on forward security. Comput. J. **64**(1), 639–652 (2019)

16. Brendel, J., Fischlin, M., Günther, F., Janson, C., Stebila, D.: Towards post-quantum security for signal's X3DH handshake. In: Dunkelman, O., Jacobson, Jr., M.J., O'Flynn, C. (eds.) SAC 2020. LNCS, vol. 12804, pp. 404–430. Springer, Cham (2021). https://doi.org/10.1007/978-3-030-81652-0_16

17. Bundesamt für Sicherheit in der Informationstechnik: BSI TR-03110. Standard (2016)

18. Bundesamt für Sicherheit in der Informationstechnik: Migration to Post Quantum Cryptography: Recommendations for action by the BSI (2020). https://www.bsi.bund.de/SharedDocs/Downloads/EN/BSI/Crypto/Migration_to_Post_Quantum_Cryptography.pdf?__blob=publicationFile&v=2

19. Byszio, F., Wirth, K.D., Nguyen, K.: Intelligent composed algorithms. Cryptology ePrint Archive, Paper 2021/813 (2021). https://eprint.iacr.org/2021/813

20. Castryck, W., Decru, T.: An efficient key recovery attack on SIDH (preliminary version). Cryptology ePrint Archive (2022)

21. Castryck, W., Lange, T., Martindale, C., Panny, L., Renes, J.: CSIDH: an efficient post-quantum commutative group action. In: Peyrin, T., Galbraith, S. (eds.) ASIACRYPT 2018, Part III. LNCS, vol. 11274, pp. 395–427. Springer, Cham (2018). https://doi.org/10.1007/978-3-030-03332-3_15

22. Dagdelen, Ö., Fischlin, M.: Security analysis of the extended access control protocol for machine readable travel documents. In: Burmester, M., Tsudik, G., Magliveras, S., Ilić, I. (eds.) ISC 2010. LNCS, vol. 6531, pp. 54–68. Springer, Heidelberg (2011). https://doi.org/10.1007/978-3-642-18178-8_6

23. Filimonov, I., Horne, R., Mauw, S., Smith, Z.: Breaking unlinkability of the ICAO 9303 standard for e-passports using bisimilarity. In: Sako, K., Schneider, S., Ryan, P.Y.A. (eds.) ESORICS 2019, Part I. LNCS, vol. 11735, pp. 577–594. Springer, Cham (2019). https://doi.org/10.1007/978-3-030-29959-0_28

24. Fischlin, M., Günther, F., Schmidt, B., Warinschi, B.: Key confirmation in key exchange: a formal treatment and implications for TLS 1.3. In: IEEE Symposium on Security and Privacy, SP 2016, pp. 452–469. IEEE Computer Society (2016)

25. Giacon, F., Heuer, F., Poettering, B.: KEM combiners. In: Abdalla, M., Dahab, R. (eds.) PKC 2018. LNCS, vol. 10769, pp. 190–218. Springer, Cham (2018). https://doi.org/10.1007/978-3-319-76578-5_7

26. Groce, A., Katz, J.: A new framework for efficient password-based authenticated key exchange. In: Proceedings of the 17th ACM Conference on Computer and Communications Security, pp. 516–525. Association for Computing Machinery (2010)

27. Heinz, D., Pöppelmann, T.: Combined fault and DPA protection for lattice-based cryptography. IACR Cryptology ePrint Archive, p. 101 (2021). https://eprint.iacr.org/2021/101

28. Hülsing, A., Butin, D., Gazdag, S., Rijneveld, J., Mohaisen, A.: XMSS: eXtended merkle signature scheme (2018)

29. Hülsing, A., et al.: SPHINCS+. Technical report, National Institute of Standards and Technology (2022). https://csrc.nist.gov/Projects/post-quantum-cryptography/selected-algorithms-2022

30. Hülsing, A., Ning, K., Schwabe, P., Weber, F., Zimmermann, P.R.: Post-quantum wireguard. In: 42nd IEEE Symposium on Security and Privacy, SP 2021, pp. 304–321. IEEE (2021)

31. International Civil Aviation Organization: ICAO doc 9303. Standard (2021). https://www.icao.int/publications/pages/publication.aspx?docnum=9303.   8th Edition

32. International Organization for Standardization/International Electrotechnical Commission: ISO/IEC 14443-4: Identification cards - contactless integrated circuit cards - proximity cards. Standard (2018)

33. International Organization for Standardization/International Electrotechnical Commission: ISO/IEC 7816-4: Identification cards - integrated circuit cards. Technical report (2020)

34. Kannwischer, M.J., et al.: Pqm4 (2022). https://github.com/mupq/pqm4/blob/master/benchmarks.md

35. Katz, J., Lindell, Y.: Introduction to Modern Cryptography, 2nd edn. CRC Press, Boca Raton (2014)

36. Katz, J., Vaikuntanathan, V.: Smooth projective hashing and password-based authenticated key exchange from lattices. In: Matsui, M. (ed.) ASIACRYPT 2009. LNCS, vol. 5912, pp. 636–652. Springer, Heidelberg (2009). https://doi.org/10.1007/978-3-642-10366-7_37

37. Krawczyk, H.: SIGMA: the 'SIGn-and-MAc' approach to authenticated Diffie-Hellman and its use in the IKE protocols. In: Boneh, D. (ed.) CRYPTO 2003. LNCS, vol. 2729, pp. 400–425. Springer, Heidelberg (2003). https://doi.org/10.1007/978-3-540-45146-4_24

38. Krawczyk, H.: Cryptographic extraction and key derivation: the HKDF scheme. In: Rabin, T. (ed.) CRYPTO 2010. LNCS, vol. 6223, pp. 631–648. Springer, Heidelberg (2010). https://doi.org/10.1007/978-3-642-14623-7_34

39. Lamport, L.: Constructing digital signatures from a one-way function. Technical Report SRI-CSL-98, SRI International Computer Science Laboratory (1979)

40. Liu, Y., Kasper, T., Lemke-Rust, K., Paar, C.: E-passport: cracking basic access control Keys. In: Meersman, R., Tari, Z. (eds.) OTM 2007. LNCS, vol. 4804, pp. 1531–1547. Springer, Heidelberg (2007). https://doi.org/10.1007/978-3-540-76843-2_30

41. Lyubashevsky, V., et al.: CRYSTALS-DILITHIUM. Technical report, National Institute of Standards and Technology (2022). https://csrc.nist.gov/Projects/post-quantum-cryptography/selected-algorithms-2022

42. MATZOV: Report on the Security of LWE: Improved Dual Lattice Attack (2022)

43. McGrew, D., Curcio, M., Fluhrer, S.: Leighton-Micali hash-based signatures. https://doi.org/10.17487/RFC8554

44. Merkle, R.C.: Secrecy, authentication and public key systems. Ph.D. thesis (1979). https://www.merkle.com/papers/Thesis1979.pdf

45. Morgner, F., von der Heyden, J.: Analyzing requirements for post quantum secure machine readable travel documents. In: Open Identity Summit 2021, pp. 205–210. Gesellschaft für Informatik e.V. (2021)

46. Mosca, M.: Cybersecurity in an era with quantum computers: will we be ready? Cryptology ePrint Archive, Paper 2015/1075 (2015). https://eprint.iacr.org/2015/1075

47. National Institute of Standards and Technology (NIST): Recommendation for stateful hash-based signature schemes, SP 800-208. Standard (2020)
48. Oder, T., Schneider, T., Pöppelmann, T., Güneysu, T.: Practical cca2-secure and masked ring-LWE implementation. IACR TCHES **2018**(1), 142–174 (2018)
49. Pradel, G., Mitchell, C.: Post-quantum certificates for electronic travel documents. In: Boureanu, I., et al. (eds.) ESORICS 2020. LNCS, vol. 12580, pp. 56–73. Springer, Cham (2020). https://doi.org/10.1007/978-3-030-66504-3_4
50. Prest, T., et al.: FALCON. Technical report, National Institute of Standards and Technology (2022). https://csrc.nist.gov/Projects/post-quantum-cryptography/selected-algorithms-2022
51. Ravi, P., Poussier, R., Bhasin, S., Chattopadhyay, A.: On configurable SCA countermeasures against single trace attacks for the NTT - a performance evaluation-study over Kyber and Dilithium on the ARM Cortex-M4. In: Batina, L., Picek, S., Mondal, M. (eds.) SPACE 2020. LNCS, vol. 12586, pp. 123–146. Springer, Cham (2020). https://doi.org/10.1007/978-3-030-66626-2_7
52. Saarinen, M.O.: Arithmetic coding and blinding countermeasures for lattice signatures - engineering a side-channel resistant post-quantum signature scheme with compact signatures. J. Cryptogr. Eng. **8**(1), 71–84 (2018)
53. Schanck, J.M., Stebila, D.: A transport layer security (TLS) extension for establishing an additional shared secret. Internet-Draft draft-schanck-tls-additional-keyshare-00, Internet Engineering Task Force (2017). https://datatracker.ietf.org/doc/draft-schanck-tls-additional-keyshare/00/. Work in Progress
54. Schwabe, P., et al.: CRYSTALS-KYBER. Technical report, National Institute of Standards and Technology (2022). https://csrc.nist.gov/Projects/post-quantum-cryptography/selected-algorithms-2022
55. Schwabe, P., Stebila, D., Wiggers, T.: Post-quantum TLS without handshake signatures. In: CCS 2020: 2020 ACM SIGSAC Conference on Computer and Communications Security, Virtual Event, USA, 9–13 November 2020, pp. 1461–1480. ACM (2020)
56. Shor, P.W.: Algorithms for quantum computation: discrete logarithms and factoring. In: 35th Annual Symposium on Foundations of Computer Science, pp. 124–134. IEEE Computer Society Press (1994)
57. Vogt, S., Funke, H.: How quantum computers threat security of PKIs and thus EIDs. In: Open Identity Summit 2021, pp. 83–94. Gesellschaft für Informatik e.V. (2021)
58. Wegman, M.N., Carter, J.L.: New hash functions and their use in authentication and set equality. J. Comput. Syst. Sci. **22**(3), 265–279 (1981)
59. Wenger, E., Chen, M., Charton, F., Lauter, K.: SALSA: attacking lattice cryptography with transformers. Cryptology ePrint Archive, Paper 2022/935 (2022). https://eprint.iacr.org/2022/935

A Study of KEM Generalizations

Bertram Poettering[1] and Simon Rastikian[1,2(✉)]

[1] IBM Research Europe – Zurich, Rüschlikon, Switzerland
{poe,sra}@zurich.ibm.com
[2] ETH Zurich, Zurich, Switzerland

Abstract. The NIST, in its recent competition on quantum-resilient confidentiality primitives, requested the submission of exclusively KEMs. The task of KEMs is to establish secure session keys that can drive, amongst others, public key encryption and TLS-like secure channels. In this work we test the KEM abstraction in the context of constructing cryptographic schemes that are not subsumed in the PKE and secure channels categories. We find that, when used to construct a key transport scheme or when used within a secure combiner, the KEM abstraction imposes certain inconvenient limits, the settling of which requires the addition of auxiliary symmetric primitives.

We hence investigate generalizations of the KEM abstraction that allow a considerably simplified construction of the above primitives. In particular, we study VKEMs and KDFEMs, which augment classic KEMs by label inputs, encapsulation handle outputs, and key derivation features, and we demonstrate that they can be transformed into KEM combiners and key transport schemes *without* requiring auxiliary components. We finally show that all four finalist KEMs of the NIST competition are effectively KDFEMs. Our conclusion is that only very mild adjustments are necessary to significantly increase their versatility.

1 Introduction

HYBRID ENCRYPTION. The contemporary approach to construct public key encryption (PKE) is via the KEM+DEM paradigm [11]: To encrypt a message $m \in \mathcal{M}$, first a key encapsulation mechanism (KEM) is used to establish a session key $k \in \mathcal{K}$, then a data encapsulation mechanism (DEM) is used to symmetrically encrypt message m with session key k. The fundamental lemma of hybrid encryption guarantees that if both KEM and DEM are secure against active adversaries, then also the resulting PKE scheme is secure against active adversaries [11].

A main advantage of constructing PKE from two separate primitives is the gain in flexibility: The KEM can be chosen to meet one specific set of conditions (e.g. related to ciphertext size/expansion, resilience against quantum adversaries, level of standardization, ROM vs. standard model, ...), and the DEM can be chosen to meet a different set of conditions (e.g. related to its performance on the

---

The full version of this article can be found at https://ia.cr/2023/272.

© The Author(s), under exclusive license to Springer Nature Switzerland AG 2023
F. Günther and J. Hesse (Eds.): SSR 2023, LNCS 13895, pp. 53–77, 2023.
https://doi.org/10.1007/978-3-031-30731-7_3

expected computing architecture, the type of underlying primitive, ...). While the KEM+DEM paradigm is now about two decades old, its attractiveness was recently confirmed when the NIST opened their call for quantum resilient cryptographic schemes, where all encryption primitive submissions were explicitly required to be of the KEM type [1].

KEY TRANSPORT. A key transport (KT) scheme is a public-key primitive that allows users to securely transport 'symmetric' keys to other users. More specifically, KT can be seen as a special case of PKE where the message space $\mathcal{M}$ is restricted to a payload key space of the form $\bar{\mathcal{K}} = \{0,1\}^\kappa$, commonly instantiated with $\kappa = 128$ or $\kappa = 256$. Standard applications of KT include OpenPGP email encryption [9] where for each email that is encrypted a fresh session key $\bar{k}$ is randomly sampled from $\bar{\mathcal{K}}$ and then transported, via KT, to all recipients of the email. The latter involves one KT operation per receiver, and implicitly represents a multi-recipient PKE construction [19].

If one wants to construct a KT scheme from a KEM, the simple approach of first establishing a session key k with the KEM and then appending the one-time pad encryption $\bar{k} \oplus k$ of $\bar{k}$ to its ciphertext is, due to the obvious malleability condition, not secure against active adversaries. Rather, it appears that a stronger encryption primitive is necessary. For instance, $\bar{k}$ could be encrypted via $c \leftarrow \mathrm{enc}_k(\bar{k})$ where enc is a DEM encapsulation routine that is secure against active adversaries. In practice, the natural options for instantiating such a DEM would be using either EtM (encrypt-then-mac, [5]) or authenticated encryption (AE/AEAD, [21]). Unfortunately, these approaches imply overheads that are inconvenient in two independent dimensions: (1) At least one auxiliary symmetric algorithm has to be agreed on and implemented (two in the case of EtM), and the effective price of this should not be underestimated.[1] (2) AE/AEAD schemes expect auxiliary inputs like nonces [22] and associated data strings [21], the processing of which requires additional resources.[2] Note that the nonce processing is demanded by the AE/AEAD interface [18], while our KT application itself wouldn't require it (and could fix the nonce to the all-zero string). The price of processing the nonce has to be paid anyway.

Starting from (a generalized form of) a KEM, this article contributes a KT construction that does not require any auxiliary symmetric algorithm. That is, our KT scheme completely removes the two overhead categories discussed above.

KEM COMBINERS. A KEM combiner merges two ingredient KEMs into a single (hybrid) KEM such that if at least one of the ingredient KEMs is secure then so is the hybrid. Interest in KEM combiners increased recently [2] with the availability of KEMs that are potentially resilient against quantum adversaries:

---

[1] Firstly, agreeing on an auxiliary component will likely require dedicated standardization efforts. Secondly, side-channel resilient implementations of cryptographic algorithms require knowledge of the target machine and hence, in the worst case, one dedicated implementation per computing architecture.

[2] For instance, the nonce handling of most AES-based AE/AEAD schemes requires one additional blockcipher invocation.

While hardness assumptions in the domain of lattices and codes can be considered less tested than RSA/DL, only the former have the potential to provide security once quantum computers become available; hence, combining a classic KEM with a lattice or code based KEM promises to achieve security in more scenarios. Similarly to above (see KT discussion), the simple construction of first letting the ingredient KEMs establish session keys k_1, k_2 independently of each other and then combining these keys to a common key via $k \leftarrow k_1 \oplus k_2$ does, due to malleability issues, not provide security against active adversaries.

KEM combiners secure against active adversaries have been investigated in [8, 15]. All known constructions require auxiliary symmetric primitives, namely either blockciphers, PRFs, or hash functions. For instance, the likely most elegant hybrid from [15] has an encapsulation routine that lets the ingredient algorithms enc_1, enc_2 establish session keys k_1, k_2 independently of each other, and then computes the hybrid key as per $k \leftarrow F(k_1, c_2) \oplus F(k_2, c_1)$, where F is an auxiliary PRF and c_1, c_2 are the ingredient KEMs' ciphertexts. Another example of a KEM combiner would derive the combined key k as per $k \leftarrow H(k_1, k_2, c_1, c_2)$, for a (quantum) random oracle H. As we discussed in the KT context, the use of auxiliary symmetric components comes with a price that should not be underestimated.

Starting from (a generalized form of) a KEM, this article contributes a KEM combiner that does not require any auxiliary symmetric algorithm.

1.1   Existing KEM Generalizations

As discussed above, neither key transport nor KEM combiners seem to be constructable from KEMs directly, i.e., without adding an auxiliary symmetric primitive of some kind. The goal of this article is to study whether a relatively small strengthening of the KEM primitive might suffice to enable the construction of key transport or KEM combiners without adding extra primitives. We are not the first authors to consider strengthenings of the KEM primitive. In the following we review three prior approaches (all of which were originally explored with an overall different focus).

LABELED PKE/KEMs. In labeled PKE [24], the encryption and decryption algorithms take, in addition to their standard inputs (public or secret key, message or ciphertext), an auxiliary label input L which may consist of an arbitrary string. Correctness is provided if and only if encryption and decryption use the same label. That is, intuitively, $\forall L, m$: $dec(sk, L, enc(pk, L, m)) = m$. The adapted security definition, which is a straightforward variant of the standard PKE security definition, implies that for $L_1 \neq L_2$ the value of $dec(sk, L_2, enc(pk, L_1, m))$ is not correlated with m. (Assuming that dec doesn't reject the ciphertext in the first place). The main application of the auxiliary label input is that it easily allows to implement domain separation. For instance, if the same PKE instance is relied on both for receiving encrypted emails and for authenticating to services (by proving the ability to decrypt challenge ciphertexts), if the labels `"enc"` and `"auth"` are used to logically separate to two applications, it is ensured that the otherwise obvious attacks are not possible.

The idea of adding a label input to the PKE interface was formalized in [24]. Translating the idea to the KEM world is immediate: Intuitively, for correctness we now would demand that $\forall L\colon enc(pk, L) = (c, k) \implies dec(sk, L, c) = k$. Also the adaptation of the security notions is straightforward.

TAGKEMs. It was observed by Abe *et al.* [3] that certain IND-CCA secure KEM constructions (e.g., in the spirit of Cramer–Shoup encryption [11]) contain an internal mechanism that authenticates ciphertexts in such a way that the decryptor can detect and reject malicious ciphertext manipulations. One idea behind their TagKEM primitive is to use the same authentication mechanism to also protect the DEM ciphertext of a KEM+DEM hybrid. To make this practical, the KEM encapsulation is split into two algorithms, enc_1 and enc_2, such that first enc_1 is executed on input the public key and with output the session key k plus some state information, then session key k is used with a DEM to encrypt the payload message $\bar{m}$ which results in a DEM ciphertext $\bar{c}$, and finally enc_2 is executed on input the state information and $\bar{c}$ as a *tag*, and with output the KEM ciphertext c. The TagKEM decapsulation routine is not split, and would recover k from sk, c and tag $\bar{c}$, so that then $\bar{m}$ can be recovered from $\bar{c}$ via DEM decapsulation.

While the TagKEM concept was specifically developed to allow the construction of efficient PKE schemes, the fact that its encapsulation routine is split and can authenticate the *use* of the session keys might find more general applications. This article will draw on a very similar concept.

We note that while labels (see above) and tags (see here) serve slightly different purposes, both of them represent arbitrary strings that are known to both sender and receiver, and significantly control the behavior of the corresponding algorithms. This concept also appears in other areas of cryptography, e.g., in the form of associated-data strings in AEAD [21], or as a tweak input for blockciphers [17]. As it will become clear in the course of this paper, it is meaningful in our generalizations to use one single term for the label/tag inputs of KEMs; we chose to consistently use the term 'label'.

KEMs WITH HANDLES. A KEM can be seen as a special form of a one-pass key establishment (KE) protocol for two parties where only one party is authenticated (via a public key). Early models for key establishment [7] define security via session transcripts that would match (or not) on both sides. To side-step drawbacks implied by this purely syntactical approach, later models, e.g. [6], adopted the idea of letting protocol instances also output an explicit *session id*, the matching of which would replace the matching of transcripts. More concretely, if participant Alice establishes session id/key pair (sid_A, k_A) and Bob establishes pair (sid_B, k_B), then, intuitively, correctness would demand that $sid_A = sid_B \implies k_A = k_B$ ("same session, same key"), while the security definition would demand that if $sid_A \neq sid_B$ then k_A, k_B are not correlated ("different session, independent key"). The main advantage of models with session id is that the concept of matching sessions is made explicit and clear, and that obviously correct protocols that couldn't be proven in the model of [7] (for purely syntactical reasons) suddenly become tractable.

Given that KEMs represent a special KE case, it makes sense to explore introducing the session id concept also to KEMs. As in the KE world, this can only increase the number of tractable constructions. However, as establishing a shared key using a KEM doesn't really involve creating a 'session', in this article we use the term 'encapsulation handle' instead of 'session id'; we often just write *handle* for short. Syntactically, a KEM supporting handles encapsulates via $(c, hd, k) \leftarrow \text{enc}(pk)$ and decapsulates via $(hd', k') \leftarrow \text{dec}(sk, c)$. The KE correctness condition translates to $hd' = hd \implies k' = k$ ("same handle, same key"), and for security we demand that if $hd' \neq hd$ then k', k are not correlated ("different handle, independent key").

We observe that the classic KEM notion also provides a handle concept, but only implicitly: In standard correctness and security definitions for KEMs [11], the ciphertext takes a dual role: (1) It conveys the information necessary for the decryptor to reconstruct the session key, and (2) it serves as a handle for the encapsulation operation: Each KEM ciphertext uniquely identifies the invocation of the encapsulation algorithm that created it. Also the "same ciphertext, same key" and "different ciphertext, independent key" principles hold for (IND-CCA secure) KEMs.

While all formalizations in this article consistently use handle based definitions for KEMs and PKE, readers unfamiliar or uncomfortable with this concept can, whenever a handle is mentioned, instead think of the ciphertext. This way of thinking *does* reduce the generality of our results, but only mildly so. We will make those cases explicit where the difference is significant.

1.2 Our Approach

The goal of this article is to find and study natural generalizations of the KEM primitive such that intuitively simple applications like key transport (KT) and KEM combiners can be constructed without having to rely on auxiliary symmetric building blocks. In our search we considered it a necessary condition that the KEM generalization wouldn't change the main character profile of a KEM too much. For instance, we insisted on the overall communication from sender to receiver remaining one-pass. In the end our search identified two different KEM generalizations, dubbed VKEM and KDFEM, that we briefly present in the upcoming paragraphs. We found in particular the KDFEM primitive suitable for our purposes.

VKEMs. In Sect. 1.1 we discussed three already existing KEM generalizations from prior work: KEMs with labels, with tags, and with handles. What we call a versatile key encapsulation mechanism (VKEM) is a KEM variant that combines all three of these approaches, in a clean and unified way, with the ultimate goal of maximum versatility: A VKEM has *both* the encapsulation and decapsulation routine split into two phases each, where the algorithms of both phases take labels on input and generate keys and handles on output. (See Fig. 4 for a high-level illustration of the syntax).

After defining the precise syntax and security of VKEMs, we study how a KEM combiner and/or KT scheme can be constructed from this primitive. The encapsulation routine of our VKEM combiner from Sect. 5 is illustrated in Fig. 1. As the red crosses suggest, the label input and the session key output of the two first-phase VKEM invocations (top left and top right) are not used. In contrast, the first-phase encapsulation handles, serving as identifiers for the respective encapsulation invocations, are fed, in form of labels, into the second phase of the *other* VKEM instance. The idea behind this cross-over is to cryptographically tie the two VKEM instances together, so that an attack against the one can be noticed, and reacted to, by the other. The hybrid KEM's key k is the XOR of the two second-phase session keys, while the hybrid's handle hd is the concatenation of the two second-phase handles. We formally confirm the security of this construction in Sect. 5.

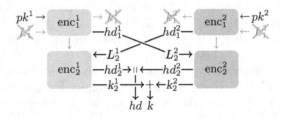

Fig. 1. Combiner of two VKEMs (left and right) to obtain one secure KEM. We only show the encapsulation process, and, for clarity, omit drawing the arrows transporting ciphertexts.

We also succeeded with transforming a VKEM into a KT scheme. The construction is a little odd for allowing empty second-phase ciphertexts and using the second-phase session keys exclusively, in the style of MAC tags, in cleartext for authentication. While this was confusing at first, we eventually noticed that the very same key transport scheme could also be instantiated with a KDFEM (see below) instead of with a VKEM, meaning that its requirements are located in the small intersection of VKEMs and KDFEMs. As the KDFEM notation is substantially cleaner when it comes to defining a KT scheme, we decided to present our KT solution and its analysis exclusively in the KDFEM setting.

KDFEMs. Our second approach to generalizing KEMs is based on the observation that many real-world KEM constructions internally derive the output session key with a dedicated key derivation function (KDF) like HKDF [16]. While KDFs allow for deriving many keys from a single seed, we are not aware of a KEM construction that would evaluate its KDF at more than one point. Our approach is to remove this restriction and to enable the evaluation of the (seeded) KDF on arbitrarily many points. Very briefly, what we refer to as a key derivation function encapsulation mechanism (KDFEM) consists of encapsulation/decapsulation algorithms $(c, st) \leftarrow \text{enc}(pk)$ and $st' \leftarrow \text{dec}(sk, c)$ and a KDF evaluation algorithm eval such that $k \leftarrow \text{eval}(st, L)$ and $k' \leftarrow \text{eval}(st', L)$ lead to the same result $k = k'$.

We observe that the KDFEM primitive allows for constructing both a KEM combiner and a KT scheme in an extremely straightforward manner: The $k \leftarrow F(k_1, c_2) \oplus F(k_2, c_1)$ construction of [15] discussed earlier can be salvaged by replacing the (auxiliary) PRF with the KDFEM's eval routine: Using our handle-based notation, the instruction becomes $k \leftarrow \text{eval}(st_1, hd_2) \oplus \text{eval}(st_2, hd_1)$. Pronto. Our key transport construction is as simple: A first eval invocation establishes a mask that is used to one-time pad encrypt the payload key, and a second eval invocation is used on the resulting ciphertext to protect its integrity in an encrypt-then-mac fashion. We formally confirm the security of these constructions in Sect. 7 and Sect. 9.

DISCUSSION. Our approach to expect of a generalized KEM that it expose a new kind of auxiliary KDF functionality may at first seem moot given that our overall goal was to *reduce* the number of auxiliary symmetric primitives (including KDFs) required to construct KEM combiners and KT. It's not. The key insight is that many KEMs already have that KDF functionality built into them, so we can re-use it for free. The cost reduction of our approach is not necessarily visible in computation time or the like, but in the removed requirement to agree on an additional primitive. Concretely, in Sect. 10 we demonstrate that all four KEM finalists of the recent NIST competition [1] can be turned into KDFEMs with almost no modification.

1.3 Related Work

We already gave numerous references to related work inline in the above paragraphs. This includes work on KEMs with labels, with tag inputs, and of primitives that establish keys together with handles. We also mentioned relevant standardization efforts like ETSI TS 103 744 [2] and the ongoing, soon-to-be completed efforts by NIST [1]. The public interest in KEM combiners is also visible in the existence of an RFC draft that explicitly targets this primitive (tolerating an auxiliary random oracle).[3]

The works of Zhang et al. [25], Dodis and Katz [13], Giacon et al. [15], as well as Bindel et al. [8] consider combiners for public key encryption and key encapsulation mechanisms. While the former two works consider PKE and their results cannot be translated to the KEM setting, the latter two combine KEMs but require additional building blocks. In this sense, they don't present solutions to our challenge.

Numerous practical protocols, including development versions of TLS and MLS, employ KEM combiners or KT schemes only implicitly. This is typically done via key mixing, using auxiliary symmetric primitives like hash functions

---

[3] https://datatracker.ietf.org/doc/draft-ounsworth-cfrg-kem-combiners/.

or KDFs. A difference to our setting is that TLS and MLS are generously using such primitives anyway, so that the advantages offered by our approach become less considerable.

2 Preliminaries

2.1 Notation

We specify scheme algorithms and security games in pseudocode. In such code we write $var \leftarrow exp$ for evaluating expression exp and assigning the result to variable var. If var is a set variable and exp evaluates to a set, we write $var \overset{\cup}{\leftarrow} exp$ shorthand for $var \leftarrow var \cup exp$. A (row) vector variable can be appended to another vector variable with the (associative) concatenation operator $\shortparallel$, and we write $var \overset{\shortparallel}{\leftarrow} exp$ shorthand for $var \leftarrow var \shortparallel exp$. We do *not* overload the $\shortparallel$ operator to also indicate string concatenation, i.e., the objects $\mathsf{a} \shortparallel \mathsf{b}$ and ab are not the same. We use $[\,]$ notation for associative arrays (i.e., the 'dictionary' data structure): Once the instruction $A[\cdot] \leftarrow exp$ initialized all items of array A to the default value exp, individual items can be accessed as per $A[idx]$, e.g., updated and extracted via $A[idx] \leftarrow exp$ and $var \leftarrow A[idx]$, respectively, for any expression idx.

To keep our games compact, we use the alias-creating operator ":=" where convenient. The instruction '$A := B$' introduces A as a symbolic alias for the expression B. This crucially differs from $A \leftarrow B$ which is an assignment that evaluates expression B and stores the result in variable A. For instance, if $D[\,]$ is a dictionary and $D["\mathtt{x}"]$ an integer entry, and an alias is created as per $A := D["\mathtt{x}"]$, then the instruction $A \leftarrow A + 1$ expands to $D["\mathtt{x}"] \leftarrow D["\mathtt{x}"] + 1$ and thus modifies the value of $D["\mathtt{x}"]$.

Unless explicitly noted, any scheme algorithm may be randomized. We use $\langle\,\rangle$ notation for stateful algorithms: If alg is a (stateful) algorithm, we write $y \leftarrow alg\langle st\rangle(x)$ shorthand for $(st, y) \leftarrow alg(st, x)$ to denote an invocation with input x and output y that updates its state st. (Depending on the algorithm, x and/or y may be missing). If in a specific context one of the output elements of an algorithm shall be ignored, we annotate this by assigning it to the symbol _. Importantly, and in contrast to most prior works, we assume that *any* algorithm of a cryptographic scheme may fail or abort, even if this is not explicitly specified in the syntax definition. This approach is inspired by how modern programming languages deal with error conditions via *exceptions*: Any code can at any time 'throw an exception' which leads to an abort of the current code and is passed on to the calling instance. In particular, if in our game definitions a scheme algorithm aborts, the corresponding game oracle immediately aborts as well (and returns to the adversary).

Security games are parameterized by an adversary, and consist of a main game body plus zero or more oracle specifications. The adversary is allowed to call any of the specified oracles. The execution of the game starts with the main game body and terminates when a '**Stop with** exp' instruction is reached, where the value of expression exp is taken as the outcome of the game. If the outcome of a game G is Boolean, we write $\Pr[G(\mathcal{A})]$ for the probability (over the random coins of G and $\mathcal{A}$) that an execution of G with adversary $\mathcal{A}$ results in the outcome 1. We define shorthand notation for specific combinations of game-ending instructions: While in computational games we write 'Win' for 'Stop with 1', in distinguishing games we write 'Win' for 'Stop with b' (where b is the challenge bit). In any case we write 'Lose' for 'Stop with 0'. Further, for a Boolean condition C, we write '**Require** C' for 'If $\neg C$: Lose', 'Penalize C' for 'If C: Lose', 'Reward C' for 'If C: Win', and '**Promise** C' for 'If $\neg C$: Win'.

Many of the oracles specified in a security game will produce information that is considered public and to be shared with the adversary. This holds for instance for a ciphertext c created within an encryption oracle. Instead of collecting such information in an explicit data structure and returning it to the adversary when the processing of the oracle finishes, we use the **Share** shortcut notation to perform the same job implicitly. (In the above case we would write 'Share c'). If required, this concept could be formalized by initializing a list $L \leftarrow \epsilon$ when the game starts, by appending the arguments of any Share instruction to this list (e.g., $L \xleftarrow{\shortmid\shortmid} c$), and to return L from any oracle query. We chose our implicit notation as it uses less symbols and makes the game mechanics more clear.

2.2 Key Establishment Games

Most of the cryptographic primitives considered in this work (KEMs, VKEMs, KDFEMs) are key establishing primitives: Their goal is to establish fresh session keys that can be used with arbitrary applications. While, not surprisingly, each such primitive is covered by individual security definitions and games, some parts of these definitions overlap and are common across all formalizations. Instead of specifying the same game components over and over again, we define and describe the common parts here and refer to them from the main body of our treatment.

In Fig. 2 we define the core part that the formalizations of all our key establishing primitives have in common. The game body (lines 00–03) initializes a secret/public key pair, invokes the adversary on input the public key, checks for trivial win conditions (see below), and terminates the game with the output provided by the adversary. The adversary can invoke a number of oracles (depending on the modeled primitive), among which are always the Reveal and Challenge oracles specified here. (Some works in the key establishment literature may refer to our Challenge oracle as the Test oracle). Both oracles provide access to a key that was priorly accepted (see lines 04,08; entries will be added to set A by other oracles). The Reveal oracle always returns the real key (stored in array K, line 06), and the Challenge oracle either returns the real key or a random key (line 10). (Array R is initialized to random keys, see the INITIALIZATIONS: line at the top of the figure).

Intuitively, if the adversary reveals a specific key, the latter becomes exposed. We record this in set X (line 05). If however the adversary tests a key by invoking the Challenge oracle, the key is thereby declared fresh. We record this in set F (line 09). It is a trivial attack to first reveal a key and then test it (or vice versa); hence, in line 02, the game aborts (Stops with 0) if this condition is identified. Based on the $\mathbf{KE}^0, \mathbf{KE}^1$ games specified in Fig. 2 (plus additional scheme specific oracles), a typical advantage of an adversary would be defined as $\mathbf{Adv}(\mathcal{A}) := |\Pr[\mathbf{KE}^0(\mathcal{A})] - \Pr[\mathbf{KE}^1(\mathcal{A})]|$.

INITIALIZATIONS: $A, X, F \leftarrow \emptyset$; $K[\cdot] \leftarrow \diamond$; $R[\cdot] \leftarrow \$(\mathcal{K})$

Game $\mathbf{KE}^b(\mathcal{A})$	Oracle Reveal(hd)	Oracle Challenge(hd)
00 $(sk, pk) \leftarrow$ gen	04 Require $hd \in A$	08 Require $hd \in A$
01 $b' \leftarrow \mathcal{A}(pk)$	05 $X \overset{\cup}{\leftarrow} \{hd\}$	09 $F \overset{\cup}{\leftarrow} \{hd\}$
02 Require $X \cap F = \emptyset$	06 $k \leftarrow K[hd]$	10 $k \leftarrow b? K[hd] : R[hd]$
03 Stop with b'	07 Return k	11 Return k

Fig. 2. Game components for general key establishment. Legend: A: accepted; X: exposed; F: fresh; K: key; R: random.

3   Key Encapsulation Mechanisms (KEM)

As a warm-up we define a KEM variant that supports encapsulation handles: Each encapsulation generates a fresh such handle, and a corresponding decapsulation operation can recover it from the ciphertext. In contrast to the established session key, the handle is considered public information. As discussed in Sect. 1.1, the handle concept is borrowed from the key establishment literature where handles reside under the name of *session id* [6].

Definition 1. *A key encapsulation mechanism (KEM) for (session) key space $\mathcal{K}$ consists of a secret key space $\mathcal{SK}$, a public key space $\mathcal{PK}$, a ciphertext space $\mathcal{C}$, an encapsulation handle space $\mathcal{HD}$, a key generation algorithm* gen $\rightarrow \mathcal{SK} \times \mathcal{PK}$, *and algorithms* enc, dec *as follows:*

$$\mathcal{PK} \rightarrow \text{enc} \rightarrow \mathcal{C} \times \mathcal{HD} \times \mathcal{K} \qquad \mathcal{SK} \times \mathcal{C} \rightarrow \text{dec} \rightarrow \mathcal{HD} \times \mathcal{K}$$

Intuitively, for correctness we demand that after $(sk, pk) \leftarrow$ gen and $(c, hd, k) \leftarrow \text{enc}(pk)$ and $(hd', k') \leftarrow \text{dec}(sk, c')$ we have (1) *handle freshness:* the handle hd output by enc is unique (doesn't collide with other handles output by enc); and (2) *key recovery:* $hd' = hd \implies k' = k$.[4] We formalize this in the following.

Definition 2. *A KEM is correct if for every considerable adversary $\mathcal{A}$ the advantage function* $\mathbf{Adv}^{\text{cor-kem}}(\mathcal{A}) := \Pr[(sk, pk) \leftarrow \text{gen}; \text{Invoke } \mathcal{A}(pk); \text{Lose}]$ *is negligible, where the adversary has access to the oracles of Fig. 3, and the*

---

[4] It might be tempting to additionally require that $c' = c \implies hd' = hd$. However, as no part of our article logically depends on such a property, we abstain from *formally demanding* it.

game variables A, K *are initialized as in Fig. 2. The KEM is secure (against active adversaries) if for every considerable adversary* $\mathcal{A}$ *the advantage function* $\mathbf{Adv}^{\mathrm{ke\text{-}kem}}(\mathcal{A}) := |\Pr[\mathbf{KE}^0(\mathcal{A})] - \Pr[\mathbf{KE}^1(\mathcal{A})]|$ *is negligible, where the* $\mathbf{KE}^0, \mathbf{KE}^1$ *games consist of the components specified in Fig. 2 and Fig. 3.*

INITIALIZATIONS: $C[\cdot] \leftarrow \diamond$

Oracle Enc()
20 $(c, hd, k) \leftarrow \mathrm{enc}(pk)$
21 $\mathrm{Accept}_E(c, hd, k)$
22 Share c, hd

Proc $\mathrm{Accept}_E(c, hd, k)$
23 Promise $hd \notin A$
24 $A \xleftarrow{\cup} \{hd\}$
25 $C[hd] \leftarrow c$
26 $K[hd] \leftarrow k$

Oracle Dec(c)
27 $(hd, k) \leftarrow \mathrm{dec}(sk, c)$
28 $\mathrm{Accept}_D(c, hd, k)$
29 Share hd

Proc $\mathrm{Accept}_D(c, hd, k)$
30 If $hd \in A$:
31   Promise $C[hd] = c$
32   Promise $K[hd] = k$
33 Else:
34   Share k

Fig. 3. KEM-specific oracles required by Definition 2. (By default ignore the gray components, in particular lines 25,31). In the $\mathbf{KE}^0, \mathbf{KE}^1$ games, the adversary can query the Reveal, Challenge oracles of Fig. 2 and the Enc, Dec oracles specified here. The $\mathrm{Accept}_E, \mathrm{Accept}_D$ procedures are invoked (exclusively) from lines 21, 28. See Sect. 2.1 for the meaning of instructions 'Share' and 'Promise'.

Note that the security definition also covers correctness (as the same Promise lines are present in both games). Observe how lines 23, 24 formalize *handle freshness* while lines 26, 30, 32 formalize the *key recovery* demand. Lines 22, 29, 34 model that ciphertexts and handles and dishonestly generated session keys are not considered secret but public information. While Definition 2, as is, specifies security against active adversaries, a strengthening to IND-CCA security can be achieved by activating the gray components including lines 25, 31. (For the results of this article, this will not be necessary).

4   Versatile Key Encapsulation: VKEM

We formalize the first of our two KEM generalizations. As discussed in Sect. 1.1, VKEMs combine and extend the features of earlier KEM generalizations: They are two-phased as in Abe *et al.* [3], they support labels as in ISO 18033-2, and they support handles as already used in Sect. 3. We illustrate the syntax of VKEMs in Fig. 4.

Definition 3. *A* versatile key encapsulation mechanism (VKEM) *for label spaces* $\mathcal{L}_1, \mathcal{L}_2$ *and (session) key spaces* $\mathcal{K}_1, \mathcal{K}_2$ *consists of a secret key space* $\mathcal{SK}$, *a public key space* $\mathcal{PK}$, *state spaces* $\mathcal{ST}_E, \mathcal{ST}_D$, *ciphertext spaces* $\mathcal{C}_1, \mathcal{C}_2$, *encapsulation handle spaces* $\mathcal{HD}_1, \mathcal{HD}_2$, *a key generation algorithm* gen $\to \mathcal{SK} \times \mathcal{PK}$, *and algorithms* $\text{enc}_1, \text{enc}_2, \text{dec}_1, \text{dec}_2$ *as follows:*

$$\mathcal{PK} \times \mathcal{L}_1 \to \text{enc}_1 \to \mathcal{C}_1 \times \mathcal{HD}_1 \times \mathcal{K}_1 \times \mathcal{ST}_E$$
$$\mathcal{ST}_E \times \mathcal{L}_2 \to \text{enc}_2 \to \mathcal{C}_2 \times \mathcal{HD}_2 \times \mathcal{K}_2$$
$$\mathcal{SK} \times \mathcal{L}_1 \times \mathcal{C}_1 \to \text{dec}_1 \to \mathcal{HD}_1 \times \mathcal{K}_1 \times \mathcal{ST}_D$$
$$\mathcal{ST}_D \times \mathcal{L}_2 \times \mathcal{C}_2 \to \text{dec}_2 \to \mathcal{HD}_2 \times \mathcal{K}_2$$

Fig. 4. Interplay of VKEM algorithms. The thick arrows are relevant for functionality/applications. The thin arrows are for technical artifacts.

In a nutshell, for correctness we demand that if the encapsulation and decapsulation algorithms are invoked and the labels and handles are consistent, then so are the established session keys. More precisely, we demand that for all $(L_1, L_2), (L_1', L_2') \in \mathcal{L}_1 \times \mathcal{L}_2$, after $(sk, pk) \leftarrow$ gen and $(c_1, hd_1, k_1, st_E) \leftarrow \text{enc}_1(pk, L_1)$ followed by $(c_2, hd_2, k_2) \leftarrow \text{enc}_2(st_E, L_2)$ and $(hd_2', k_1', st_D) \leftarrow \text{dec}_1(sk, L_1', c_1')$ followed by $(hd_2', k_2') \leftarrow \text{dec}_2(st_D, L_2', c_2')$, we have (1) *handle freshness:* the handles hd_1, hd_2 output by $\text{enc}_1, \text{enc}_2$ are unique (don't collide with other handles output by enc_1 and enc_2); (2) *history matching:* $hd_1' = hd_1 \implies L_1' = L_1$ and $hd_2' = hd_2 \implies (L_1', hd_1', L_2') = (L_1, hd_1, L_2)$; and (3) *key recovery:* $hd_1' = hd_1 \implies k_1' = k_1$ and $hd_2' = hd_2 \implies k_2' = k_2$.[5] Before we formalize this, note that history matching is equivalent with the possibly more intuitive demand for (2') *handle divergence:* $L_1' \neq L_1 \implies hd_1' \neq hd_1$ and $(L_1', hd_1', L_2') \neq (L_1, hd_1, L_2) \implies hd_2' \neq hd_2$.

The oracles required by our formal definitions of correctness and security are considerably more involved than those for KEMs in Fig. 3. This is primarily because the splitting of enc, dec into two phases requires infrastructure for session management: In practice, multiple enc/dec sessions might be invoked in parallel, meaning that an expressive definition has to support concurrency. We provide further discussion after the definition.

---

[5] Analogously to Footnote 4, it might be tempting to additionally require $c_1' = c_1 \implies hd_1' = hd_1$ and $(c_1', c_2') = (c_1, c_2) \implies hd_2' = hd_2$. However, as no part of our article logically depends on such a property, we once more abstain from *formally demanding* it.

Definition 4. *A VKEM is correct if for every considerable adversary $\mathcal{A}$ the advantage function $\mathbf{Adv}^{\mathrm{cor-vkem}}(\mathcal{A}) := \Pr[(sk, pk) \leftarrow \mathrm{gen}; \mathrm{Invoke}\ \mathcal{A}(pk); \mathrm{Lose}]$ is negligible, where the adversary has access to the oracles of Fig. 5, and the game variables* A, K *are initialized as in Fig. 2. The VKEM is secure (against active adversaries) if for every considerable adversary $\mathcal{A}$ the advantage function $\mathbf{Adv}^{\mathrm{ke-vkem}}(\mathcal{A}) := |\Pr[\mathbf{KE}^0(\mathcal{A})] - \Pr[\mathbf{KE}^1(\mathcal{A})]|$ is negligible, where the $\mathbf{KE}^0, \mathbf{KE}^1$ games consist of the components specified in Fig. 2 and Fig. 5.*

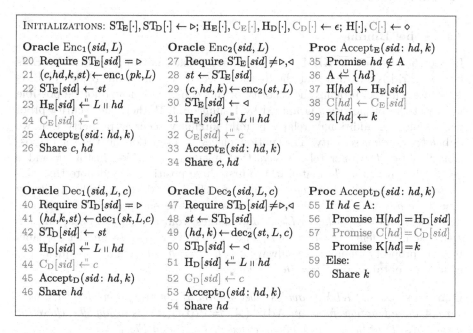

Fig. 5. VKEM-specific oracles required by Definition 4. (By default ignore the gray components). In the $\mathbf{KE}^0, \mathbf{KE}^1$ games, the adversary can query the Reveal, Challenge oracles of Fig. 2 and the $\mathrm{Enc}_1, \mathrm{Enc}_2, \mathrm{Dec}_1, \mathrm{Dec}_2$ oracles specified here. The $\mathrm{Accept}_E, \mathrm{Accept}_D$ procedures are invoked (exclusively) from lines 25, 33, 45, 53. See Sect. 2.1 for the meaning of instructions 'Share' and 'Promise' and 'Require'.

In Fig. 5 we store the states of enc/dec sessions in the arrays $\mathrm{ST}_E, \mathrm{ST}_D$, and use the $\rhd, \lhd$ symbols to identify freshly initialized and completed sessions. See lines 20, 22, 27, 28, 30, 40, 42, 47, 48, 50. Note that the adversary can freely refer to any session via a self-chosen identifier sid.[6] We further record the input-output history of sessions in arrays H_E and H_D. More precisely, every completed

---

[6] This notion of session id has nothing to do with the one used in the key exchange literature and mentioned in Sect. 1.1. In the context of Fig. 5, session ids are not visible by any protocol algorithm. Their function is exclusively to make sessions individually addressable by the adversary.

VKEM encapsulation or decapsulation operation defines a history h of the form $h = L_1 \parallel hd_1 \parallel L_2 \parallel hd_2$ that records the public information (here: the involved labels and established handles) logically associated with the established session keys k_1, k_2. These histories are recorded in lines 23, 31, 43, 51. Note how lines 37, 56 implement *history matching/handle divergence* and lines 39, 58 implement *key recovery*. While Definition 4, as is, specifies security against active adversaries, a strengthening to IND-CCA security can be achieved by activating the gray components including lines 24, 32, 38, 44, 52, 57. (For the results of this article, this will not be necessary).

4.1 Label Binding

In Sect. 5 we specify a KEM combiner that transforms two ingredient VKEMs into a hybrid KEM such that the hybrid is secure if at least one of the VKEMs is. As we will see, proving the security of this construction will not be possible with just the properties guaranteed by Definition 4. Rather, the security proof will require an additional, relatively mild auxiliary security property that we dub *label binding* security. This notion places a restriction on the set of possible histories h. Concretely, it says that if an encapsulation history h and a decapsulation history h' match in the first three positions (we denote this condition with $h \doteq h'$), then they actually match fully. More precisely, if history $h = L_1 \parallel hd_1 \parallel L_2 \parallel hd_2$ emerges from a complete encapsulation invocation, and history $h' = L_1' \parallel hd_1' \parallel L_2' \parallel hd_2'$ emerges from a complete decapsulation invocation, we define $h \doteq h' \iff L_1 \parallel hd_1 \parallel L_2 = L_1' \parallel hd_1' \parallel L_2'$ and let the label binding property demand that always $h \doteq h' \implies h = h'$. As a consequence, of course, we obtain $h \doteq h' \implies hd_2 = hd_2'$.

Definition 5. *A VKEM provides label binding if for every considerable adversary $\mathcal{A}$ the advantage function $\mathbf{Adv}^{\mathrm{lb}}(\mathcal{A}) := \Pr[\mathbf{LB}(\mathcal{A})]$ is negligible, where the game consists of the components specified in Fig. 5 and Fig. 6.*

4.2 Constructions

VKEMs condense concepts explored in several lines of prior work into a single primitive. Many interesting constructions in the spirit of the same prior work will hence exist. As we are specifically interested in what one can do with VKEMs, we briefly exemplify the primitive in the full version [20] and leave a more detailed study of VKEM instantiations for future research. Our construction combines a regular KEM with a PRF and is thus very efficient.

```
INITIALIZATIONS: A ← ∅; K[·] ← ⋄

Game LB(𝒜)
00  (sk, pk) ← gen
01  Invoke 𝒜(pk)
02  For all h ∈ H_E[·] with |h| = 4:
03      For all h' ∈ H_D[·] with |h'| = 4:
04          Promise h ≐ h'  ⟹  h = h'
05  Stop with 0
```

Fig. 6. Game required by Definition 5 to define label binding. The adversary can query the $\mathrm{Enc}_1, \mathrm{Enc}_2, \mathrm{Dec}_1, \mathrm{Dec}_2$ oracles specified in Fig. 5.

5   KEM Combiner from VKEMs

We present a combiner that constructs a KEM from two VKEMs. The combiner is generic, in the sense that it allows running any two (correct) VKEMs such that, as long as one of the VKEMs meets **KE** security definition (strong) and the other meets the **LB** definition (weak), then the overall combined scheme forms a **KE** secure (and correct) KEM. The label-binding property is crucial for proving the combiner secure. The reason is that the combined instances cross the first phase handles to exchange information about the other VKEM (see Fig. 1 for an illustration). Intuitively, this prevents attacks against the first phase part of weak VKEM. Adding label-binding prevents malleability attacks against the second phase of the weak VKEM. The full specification of the combiner is in Fig. 7.

```
Proc gen                          Proc enc(pk)                                          Proc dec(sk, c)
00  (sk¹, pk¹) ← gen¹             05  (c₁¹, hd₁¹, _, st¹) ← enc₁¹(pk¹, ⋄)               13  (hd₁¹, _, st¹) ← dec₁¹(sk¹, ⋄, c₁¹)
01  (sk², pk²) ← gen²             06  (c₁², hd₁², _, st²) ← enc₁²(pk², ⋄)               14  (hd₁², _, st²) ← dec₁²(sk², ⋄, c₁²)
02  sk := (sk¹, sk²)              07  (c₂¹, hd₂¹, k₂¹) ← enc₂¹(st¹, hd₁²)               15  (hd₂¹, k₂¹) ← dec₂¹(st¹, hd₁², c₂¹)
03  pk := (pk¹, pk²)              08  (c₂², hd₂², k₂²) ← enc₂²(st², hd₁¹)               16  (hd₂², k₂²) ← dec₂²(st², hd₁¹, c₂²)
04  Return sk, pk                 09  c := (c₁¹, c₂¹, c₁², c₂²)                         17  hd ← (hd₂¹, hd₂²)
                                  10  hd ← (hd₂¹, hd₂²)                                 18  k ← k₂¹ + k₂²
                                  11  k ← k₂¹ + k₂²                                     19  Return hd, k
                                  12  Return c, hd, k
```

Fig. 7. KEM combiner from two VKEM schemes. The instantiated combiner runs a single time both encapsulation/decapsulation chains and crosses over the handles as depicted in Fig. 1. We assume $\{\diamond\} \subseteq \mathcal{L}_1^1 = \mathcal{L}_1^2$ and $\mathcal{HD}_1^2 \subseteq \mathcal{L}_2^1$ and $\mathcal{HD}_1^1 \subseteq \mathcal{L}_2^2$. We let $\mathcal{HD} = \mathcal{HD}_2^1 \times \mathcal{HD}_2^2$.

Theorem 1. *Let* $\mathrm{VKEM}^1 := (\mathrm{gen}^1, \mathrm{enc}_1^1, \mathrm{enc}_2^1, \mathrm{dec}_1^1, \mathrm{dec}_2^1)$ *and* $\mathrm{VKEM}^2 := (\mathrm{gen}^2, \mathrm{enc}_1^2, \mathrm{enc}_2^2, \mathrm{dec}_1^2, \mathrm{dec}_2^2)$ *be two VKEMs. Let* $\mathrm{C} := (\mathrm{gen}, \mathrm{enc}, \mathrm{dec})$ *be the KEM* *constructed by combining them according to Fig. 7. For all adversaries $\mathcal{A}$ attacking the security of the KEM there exist adversaries $\mathcal{B}_1, \mathcal{B}_2$ attacking the security of* $\mathrm{VKEM}^1, \mathrm{VKEM}^2$, *respectively, and adversaries $\mathcal{C}_1, \mathcal{C}_2$ attacking the label binding of* $\mathrm{VKEM}^1, \mathrm{VKEM}^2$, *respectively, such that*

$$\mathbf{Adv}^{\mathrm{ke\text{-}kem}}(\mathcal{A}) \leq \mathbf{Adv}^{\mathrm{ke\text{-}vkem}}(\mathcal{B}_1) + \mathbf{Adv}^{\mathrm{lb}}(\mathcal{C}_2)$$

and

$$\mathbf{Adv}^{\mathrm{ke\text{-}kem}}(\mathcal{A}) \leq \mathbf{Adv}^{\mathrm{ke\text{-}vkem}}(\mathcal{B}_2) + \mathbf{Adv}^{\mathrm{lb}}(\mathcal{C}_1)$$

where the security definitions are those of Definition 2 and Definition 4 and Definition 5.

We give an overview of the proof; the details can be found in the full version [20]. Starting with the KEM security game instantiated with the algorithms of Fig. 7, we add a Promise instruction that lets adversary $\mathcal{A}$ 'win' in case its actions break label binding, i.e., if $h \doteq h'$ yet $h \neq h'$ for an encapsulation history h and a decapsulation history h'. This game hop comes at the cost of $\mathbf{Adv}^{\mathrm{lb}}(\mathcal{C})$ for some adversary $\mathcal{C}$ derived from $\mathcal{A}$. Once the condition is taken care of, the history h' of every decapsulation query has either $h' = h$ for a prior h (and is then trivial to reply to), or the labels and first-stage handle of h' are sufficiently different from any prior h such that the access rules in Fig. 5 allow for straightforwardly replying to the query in a reduction by using the session keys released by the game's line 60. That is, the remaining advantage of $\mathcal{A}$ is $\mathbf{Adv}^{\mathrm{ke\text{-}vkem}}(\mathcal{B})$ for some adversary $\mathcal{B}$ derived from $\mathcal{A}$.

6   KDF Encapsulation Mechanisms: KDFEM

We formalize the second of our two KEM generalizations. As discussed in Sect. 1.1, KDFEMs don't output session keys directly, but instead establish keyed KDF instances. These KDF instances deterministically map a domain $\mathcal{L}$ to a range $\mathcal{K}$, and can be used to derive an arbitrary number of session keys.

Definition 6. *A KDF encapsulation mechanism (KDFEM) for label space $\mathcal{L}$ and (session) key space $\mathcal{K}$ consists of a secret key space $\mathcal{SK}$, a public key space $\mathcal{PK}$, a state space $\mathcal{ST}$, a ciphertext space $\mathcal{C}$, an encapsulation handle space $\mathcal{HD}$, a key generation algorithm* $\mathrm{gen} \rightarrow \mathcal{SK} \times \mathcal{PK}$, *and algorithms* $\mathrm{enc, dec, eval}$ *as follows:*

$$\mathcal{PK} \rightarrow \mathrm{enc} \rightarrow \mathcal{C} \times \mathcal{HD} \times \mathcal{ST} \qquad \mathcal{SK} \times \mathcal{C} \rightarrow \mathrm{dec} \rightarrow \mathcal{HD} \times \mathcal{ST} \qquad \mathcal{ST} \times \mathcal{L} \rightarrow \mathrm{eval} \rightarrow \mathcal{K}$$

Intuitively, for correctness we demand that after $(sk, pk) \leftarrow \mathrm{gen}$ and $(c, hd, st) \leftarrow \mathrm{enc}(pk)$ and $k \leftarrow \mathrm{eval}(st, L)$ and $(hd', st') \leftarrow \mathrm{dec}(sk, c')$ and $k' \leftarrow \mathrm{eval}(st, L')$ we have (1) *handle freshness:* the handle hd output by enc is unique (doesn't collide with other handles output by enc); and (2) *key recovery:* $hd' = hd \wedge L' = L \implies k' = k.$[7] We formalize this in the following.

---

[7] Analogously to Footnotes 4 and 5, it might be tempting to additionally require that $c' = c \implies hd' = hd$. However, as no part of our article logically depends on such a property, we once more abstain from *formally demanding* it.

Definition 7. *A KDFEM is correct if for every considerable adversary $\mathcal{A}$ the advantage function* $\mathbf{Adv}^{\mathrm{cor-kdfem}}(\mathcal{A}) := \Pr[(sk, pk) \leftarrow \mathrm{gen};\ \mathrm{Invoke}\ \mathcal{A}(pk);\ \mathrm{Lose}]$ *is negligible, where the adversary has access to the oracles of Fig. 8 and the game variables* A, K *are initialized as in Fig. 2. The KDFEM is secure (against active adversaries) if for every considerable adversary $\mathcal{A}$ the advantage function* $\mathbf{Adv}^{\mathrm{ke-kdfem}}(\mathcal{A}) := |\Pr[\mathbf{KE}^0(\mathcal{A})] - \Pr[\mathbf{KE}^1(\mathcal{A})]|$ *is negligible, where the* $\mathbf{KE}^0, \mathbf{KE}^1$ *games consist of the components specified in Fig. 2 and Fig. 8.*

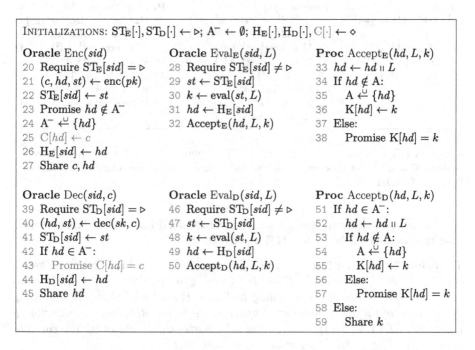

INITIALIZATIONS: $\mathrm{ST_E}[\cdot], \mathrm{ST_D}[\cdot] \leftarrow \triangleright$; $\mathrm{A}^- \leftarrow \emptyset$; $\mathrm{H_E}[\cdot], \mathrm{H_D}[\cdot], \mathrm{C}[\cdot] \leftarrow \diamond$

Oracle Enc(*sid*)
20   Require $\mathrm{ST_E}[sid] = \triangleright$
21   $(c, hd, st) \leftarrow \mathrm{enc}(pk)$
22   $\mathrm{ST_E}[sid] \leftarrow st$
23   Promise $hd \notin \mathrm{A}^-$
24   $\mathrm{A}^- \xleftarrow{\cup} \{hd\}$
25   $\mathrm{C}[hd] \leftarrow c$
26   $\mathrm{H_E}[sid] \leftarrow hd$
27   Share c, hd

Oracle $\mathrm{Eval_E}(sid, L)$
28   Require $\mathrm{ST_E}[sid] \neq \triangleright$
29   $st \leftarrow \mathrm{ST_E}[sid]$
30   $k \leftarrow \mathrm{eval}(st, L)$
31   $hd \leftarrow \mathrm{H_E}[sid]$
32   $\mathrm{Accept_E}(hd, L, k)$

Proc $\mathrm{Accept_E}(hd, L, k)$
33   $hd \leftarrow hd \parallel L$
34   If $hd \notin \mathrm{A}$:
35     $\mathrm{A} \xleftarrow{\cup} \{hd\}$
36     $\mathrm{K}[hd] \leftarrow k$
37   Else:
38   Promise $\mathrm{K}[hd] = k$

Oracle Dec(*sid*, *c*)
39   Require $\mathrm{ST_D}[sid] = \triangleright$
40   $(hd, st) \leftarrow \mathrm{dec}(sk, c)$
41   $\mathrm{ST_D}[sid] \leftarrow st$
42   If $hd \in \mathrm{A}^-$:
43   Promise $\mathrm{C}[hd] = c$
44   $\mathrm{H_D}[sid] \leftarrow hd$
45   Share hd

Oracle $\mathrm{Eval_D}(sid, L)$
46   Require $\mathrm{ST_D}[sid] \neq \triangleright$
47   $st \leftarrow \mathrm{ST_D}[sid]$
48   $k \leftarrow \mathrm{eval}(st, L)$
49   $hd \leftarrow \mathrm{H_D}[sid]$
50   $\mathrm{Accept_D}(hd, L, k)$

Proc $\mathrm{Accept_D}(hd, L, k)$
51   If $hd \in \mathrm{A}^-$:
52     $hd \leftarrow hd \parallel L$
53   If $hd \notin \mathrm{A}$:
54      $\mathrm{A} \xleftarrow{\cup} \{hd\}$
55      $\mathrm{K}[hd] \leftarrow k$
56   Else:
57   Promise $\mathrm{K}[hd] = k$
58   Else:
59   Share k

Fig. 8. KDFEM-specific oracles required by Definition 7. (By default ignore the gray components). In the $\mathbf{KE}^0, \mathbf{KE}^1$ games, the adversary can query the Reveal, Challenge oracles of Fig. 2 and the Enc, $\mathrm{Eval_E}$, Dec, $\mathrm{Eval_D}$ oracles specified here. The $\mathrm{Accept_E}$, $\mathrm{Accept_D}$ procedures are invoked (exclusively) from lines 32, 50. See Sect. 2.1 for the meaning of instructions 'Share' and 'Promise' and 'Require'.

In Fig. 8, the session management is organized in the same way as in Fig. 5. A novelty is the splitting of set A into two: Set A^- indicates the set of (pre-)accepted enc, dec operations (lines 23, 24, 51) and set A indicates the accepted KDF evaluations (lines 34, 35, 53, 54). (The latter matches precisely the spirit of our KEM/VKEM formalizations in Sect. 3 and Sect. 4). As in our KEM/VKEM formalizations, while Definition 7, as is, specifies security against active adversaries, a strengthening to IND-CCA security can be achieved by activating the gray components in Fig. 8. (As before, for the results of this article, this will not be necessary).

7 KEM Combiner from KDFEMs

We present a combiner that generically constructs a KEM from two KDFEMs. We specify the details in Fig. 9. The idea is to derive session keys as per $k \leftarrow f_1(hd_2) + f_2(hd_1)$ where f_1, f_2 represent the keyed KDF instances of the two KDFEMs. Note that, similarly to Fig. 1, the handles of the two instances are crossed.

Proc gen	**Proc enc(pk)**	**Proc dec(sk, c)**
00 $(sk^1, pk^1) \leftarrow gen^1$	05 $(c^1, hd^1, st^1) \leftarrow enc^1(pk^1)$	13 $(hd^1, st^1) \leftarrow dec^1(sk^1, c^1)$
01 $(sk^2, pk^2) \leftarrow gen^2$	06 $(c^2, hd^2, st^2) \leftarrow enc^2(pk^2)$	14 $(hd^2, st^2) \leftarrow dec^2(sk^2, c^2)$
02 $sk := (sk^1, sk^2)$	07 $k^1 \leftarrow eval^1(st^1, hd^2)$	15 $k^1 \leftarrow eval^1(st^1, hd^2)$
03 $pk := (pk^1, pk^2)$	08 $k^2 \leftarrow eval^2(st^2, hd^1)$	16 $k^2 \leftarrow eval^2(st^2, hd^1)$
04 Return sk, pk	09 $c := (c^1, c^2)$	17 $hd \leftarrow (hd^1, hd^2)$
	10 $hd \leftarrow (hd^1, hd^2)$	18 $k \leftarrow k^1 + k^2$
	11 $k \leftarrow k^1 + k^2$	19 Return hd, k
	12 Return c, hd, k	

Fig. 9. A KEM combiner from two KDFEM schemes. The combiner crosses handles in lines 07 and 08 during encapsulation, and in lines 15 and 16 during decapsulation. We let $\mathcal{HD} = \mathcal{HD}^1 \times \mathcal{HD}^2$.

Our security theorem states that if one of the KDFEMs meets **KE** security, then the combined scheme is a **KE** secure KEM.

Theorem 2. *Let* $KDFEM^1 := (gen^1, enc^1, dec^1, eval^1)$ *and* $KDFEM^2 := (gen^2, enc^2, dec^2, eval^2)$ *be two KDFEMs. Let* C $:= (gen, enc, dec)$ *be the KEM constructed by combining them according to Fig. 9. For all adversaries $\mathcal{A}$ attacking the security of the KEM there exist adversaries $\mathcal{B}_1, \mathcal{B}_2$ attacking the security of $KDFEM^1, KDFEM^2$, respectively, and adversaries $\mathcal{C}_1, \mathcal{C}_2$ attacking the correctness of $KDFEM^1, KDFEM^2$, respectively, such that*

$$\mathbf{Adv}^{\mathrm{ke-kem}}(\mathcal{A}) \leq \mathbf{Adv}^{\mathrm{ke-kdfem}}(\mathcal{B}_1) + \mathbf{Adv}^{\mathrm{cor-kdfem}}(\mathcal{C}_2)$$

and

$$\mathbf{Adv}^{\mathrm{ke-kem}}(\mathcal{A}) \leq \mathbf{Adv}^{\mathrm{ke-kdfem}}(\mathcal{B}_2) + \mathbf{Adv}^{\mathrm{cor-kdfem}}(\mathcal{C}_1)$$

where the security definitions are those of Definition 2 and Definition 7.

The proof is of the same flavor as the one in Sect. 5. The details can be found in the full version [20].

8 Key Transport

A key transport scheme can be seen as a PKE scheme that is specialized on encrypting short constant-length symmetric keys from some key space $\mathcal{K}$. Typically we have $\mathcal{K} = \{0, 1\}^\kappa$ for $\kappa = 128$ or $\kappa = 256$. In this section we specify its syntax and security. We provide a construction in Sect. 9.

Definition 8. *A key transport* (KT) *scheme for a payload key space* $\mathcal{K}$ *consists of a secret key space* $\mathcal{SK}$, *a public key space* $\mathcal{PK}$, *a ciphertext space* $\mathcal{C}$, *an encryption handle space* $\mathcal{HD}$, *a key generation algorithm* gen $\rightarrow \mathcal{SK} \times \mathcal{PK}$, *and algorithms* enc, dec *as follows:*

$$\mathcal{PK} \times \mathcal{K} \rightarrow \text{enc} \rightarrow \mathcal{C} \times \mathcal{HD} \qquad\qquad \mathcal{SK} \times \mathcal{C} \rightarrow \text{dec} \rightarrow \mathcal{HD} \times \mathcal{K}$$

Intuitively, for correctness we demand that after $(sk, pk) \leftarrow$ gen and $(c, hd) \leftarrow$ enc(pk, k) and $(hd', k') \leftarrow$ dec(sk, c') we have (1) *handle freshness:* the handle hd output by enc is unique (doesn't collide with other handles output by enc); and (2) *payload key recovery:* $hd' = hd \implies k' = k$.[8]

A formal version of these demands is covered by Definition 9. Our security definition is simulation based. In a nutshell, we say that a KT scheme is secure if there exists a simulator that behaves precisely like (read: indistinguishably from) the real scheme, just that it never sees the payload keys that it is meant to transport. If no adversary can tell apart whether it interacts with the real scheme or such a simulator, it also cannot learn information about the transported keys.

We start with defining the syntax of a simulator that fits the specification of Definition 8: A simulator for a KT scheme consists of a state space $\mathcal{ST}$ and algorithms

$$\mathcal{PK} \rightarrow \text{sim}_E\langle \mathcal{ST} \rangle \rightarrow \mathcal{C} \times \mathcal{HD} \qquad\qquad \mathcal{SK} \times \mathcal{C} \rightarrow \text{sim}_D\langle \mathcal{ST} \rangle \rightarrow \mathcal{HD} \times \mathcal{K} \ ,$$

where the $\langle \mathcal{ST} \rangle$ notation suggests that the algorithms are stateful with the common state space $\mathcal{ST}$.

Definition 9. *A KT scheme is correct and secure (against active adversaries) if there exists a simulator such that for every considerable adversary* $\mathcal{A}$ *the advantage function* $\mathbf{Adv}^{\text{ind}}(\mathcal{A}) := |\Pr[\mathbf{IND}^0(\mathcal{A})] - \Pr[\mathbf{IND}^1(\mathcal{A})]|$ *is negligible, where the games are in Fig. 10.*

Note how lines 04, 05 formalize *handle freshness* while lines 07, 12, 14, 15 formalize the *payload key recovery* demand. (In the $b = 1$ case there is no payload key, hence the conditioning in line 14). Lines 03, 11, 17 model that ciphertexts and handles and the payload keys of dishonestly generated ciphertexts are not considered secret but public information. As in our KEM/VKEM/KDFEM formalizations, while Definition 9, as is, specifies security against active adversaries, a strengthening to IND-CCA security can be achieved by activating the gray components in Fig. 10. (As before, for the results of this article, this will not be necessary).

---

[8] Analogously to Footnotes 4 and 5, it might be tempting to additionally require that $c' = c \implies hd' = hd$. However, as no part of our article logically depends on such a property, we once more abstain from *formally demanding* it.

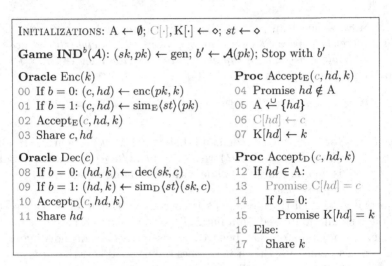

INITIALIZATIONS: $A \leftarrow \emptyset$; $C[\cdot], K[\cdot] \leftarrow \diamond$; $st \leftarrow \diamond$

Game $\text{IND}^b(\mathcal{A})$: $(sk, pk) \leftarrow \text{gen}$; $b' \leftarrow \mathcal{A}(pk)$; Stop with b'

Oracle Enc(k)
00 If $b = 0$: $(c, hd) \leftarrow \text{enc}(pk, k)$
01 If $b = 1$: $(c, hd) \leftarrow \text{sim}_E\langle st \rangle(pk)$
02 $\text{Accept}_E(c, hd, k)$
03 Share c, hd

Proc $\text{Accept}_E(c, hd, k)$
04 Promise $hd \notin A$
05 $A \overset{\cup}{\leftarrow} \{hd\}$
06 $C[hd] \leftarrow c$
07 $K[hd] \leftarrow k$

Oracle Dec(c)
08 If $b = 0$: $(hd, k) \leftarrow \text{dec}(sk, c)$
09 If $b = 1$: $(hd, k) \leftarrow \text{sim}_D\langle st \rangle(sk, c)$
10 $\text{Accept}_D(c, hd, k)$
11 Share hd

Proc $\text{Accept}_D(c, hd, k)$
12 If $hd \in A$:
13   Promise $C[hd] = c$
14   If $b = 0$:
15   Promise $K[hd] = k$
16 Else:
17   Share k

Fig. 10. Games $\text{IND}^0, \text{IND}^1$ as required by Definition 9. (By default ignore the gray components). The adversary can query the Enc, Dec oracles. The $\text{Accept}_E, \text{Accept}_D$ procedures are invoked (exclusively) from lines 02, 10.

9 Key Transport from KDFEMs

We demonstrate how an efficient key transport (KT) scheme can be derived from a KDFEM. The details of our construction are in Fig. 11. We prove that if the KDFEM is secure then so is the KT scheme.

Intuitively, our transform follows an encrypt-then-mac approach. The KT encryption algorithm invokes the KDFEM encapsulation algorithm once and the KDF evaluation algorithm twice. The first KDF evaluation creates a mask with which the transported key is one-time pad encrypted, and the second KDF evaluation is used to create a MAC tag for the resulting ciphertext. The KT decryption algorithm reverses this, and rejects all ciphertexts that have a wrong MAC tag.

Theorem 3. *Let* KDFEM $:= (\overline{\text{gen}}, \overline{\text{enc}}, \overline{\text{dec}}, \overline{\text{eval}})$ *be a KDFEM. Let* KT $:= (\text{gen}, \text{enc}, \text{dec})$ *be the KT scheme constructed from it according to Fig. 11. Then there exists a simulator for* KT *such that for all adversaries $\mathcal{A}$ attacking the security of the KT scheme there exists an adversary $\mathcal{B}$ attacking the security of the KDFEM such that*

$$\text{Adv}^{\text{ind}}(\mathcal{A}) \leq \text{Adv}^{\text{ke-kdfem}}(\mathcal{B}) + \frac{q}{|\mathcal{K}| - q}$$

where q denotes the number of decryption queries that $\mathcal{A}$ is allowed to pose, and the security games are those of Definition 7 and Definition 9.

The proof can be found in the full version [20]. In the following we provide some intuition. We first fix the simulator such that sim_E runs $\overline{\text{enc}}$ to establish the

Proc gen	**Proc** enc(pk, k)	**Proc** dec(sk, c)
00 $(sk, pk) \leftarrow \overline{\text{gen}}$	02 $(\bar{c}, \bar{hd}, st) \leftarrow \overline{\text{enc}}(pk)$	09 $(\bar{hd}, st) \leftarrow \overline{\text{dec}}(sk, \bar{c})$
01 Return sk, pk	03 $\mu \leftarrow \overline{\text{eval}}(st, \diamond)$	10 $\tau' \leftarrow \overline{\text{eval}}(st, \bar{k})$
	04 $\bar{k} \leftarrow k + \mu$	11 if $\tau = \tau'$:
	05 $\tau \leftarrow \overline{\text{eval}}(st, \bar{k})$	12 $\quad \mu \leftarrow \overline{\text{eval}}(st, \diamond)$
	06 $c := (\bar{c}, \bar{k}, \tau)$	13 $\quad k \leftarrow \bar{k} - \mu$
	07 $hd \leftarrow \bar{hd} \,_{\shortparallel}\, \bar{k}$	14 $\quad hd \leftarrow \bar{hd} \,_{\shortparallel}\, \bar{k}$
	08 Return c, hd	15 $\quad$ Return hd, k
		16 else: Abort

Fig. 11. Key transport built from KDFEM algorithms. The input key is masked by μ. A tag τ is generated for the masked key $\bar{k}$ in line 05. Line 16 aborts when the tag in the ciphertext is deemed unauthentic.

KDFEM ciphertext and handle, and then picks values $\bar{k}, \tau$ uniformly at random, while sim_D decrypts ciphertexts using the secret key except for authentic ciphertexts which it can recognize based on their KDFEM handle and the tabulated values $\bar{k}, \tau$.

Given this simulator, the reduction from KT security to KDFEM security is straightforward, as all KDFEM algorithm invocations can be replaced by corresponding oracle calls. The term $q/(|\mathcal{K}| - q)$ of the theorem statement comes from the encrypt-then-MAC design and covers adversaries that try to find valid MAC tags by guessing them. (With one attempt per decryption query, hence the factor q; note that set $\mathcal{K}$ coincides with the universe of MAC tag).

10 NIST KEM Candidates

We demonstrate that the four NIST post-quantum KEM finalists (CRYSTALS-KYBER[9] [23], Classic McEliece [4], SABER [12] and NTRU [10]) are almost (post-quantum secure) KDFEMs. More precisely, only mild tweaks are required to turn them into KDFEMs. Two challenges have to be resolved for this:

1. The NIST KEMs don't natively support handles. Our KDFEM interpretations need to introduce them, such that each enc invocation outputs a fresh handle, and such that any corresponding dec invocation recovers it.
2. The two KEM algorithms (encapsulation and decapsulation) need to be broken into three KDFEM algorithms (encapsulation, decapsulation, evaluation).

We address the first challenge by exploiting that the NIST KEMs are CCA secure so that we can simply use the ciphertexts as handles. More compact solutions for the handle may exist, for instance inspired by the approach of [14] that hashes an unpredictable part of the ciphertext. The second point is addressed by observing a common structure of the NIST KEMs that is illustrated in Fig. 12.

---

[9] CRYSTALS-KYBER has been selected as a winner by the NIST on July 5, 2022.

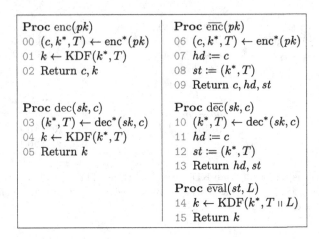

Proc enc(pk)
00 $(c, k^*, T) \leftarrow$ enc$^*(pk)$
01 $k \leftarrow$ KDF(k^*, T)
02 Return c, k

Proc $\overline{\text{enc}}$(pk)
06 $(c, k^*, T) \leftarrow$ enc$^*(pk)$
07 $hd := c$
08 $st := (k^*, T)$
09 Return c, hd, st

Proc dec(sk, c)
03 $(k^*, T) \leftarrow$ dec$^*(sk, c)$
04 $k \leftarrow$ KDF(k^*, T)
05 Return k

Proc $\overline{\text{dec}}$(sk, c)
10 $(k^*, T) \leftarrow$ dec$^*(sk, c)$
11 $hd := c$
12 $st := (k^*, T)$
13 Return hd, st

Proc $\overline{\text{eval}}$(st, L)
14 $k \leftarrow$ KDF$(k^*, T \parallel L)$
15 Return k

Fig. 12. The left-hand side represents a high level abstraction of the encapsulation and decapsulation algorithms of all four NIST post-quantum candidates. Each of these algorithms can be seen as a succession of core steps (denoted with enc* or dec*) that output a pre-key k^*, some additional terms T, and a ciphertext in the case of enc*. Both algorithms end with a key derivation step denoted with KDF. The right-hand side shows how we transform the KEMs into the KDFEM setting. Note that the KDF step is outsourced into a separate procedure, which adds the label input to the information in T. Note also that the KEM ciphertexts are used as handles.

In the remaining part of this section we provide the details of how the four NIST KEMs can be turned into KDFEMs. For concreteness we use the symbols from the documents provided by the KEMs' authors. While their notation differs from ours in many cases, the overall concepts remain sufficiently visible.

CRYSTALS-KYBER. Considering page 10 of the specification document [23], we build the generation algorithm exactly as in Algorithm 7. The encapsulation algorithm $\overline{\text{enc}}$ is constructed from lines 1–4 and returns $(c, hd, (\bar{K}, H(c)))$ where hd is actually c. The decapsulation $\overline{\text{dec}}$ is the same except for line 8 that should now return $(hd, (\bar{K}', H(c)))$ and line 10 that should return $(hd, (z, H(c)))$. The $\overline{\text{eval}}$ function is simply the KDF where the label is appended to the state.

CLASSIC MCELIECE. We build $\overline{\text{gen}}$ similarly as in page 9 of the specification document [4]. $\overline{\text{enc}}$ is described as in lines 1 and 2 from the encapsulation section on page 10 and $\overline{\text{dec}}$ as in lines 1–3 from the decapsulation section. Recall that in $\overline{\text{enc}}$ and $\overline{\text{dec}}$, the ciphertext is assigned to the handle. $\overline{\text{eval}}$ computes the hash H of the state appended to the label.

SABER. $\overline{\text{gen}}$ should be the same as the generation algorithm described in page 10 of the specification document [12]. $\overline{\text{enc}}$ represents lines 1–3 of the encapsulation figure with the returned value being $(c, hd, (\mathcal{H}(c), \hat{K}))$. $\overline{\text{dec}}$ is similar to the one presented in lines 1–7 of Algorithm 6 but with the exception that line 5 returns $(hd, (\mathcal{H}(c), \hat{K}'))$ and line 7 returns $(hd, (\mathcal{H}(c), z))$. Finally, $\overline{\text{eval}}$ computes the hash $\mathcal{H}$ of the state appended to the label.

NTRU. This case is very similar to the previous ones: $\overline{gen}$ is described similarly as in Sect. 1.12.1 [10], $\overline{enc}$ is set to execute lines 1, 2, 3 and 5 of Sect. 1.12.2 with the handle being the ciphertext. $\overline{enc}$ returns the tuple (packed_ciphertext, hd, st) where $st :=$ bytes_to_bits($packed\_rm, 8 \cdot$ dpke_plaintext_bytes). $\overline{dec}$ shall execute lines 1, 2, 4 and 5 but with the output being (hd, st) if $fail = 0$, and (hd, st') otherwise where $st' :=$ bytes_to_bits(prf_key, prf_key_bits) $\|$ bytes_to_bits($packed\_ciphertext, 8 \cdot$ kem_ciphertext_bytes). $\overline{eval}$ is now simply executing the function Hash over the state concatenated with the label.

11 Conclusion

The current efforts by NIST and other bodies to standardize quantum-resilient KEMs have a huge impact on the next decades of practical cryptography. This is not only because the new schemes have the potential to protect us from possible future threats, but also because of the conceptual change of considering KEMs instead of PKE schemes as the more fundamental building block. (Prior confidentiality standards like OAEP and IES and ECIES tended to formalize PKE, not KEM; this is now reversed). It is of utmost importance to get this PKE → KEM transition right: History has shown that any detail that can be misunderstood by practitioners might be gotten wrong eventually, with severe security issues as a consequence.

While cryptographic theory has found the classic KEM concept to be the most versatile abstraction, practical needs suggest that KEMs should be a little stronger than theory assumes. Our research explores two avenues to provide such a strengthening. We test our newly proposed primitives, VKEM and KDFEM, with benchmarks in the important domains of KEM combiners and key transport. We found in particular the KDFEM approach promising, as (1) the concept is simple and the constructions of combiners and key transports are immediate; and (2) all four NIST finalist KEMs require only minimal modifications to meet our KDFEM syntax and security. We hope that our work helps informing future standardization efforts.

Acknowledgment. Many valuable comments of anonymous SSR'23 reviewers helped improving this article. This research was partially funded by armasuisse Science and Technology (Project Nr. CYD-C-2020010).

References

1. Submission Requirements and Evaluation Criteria for the Post-Quantum Cryptography Standardization Process. Technical report, NIST (2016). https://csrc.nist.gov/CSRC/media/Projects/Post-Quantum-Cryptography/documents/call-for-proposals-final-dec-2016.pdf
2. CYBER; Quantum-safe Hybrid Key Exchanges. Technical Specification TS 103 744, ETSI (2020). https://www.etsi.org/deliver/etsi_ts/103700_103799/103744/01.01.01_60/ts_103744v010101p.pdf

3. Abe, M., Gennaro, R., Kurosawa, K., Shoup, V.: Tag-KEM/DEM: a new framework for hybrid encryption and a new analysis of Kurosawa-Desmedt KEM. In: Cramer, R. (ed.) EUROCRYPT 2005. LNCS, vol. 3494, pp. 128–146. Springer, Heidelberg (2005). https://doi.org/10.1007/11426639_8

4. Albrecht, M.R., et al.: Classic McEliece. Technical report, National Institute of Standards and Technology (2020). https://csrc.nist.gov/projects/post-quantum-cryptography/post-quantum-cryptography-standardization/round-3-submissions

5. Bellare, M., Namprempre, C.: Authenticated encryption: relations among notions and analysis of the generic composition paradigm. In: Okamoto, T. (ed.) ASIACRYPT 2000. LNCS, vol. 1976, pp. 531–545. Springer, Heidelberg (2000). https://doi.org/10.1007/3-540-44448-3_41

6. Bellare, M., Pointcheval, D., Rogaway, P.: Authenticated key exchange secure against dictionary attacks. In: Preneel, B. (ed.) EUROCRYPT 2000. LNCS, vol. 1807, pp. 139–155. Springer, Heidelberg (2000). https://doi.org/10.1007/3-540-45539-6_11

7. Bellare, M., Rogaway, P.: Entity authentication and key distribution. In: Stinson, D.R. (ed.) CRYPTO 1993. LNCS, vol. 773, pp. 232–249. Springer, Heidelberg (1994). https://doi.org/10.1007/3-540-48329-2_21

8. Bindel, N., Brendel, J., Fischlin, M., Goncalves, B., Stebila, D.: Hybrid key encapsulation mechanisms and authenticated key exchange. In: Ding, J., Steinwandt, R. (eds.) PQCrypto 2019. LNCS, vol. 11505, pp. 206–226. Springer, Cham (2019). https://doi.org/10.1007/978-3-030-25510-7_12

9. Callas, J., Donnerhacke, L., Finney, H., Shaw, D., Thayer, R.: OpenPGP message format. RFC 4880, RFC Editor (2007). https://doi.org/10.17487/RFC4880, https://www.rfc-editor.org/info/rfc4880

10. Chen, C., et al.: NTRU. Technical report, National Institute of Standards and Technology (2020). https://csrc.nist.gov/projects/post-quantum-cryptography/post-quantum-cryptography-standardization/round-3-submissions

11. Cramer, R., Shoup, V.: Design and analysis of practical public-key encryption schemes secure against adaptive chosen ciphertext attack. SIAM J. Comput. 33(1), 167–226 (2003)

12. D'Anvers, J.P., et al.: SABER. Technical report, National Institute of Standards and Technology (2020). https://csrc.nist.gov/projects/post-quantum-cryptography/post-quantum-cryptography-standardization/round-3-submissions

13. Dodis, Y., Katz, J.: Chosen-ciphertext security of multiple encryption. In: Kilian, J. (ed.) TCC 2005. LNCS, vol. 3378, pp. 188–209. Springer, Heidelberg (2005). https://doi.org/10.1007/978-3-540-30576-7_11

14. Duman, J., Hövelmanns, K., Kiltz, E., Lyubashevsky, V., Seiler, G.: Faster lattice-based KEMs via a generic Fujisaki-Okamoto transform using prefix hashing. In: Vigna, G., Shi, E. (eds.) ACM CCS 2021, pp. 2722–2737. ACM Press (2021). https://doi.org/10.1145/3460120.3484819

15. Giacon, F., Heuer, F., Poettering, B.: KEM combiners. In: Abdalla, M., Dahab, R. (eds.) PKC 2018. LNCS, vol. 10769, pp. 190–218. Springer, Cham (2018). https://doi.org/10.1007/978-3-319-76578-5_7

16. Krawczyk, H.: Cryptographic extraction and key derivation: the HKDF scheme. In: Rabin, T. (ed.) CRYPTO 2010. LNCS, vol. 6223, pp. 631–648. Springer, Heidelberg (2010). https://doi.org/10.1007/978-3-642-14623-7_34

17. Liskov, M., Rivest, R.L., Wagner, D.: Tweakable block ciphers. J. Cryptol. 24(3), 588–613 (2011). https://doi.org/10.1007/s00145-010-9073-y

18. McGrew, D.: An interface and algorithms for authenticated encryption. RFC 5116, RFC Editor (2008). https://doi.org/10.17487/RFC5116, https://www.rfc-editor.org/info/rfc5116

19. Pinto, A., Poettering, B., Schuldt, J.C.N.: Multi-recipient encryption, revisited. In: Moriai, S., Jaeger, T., Sakurai, K. (eds.) ASIACCS 2014, pp. 229–238. ACM Press (2014)

20. Poettering, B., Rastikian, S.: A study of KEM generalizations. Cryptology ePrint Archive, Paper 2023/272 (2023). https://eprint.iacr.org/2023/272

21. Rogaway, P.: Authenticated-encryption with associated-data. In: Atluri, V. (ed.) ACM CCS 2002, pp. 98–107. ACM Press (2002). https://doi.org/10.1145/586110.586125

22. Rogaway, P.: Nonce-based symmetric encryption. In: Roy, B., Meier, W. (eds.) FSE 2004. LNCS, vol. 3017, pp. 348–358. Springer, Heidelberg (2004). https://doi.org/10.1007/978-3-540-25937-4_22

23. Schwabe, P., et al.: CRYSTALS-KYBER. Technical report, National Institute of Standards and Technology (2020). https://csrc.nist.gov/projects/post-quantum-cryptography/post-quantum-cryptography-standardization/round-3-submissions

24. Shoup, V.: A proposal for an ISO standard for public key encryption. Technical report, Version 2.1, IBM Zurich Research Lab (2001). https://www.shoup.net/papers/iso-2_1.pdf

25. Zhang, R., Hanaoka, G., Shikata, J., Imai, H.: On the security of multiple encryption or CCA-security+CCA-security=CCA-security? In: Bao, F., Deng, R., Zhou, J. (eds.) PKC 2004. LNCS, vol. 2947, pp. 360–374. Springer, Heidelberg (2004). https://doi.org/10.1007/978-3-540-24632-9_26

Vision Paper: Do We Need to Change Some Things?

Open Questions Posed by the Upcoming Post-quantum Migration to Existing Standards and Deployments

Panos Kampanakis[(✉)] and Tancrède Lepoint[ⓘ]

Amazon Web Services, Seattle, USA
{kpanos,tlepoint}@amazon.com

Abstract. Cryptographic algorithms are vital components ensuring the privacy and security of computer systems. They have constantly improved and evolved over the years following new developments, attacks, breaks, and lessons learned. A recent example is that of quantum-resistant cryptography, which has gained a lot of attention in the last decade and is leading to new algorithms being standardized today. These algorithms, however, present a real challenge: they come with strikingly different size and performance characteristics than their classical counterparts. At the same time, common foundational aspects of our transport protocols have lagged behind as the Internet remains a very diverse space in which different use-cases and parts of the world have different needs.

This vision paper motivates more research and possible standards updates related to the upcoming quantum-resistant cryptography migration. It stresses the importance of amplification reflection attacks and congestion control concerns in transport protocols and presents research and standardization takeaways for assessing the impact and the efficacy of potential countermeasures. It emphasizes the need to go beyond the standardization of key encapsulation mechanisms in order to address the numerous protocols and deployments of public-key encryption while avoiding pitfalls. Finally, it motivates the critical need for research in anonymous credentials and blind signatures at the core of numerous deployments and standardization efforts aimed at providing privacy-preserving trust signals.

Keywords: Post-quantum · Amplification Protection · Congestion Control · Public-key Encryption · Anonymous Authentication

1 Introduction

Rapid advances in quantum computing [49] have motivated the need to replace current cryptographic schemes based on the believed hardness of traditional number-theoretic problems, such as integer factorization and discrete logarithms. Since 2016, the National Institute of Standards and Technology (NIST)

© The Author(s), under exclusive license to Springer Nature Switzerland AG 2023
F. Günther and J. Hesse (Eds.): SSR 2023, LNCS 13895, pp. 78–102, 2023.
https://doi.org/10.1007/978-3-031-30731-7_4

is running an open Post-Quantum Cryptography standardization process [73] to standardize quantum-resistant key encapsulation mechanisms (KEMs) and digital signatures. In July 2022, NIST completed the third round of the process, and selected Kyber [87] as KEM, and Dilithium [64], Falcon [78], and SPHINCS+ [42] as digital signatures, to become the first NIST post-quantum standards (expected 2024).[1] While these primitives provide the same core functionalities as their classical counterparts, they feature strikingly different size and performance characteristics. Table 1 summarizes the public key, ciphertext, and signature sizes of NIST future post-quantum standards, as well as current NIST standards ECDH P-384, ECDSA P-384, and RSA-3072.

Table 1. Classical and post-quantum cryptographic schemes selected by NIST for standardization, ordered by ciphertext/signature size.

Algorithm	Quantum-safe	Public Key	Ciphertext/Signature
ECDH P-384	✗	48	48
Kyber-512	✓	800	768
Kyber-768	✓	1184	1088
ECDSA P-384	✗	48	96
RSA-3072	✗	387	384
Falcon-512	✓	897	666
Dilithium-2	✓	1312	2420
Falcon-1024	✓	1793	1280
Dilithium-3	✓	1952	3293
SPHINCS+-128s	✓	32	7856
SPHINCS+-192s	✓	48	16224

Other standardization organizations have also been working on introducing post-quantum algorithms to existing protocols and standards [94,99] and focusing on post-quantum migration challenges and solutions.[2] Additionally, a few Internet Engineering Task Force (IETF) RFC drafts are already introducing these algorithms in IETF standards [39,41,68,69,95,100]. In February 2023, the IETF created PQUIP[3], a working group focused on the use of post-quantum cryptography in protocols. Similarly, the European Telecommunications Standards Institute has formed a Quantum-Safe Working Group [28] that aims to make assessments and recommendations on the various proposals from industry and academia regarding real-world deployments of quantum-safe cryptography.

The integration of post-quantum key encapsulation mechanisms and signatures will affect existing protocols due to their size. For example, using post-quantum cryptography could increase the number of packets which in turns

---

[1] The standardization process continues with a fourth round for alternates key encapsulation mechanisms (BIKE [9], Classic McEliece [4], HQC [3], and SIKE [47]), and a new call for proposal for digital signatures.

[2] https://www.nccoe.nist.gov/crypto-agility-considerations-migrating-post-quantum-cryptographic-algorithms.

[3] https://datatracker.ietf.org/wg/pquip/about/.

could increase the loss probability in constrained conditions [74]. Post-quantum certificate chains could exceed any certificate chain size that our applications see today. Post-quantum signatures in TLS could lead to connection establishment slowdowns [11,56,91,92]. QUIC would also see challenges with post-quantum signatures related to its amplification protection feature [55]. Most of the transport protocols used today were designed decades ago under different network conditions with different sizes in mind.

Our Contributions. In this work, we emphasize several areas and gaps requiring research and standardization to make the post-quantum migration successful.

1. In Sect. 2, we discuss how post-quantum authentication will increase the amplification reflection attack risk for UDP-based secure transport protocols, and survey potential amplification protection trade-offs for QUIC, DTLS, and others (Sect. 2.1). We propose further investigations to identify current protocol use-case behavior in order to find the best option for standardization.
2. We focus on congestion control in Sect. 2.2; we point out that the initial congestion window value in common secure transport protocols may be already too small for today and could introduce connection slowdowns in a post-quantum world. We suggest a re-evaluation of the initial value as done by Chi et al. a decade ago for RFC 6928. We also stress the potential impact of such a change on various parts of the world due the heavier additional post-quantum handshake data.
3. In Sect. 3, we identify and discuss the need for standardization of quantum-safe public-key encryption, and in particular that of hybrid public key encryption and key wrapping.
4. We identify the need for research in areas like quantum-safe password-authenticated key exchange (Sect. 4), oblivious pseudorandom functions, blind signatures (Sect. 5), and other cryptographic standards which do not have the community or the forum to introduce quantum-safe algorithms (Sect. 6).

2   Transport Protocol Implications

This section discusses implications of the post-quantum migration on transport protocols, and, in particular, talks about the increased concerns around amplification attacks (Sect. 2.1) and congestion control (Sect. 2.2).

2.1   Amplification Attacks

Amplification attacks are distributed denial of service (DDoS) attacks exploiting a disparity in resource consumption between an attacker and a target system. When a small request triggers a large response, an attacker performing many such requests can disrupt a target system which receives high volumes of response data. To further increase the impact, attackers can perform amplification reflection attacks that leverage a reflector entity which inadvertently serves

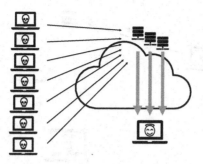

Fig. 1. Attackers spoofing multiple small requests can trigger big responses by the reflector and deploy reflection amplification DDoS to the victim.

in amplifying multiple requests spoofed from a victim's address. Figure 1 shows a typical amplification reflection.

In [67], Majkowski presents historical amplification reflection attacks and explains how attackers managed to trigger Gbps of traffic over multiple protocols. These attacks were successful with protocols where the source address is not validated and thus can be spoofed. Such protocols are usually UDP-based, like DNS or NTP. CISA created an alert for UDP-based amplification[4] describing the amplifications factors for each protocol of concern. MITRE maintains a Common Enumeration Weakness about them[5] referencing common vulnerabilities created in relation to previous DDoS amplifications attacks (e.g., CVE-1999-1379, CVE-1999-0513, CVE-2000-0041, CVE-1999-1066, CVE-2013-5211).

Such attacks were observed widely a decade ago with DNS[6]. In one of the largest amplification attacks, attackers employed open DNS recursors which responded to anyone on the Internet to initiate very large amounts of data towards https://www.spamhaus.org/ [79]. The attacks peaked at 90Gbps on the victim's system and at 300Gbps on the Tier 1 provider. The amplification factor was 100× by using 21.7 million mis-configured recursors and a UDP protocol.

The impact of an amplification attack grows as the amplification factor increases, i.e., the more data the attacker can trigger in the response with a small, cheap request, the more damage it can cause the victim. In [84], Rossow proposes to quantify the amplification by introducing the notions of bandwidth amplification factor (BAF) and packet amplification factor (PAF). They also investigate the efficiency of discovering amplifiers, and the most amplifying protocols (which include common UDP protocols).

Some protocols offer anti-amplification mechanisms which mandate the validation of the source before sending the whole large response. For example, Fig. 2 shows how the reflector can send part of the data and wait for an `Acknowledgement` before sending the rest of it. These mechanisms introduce

---

[4] https://www.cisa.gov/uscert/ncas/alerts/TA14-017A.

[5] https://cwe.mitre.org/data/definitions/406.html.

[6] https://www.cisa.gov/uscert/ncas/alerts/TA13-088A.

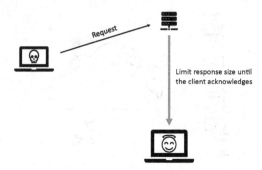

Fig. 2. Amplification Protection where the reflector limits the size of the response from a not-yet-validated source and waits for an `Acknowledgement` to limit the impact of a potential reflection amplification attack.

a round-trip while the sender is waiting for the `ACK` which slows down the connection. Thus, service providers sometimes do not honor them [72]. Additional countermeasures include address spoofing protections deployed at the network level, which validate the source address based on routing information or routing firewall rules, but these are not always available or effective. Furthermore, some of the most commonly exploited amplifying protocols, such as DNS, have seen hardened deployments over time which improved their security and made amplification reflection harder.

Below we discuss specific protocols and the potential impact quantum-safe algorithms would have on their amplification potential.

QUIC. QUIC is a UDP-based encrypted transport protocol, at the core of HTTP/3, designed for performance. It is specified in a set of IETF standards ratified in May 2021 [98]. QUIC protects its UDP datagrams by using encryption and authentication keys established in a TLS 1.3 handshake carried over QUIC transport. QUIC also offers amplification protection by mandating that a sender can send up to 3× the size of the request for non-validated addresses (which could be spoofed). Figure 3 shows QUIC's amplification protection.

In typical QUIC deployments, 3× the request size amounts to approximately ≈4 kB. Unfortunately, it is not uncommon for a certificate chain along with the leaf certificate on the Web to exceed that limit, which would trigger QUIC's amplification protection and add a round-trip to common HTTP/3 connections. As a consequence, many QUIC servers do not honor the amplification window. Nawrocki et al. [72] investigated common servers like Cloudflare and Google which exceed the window up to an amplification BAF factor of 10. Meta's servers exceed it by an even more significant amount.

In a post-quantum world, when using the general purpose Dilithium signature scheme, the `ServerHello`, `Certificate` and `CertificateVerify` messages could add up to 15-17kB for the lowest security level. Depending on the digital signature algorithm, parameters, and length of the certificate chain, the post-

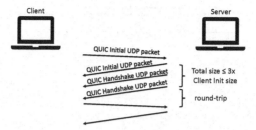

Fig. 3. Amplification Protection in QUIC where the server returns 3× the size of the QUIC client `Init` packet and waits for a response before sending more data.

quantum migration could easily make the BAF ranging from 5 to 20 in typical settings. In [55], Kampanakis et al. discuss how the post-quantum signature schemes selected by NIST will all exceed the amplification window and incur at least a round-trip. Figure 4 experimentally shows this for classical RSA-2048 and post-quantum (PQ) certificate chains, illustrating further the impact post-quantum authentication has on QUIC amplification protection. If QUIC implementers do not honor the amplification protection window today to prevent the extra round-trip [72], will they do the same in a post-quantum world where the amount of data returned from the server is significantly higher? If the servers not honoring the amplification protection introduce some amplification reflection attack risk today [72], that risk will multiply with post-quantum signatures in the future. In typical high profile attacks of the past, millions of mis-configured open DNS resolvers ended up generating Gbps of traffic with amplification factors between 50–100. Locking down these servers was relatively easy. In a future world, thousands or more of QUIC servers could theoretically serve as amplification reflectors with sizeable amplification factors. Locking them down by identifying illegitimate traffic may not be trivial as they could be serving clients from all over the world.

There are different approaches to addressing the 3× amplification window issue with post-quantum authentication in QUIC. Each of them has advantages and disadvantages. The options are:

– Increase the 3× amplification window to a level that will not incur round-trips for the post-quantum case. That could mean >15× amplification windows which certainly increase the amplification factor.
– Trim the "authentication data" sent in the handshake. That can include using session resumption [98, Sec. 4.5], [80, Sec. 2.2] or suppressing intermediate CA certificates by caching them [55,97]. These could alleviate the size of the server response and the amplification factor. A similar option could be certificate compression [34], but that would not improve the size much as the certificate bloat comes from random data (public key, signature).
– Use address validation tokens for every post-quantum authentication. QUIC validation tokens are opaque values which enable the server to confirm it has seen the client address. Tokens add a round-trip and may negatively affect

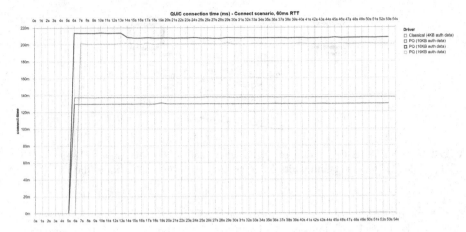

Fig. 4. QUIC connection time (ms) for classical ≈4 kB RSA-2048, 10 kB PQ certificate chains, 18kB Dilithium-2, and 22 kB Dilithium-3 certificate chains. In these experiments the client was creating 1,000 sequential connections. The client-server rount-trip was 60ms. The measurements were collected using s2n-quic's netbench benchmarking tool. s2n-quic is AWS' QUIC library. We can see that all experiments include one round-trip due to QUIC's amplification protection. The 18 and 22 kB certificate chain connections include one additional round-trip due to QUIC's initial congestion window (see Sect. 2.2). Note that captures showed that the 10 kB chain connection times are a fraction of 1 ms slower than the classical RSA 4 kB ones, whereas network condition variability made them measure a few milliseconds faster in the experiment.

performance unless the client revisits the server for the lifetime of the token. We are not aware of any work that studies the use of QUIC tokens on the Internet and how frequently clients revisit servers. Another option could be for the client to include a new extension requesting a token only when supporting post-quantum signatures and for servers that it knows it visits often. As a less aggressive measure, servers could start sending tokens only when suspecting amplification reflection attacks.

– Artificially increase the ClientHello size so that the quantum-safe authentication data fits in the amplification window. Increasing the ClientHello means we will be unnecessarily wasting resources or bandwidth.

In short, post-quantum authentication introduces performance complications with QUIC amplification. We propose the following research investigations and standardization takeaways:

Takeway 1. Study the use of address validation tokens in QUIC and identify if server implementations use them and when. Evaluate their overall effectiveness by quantifying the frequency of revisiting servers for the lifetime of a token. Optimize the lifetime of tokens based on total traffic and client revisits.

Takeway 2. Evaluate the amplification protection options and standardize the best one for post-quantum signature sizes. Trimming the authentication data and leveraging tokens seem to be the most natural options. As [72] demonstrated, $3\times$ is not enough even for classical signatures, thus a more realistic amplification protection limit should also be identified.

DTLS 1.2, 1.3. DTLS 1.3 is TLS' counterpart over UDP. It was recently standardized and is susceptible to amplification attacks because the server authentication data is disproportionately larger than the `ClientHello`. The DTLS 1.3 standard [83] addresses amplification similarly to QUIC. It recommends, but does not mandate, that *"a server SHOULD limit the amount of data it sends toward a client address to $3\times$ the amount of data sent by the client before it verifies that the client is able to receive data at that address"*. Moreover, it recommends, not mandates, the use of a cookie to validate the source address. We are not aware of any work that investigates if DTLS 1.3 implementations honor these optional amplification protections discussed in the standard.

Like TLS 1.3 and QUIC, DTLS 1.3 post-quantum authentication data size will significantly increase, which will have implications to its amplification potential. DTLS 1.3 servers could theoretically serve as amplification reflectors with sizeable amplification factors.

DTLS 1.2 [81] would suffer the same challenges with amplification and post-quantum certificates. So far, only (D)TLS 1.3 is being planned for post-quantum standardization in the IETF's TLS WG. Thus, we consider DTLS 1.2 out of scope for this work at this time.

To address some of the open questions for amplifications in post-quantum DTLS 1.3, we propose the following research investigations and standardization takeaways:

Takeway 3. Study how server DTLS 1.3 implementations behave when the certificate chain exceeds $3\times$ the client request (like [72] did for QUIC). Also consider if an amplification protection mechanism should become mandatory in DTLS 1.3.

Takeway 4. Investigate the DTLS 1.3 use-cases that would benefit from key exchange cookies when post-quantum certificates exceed the amplification window. These will depend on the frequency of clients communicating with the same server over the lifetime of the cookie.

Takeway 5. Evaluate the amplification protection options and standardize the best one for post-quantum signatures in DTLS 1.3. These options resemble the ones in QUIC and include increasing the window, using exchange cookies when post-quantum certificates are used and limiting the authentication data in the handshake. A more realistic amplification protection window should also be identified.

DNSSEC. DNS is a protocol widely used for name resolution. It runs over UDP. As we already discussed, it has traditionally been a good candidate for amplification reflection attacks. In a DNS amplification, the EDNS0 extension has been used to include large messages. A DNS request of about 50B could elicit response sizes of up to 4 kB which results to a 80× BAF [67]. Although widely effective in the past [79], DNS amplification reflections have become less common as there are fewer open resolvers and protections against them are well established [67].

DNSSEC is a standard for authenticating DNS responses to prevent DNS spoofing attacks. Unfortunately, the post-quantum signatures selected by NIST would not fit in a single packet, and fragmentation is not an option for DNSSEC [71]. To address the issue, Goertzen et al. [35] propose ARRF, a method of fragmenting DNS resource records at the application layer based on client acknowledgments. Sequentially sending each fragment after an acknowledgement would slow down getting the full response. That is why [35] describes a mode for requesting the fragments in parallel after acknowledging the first fragment. Although the BAF is high due to the size of the signed record, such an approach would not increase the PAF per DNSSEC RRSIG record. Requiring the server to keep track of the fragments until they are received by the requester adds some burden on DNS servers today which are stateless. Alternatively, Fregly et al. [29] recently proposed a Merkle-tree structure which can shrink these signatures to manageable sizes.

To address some of the amplification concerns for post-quantum DNSSEC, we propose the following standardization takeaway:

Takeway 6. Identify, evaluate and standardize an amplification-resistant solution for post-quantum DNSSEC in IETF's DNSOP working group.

TLS 1.2, 1.3. TLS is the status quo for encrypting communications on the Internet. TLS is not susceptible to the same amplification reflection risks because TCP validates the source address before the TLS negotiation. However, post-quantum TLS still induces an amplification risk as the data sent by the client and server are unbalanced in size.

For example, in a TLS 1.3 negotiation, a client could send a ClientHello to negotiate quantum-safe key exchanges without including a post-quantum key_share. If the server supported post-quantum key exchange, it would respond with a HelloRetryRequest and a post-quantum key_share which could add up to a few kB depending on the post-quantum KEM. Thus, with a very small

`ClientHello`, the client could trigger a relatively big response (5–8× BAF). This response would not be nearly as big as the post-quantum certificate chain from the server which has a higher amplification factor. We consider the amplification concern for TLS 1.3 to only be a denial of service risk for the server and client's edge capacity, not a reflection attack against a victim. Such attacks have not been seen widely in the past because they affect both the attacker and the victim and they are easy to identify and protect against.

In TLS 1.2, the client could trigger a big quantum-safe certificate chain and `Server Key Exchange` from the server. Figure 5 shows the `Server Key Exchange`, `Certificate` and `CertificateVerify` messages which could add to 20kB with a very small `ClientHello` (100× BAF) which is significant. So far, only TLS 1.3 is being planned for post-quantum standardization in the IETF's TLS WG. Thus, we consider TLS 1.2 amplifications out of scope for this work at this time.

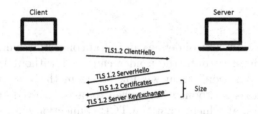

Fig. 5. Amplification in TLS 1.2 where the server returns a potentially large post-quantum certificate chain and ephemeral public key while the client has only sent a small `ClientHello`. The client address is still validated by the TCP handshake.

IKEv2. IKEv2 [60] is another protocol running over UDP. It is used to negotiate keys, authenticate and establish Security Associations between IPsec VPN peers. CERT/CC published vulnerability VU#419128[7] about how IKEv2 implementations could amplify requests by 9× based on a whitepaper by Chad Seaman from Akamai in 2016. The work had discovered IKEv2 implementations where the responder kept re-sending `IKE_SA_INIT` messages after not receiving an `IKE_AUTH` by the initiator. The study found thousands of servers replied 21 times or more per initiator `IKE_SA_INIT` message, and some servers responded thousands of times. IKEv2 specifies that the *"responder MUST never retransmit a response unless it receives a retransmission of the request"*. Thus, the behavior of these responders was violating the standard.

Post-quantum IKEv2 may need to fragment `IKE_SA_INIT` messages as the post-quantum KEM public key or ciphertext may not fit in one packet. RFC 9242 [93] specifies the `IKE_INTERMEDIATE` exchange which can carry and fragment post-quantum key exchanges after performing a classical key exchange with

---

[7] https://www.kb.cert.org/vuls/id/419128.

IKE_SA_INIT. The quantum-safe response by the server could be significantly bigger than the classical IKE_SA_INIT but given that the IKE_INTERMEDIATE exchange occurs after IKE_SA_INIT there is no additional amplification reflection possibility. Moreover, Kyber offers a balance between the public key and ciphertext which means there is no additional amplification factor introduced. Even if implementers haven't addressed the IKEv2 amplification vulnerability from 2016, post-quantum algorithms do not bring any additional amplification concerns to IKEv2.

2.2   Congestion Control

Congestion control algorithms aim to transfer data fast without overwhelming the network. Generally, they do that by offering a initial congestion window value which is the starting point. The sender ramps up sending data as long as it is successful and slows down after it sees failures (which could be because of congestion).

TCP. TCP congestion control defines an initial congestion window (initcwnd) size which is the limit of data the sender can send without receiving an ACK from the receiver. The congestion window starts in the slow-start phase from initcwnd and increases exponentially when data is received successfully until a packet loss occurs, at which point the TCP connection enters the congestion avoidance phase. Figure 6 shows the sender filling up a window with 10 segments and waiting for an ACK before continuing the slow-start phase and doubling the congestion window.

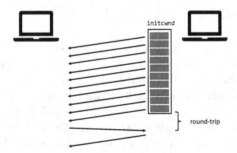

Fig. 6. After filling the initcwnd, the sender waits for a full round-trip for an Acknowledgement before resuming sending data.

The TCP initcwnd has historically been changing over time as networks evolve. It originally started at 1 Maximum TCP Segment Size (MSS) [96], and then increased to 2 MSS [76] and to 4 MSS [75]. A decade ago, after careful evaluation and research [25], RFC 6928 [19] updated initcwnd to 10 MSS. There was also a proposal [101] to introduce a mechanism to dynamically update the initial congestion window by tracking connections. This idea never got adopted.

Asia Pacific Network Information Centre's (APNIC) 2018 survey [86] showed that 80% of the Alexa Top 1M servers used `initcwnd` = 10 MSS, but there were thousands that exceeded it. Today's Content Delivery Network (CDN) providers often use `initcwnd` much higher than 10 MSS to maximize their content performance [77]. CDNs increase their starting window based on performance optimizations and content measurements of their networks, but it is unlikely they use broad Internet data to measure the effect on the rest of the Internet.

Post-quantum authentication will interfere with TCP's `initcwnd`. A certificate chain with quantum-safe signatures and public keys will exceed 10 MSS. Sikeridis et al. investigated the issue and showed that post-quantum signatures would introduce a round-trip [92]. Westerbaan simulated post-quantum authentication in TLS with `initcwnd` = 30 MSS [11], and showed that tweaking the `initcwnd` value could prevent a round-trip but would not address constrained networks, buggy servers or middle-boxes which are affected by the overall size of post-quantum signatures. A discussion[8] in NIST's pqc-forum mailing list brought up the topic of increasing the window to alleviate the issue given that CDNs already do it.

Significantly increasing the default TCP `initcwnd` value in every Internet server that wants to enable post-quantum TLS authentication should not be done lightly as it could have adverse effects on TCP Congestion Control. We consider it as a potential improvement that should be carefully studied at a large scale before deployment. For example, the last increase to 10 MSS received thorough analysis and investigation; RFC 6928 [19, Appendix A] discusses concerns which include fairness and effects on slow networks and developing regions.

To address some of these open questions, we propose the following research investigations and standardization takeaway:

Takeway 7. Consider increasing the TCP initial congestion window to `initcwnd` =20-25MSS. A similar exercise to [86] should reveal what values are commonly used today and how much the industry has tweaked the standard. We could also continuously monitor `initcwnd` trends by probing random addresses on the Internet like in [86]. After carefully researching the `initcwnd` optimal values for the Internet like in [25] to ensure the concerns in [19, Appendix A] are addressed, we could standardize a new `initcwnd` value.

QUIC Congestion Control. QUIC has its own congestion control which is similar to TCP's (RFC 6928 [19]). [46] states that *"endpoints SHOULD use an initial congestion window of ten times the maximum size (max_ datagram_ size), while limiting the window to the larger of 14,720 bytes or twice the maximum datagram size"*. It is clear that QUIC will suffer from the same connection slowdown with quantum-safe authentication as TCP due to the initial congestion

---

[8] https://groups.google.com/a/list.nist.gov/g/pqc-forum/c/2ak2U_MxyrQ/m/L-kQ-SubBwAJ.

window. RFC 6928 also says that "*Though the anti-amplification limit can prevent the congestion window from being fully utilized and therefore slow down the increase in congestion window, it does not directly affect the congestion window.*". QUIC can be slowed down by both the amplification window (Sect. 2.1) and the initial congestion window, whichever is the lowest. Figure 4 experimentally shows this for classical RSA-2048 and post-quantum (PQ) certificate chains. Other than the standard, alternate congestion control algorithms have also been proposed for QUIC such as CUBIC (RFC 8312).

To address the congestion window issue with post-quantum QUIC, we propose the following research investigation and standardization takeaways:

Takeway 8. Evaluate if QUIC implementations and deployments honor the initial congestion window. If they do not honor it, that may mean that addressing the amplification protection issue (Sect. 2.1) will be enough to enable the transition to post-quantum authentication.

Takeway 9. Consider updating the QUIC standard to support bigger initial congestion window values after carefully investigating its impact as with TCP's initcwnd above.

DTLS Congestion Control. DTLS does not specify a congestion control algorithm and leaves it to the transport protocol. [83] states that "*some transports provide congestion control for traffic carried over them. If the congestion window is sufficiently narrow, DTLS handshake retransmissions may be held rather than transmitted immediately, potentially leading to timeouts and spurious retransmission. When DTLS is used over such transports, care should be taken not to overrun the likely congestion window.*". It also acknowledges that large certificate chains can lead to congestion and recommends sending part of the chain and waiting for a response packet. It then proposes extensions that will alleviate the data size sent.

While DTLS calls out potential congestion issues with large server responses, it does not mandate any specific countermeasure. It is uncertain if implementations honor the suggestions. If they honor them, a transition to post-quantum certificates could slow down DTLS connections. To address some of these open questions, we propose the following research investigation takeaway:

Takeway 10. Research if DTLS implementations and deployments honor the congestion avoidance suggestions in [83, Sec. 5.8.3]. If these introduce a round-trip to the post-quantum certificate scenario, investigate what value would be optimal and how it would interfere with the DTLS amplification protection investigation takeaway in Sect. 2.1.

IKEv2. IKEv2 communications consist of pairs of messages where the initiator initiates an exchange and the responder responds. The specification [60] does not define any congestion control. It recognizes that retransmissions could affect congestion and mandates exponential backoffs and Explicit Congestion Notification (ECN) support to alleviate it.

Post-quantum IKEv2 would include large `IKE_INTERMEDIATE` (RFC 9242 [93]) and `IKE_AUTH` messages which could exacerbate the problem. It would be interesting to investigate how broad exponential backoff and ECN support is in IKEv2 implementations, but given that IKEv2 negotiations happen only when bringing up a tunnel and constitute a very small percentage of Internet traffic, we do not believe post-quantum IKEv2 could affect congestion on the Internet.

3 Public Key Encryption and Key Wrapping

In its post-quantum standardization call for proposals, NIST asked for public-key encryption (PKE), KEM, and digital signatures schemes, and said *"As the KEM and public-key encryption functionalities can generally be interconverted, unless the submitter specifies otherwise, NIST will apply standard conversion techniques to convert between schemes if necessary."* Indeed, almost all of the KEM candidates submitted first apply some variant of the Fujisaki–Okamoto (FO) transform [24,30,31] on a weakly-secure "base" PKE scheme to construct the resulting KEM. This blueprint holds in particular for Kyber which defines an IND-CPA secure PKE [87, Sec. 1.2], and uses a tweaked FO transform to create the IND-CCA2-secure KEM [87, Sec. 1.3].

The generic reverse construction follows the KEM-DEM paradigm [89] (a.k.a, hybrid encryption). The recipient public key is used as input of the encapsulation function of the KEM to create a ciphertext and shared key, and the data is encrypted using the shared key in a data-encapsulation mechanism (DEM) — often instantiated with an AEAD scheme such as AES-GCM. Albeit these generic transformations give a nice theoretical framework to work with, we believe that standardizing public-key encryption will necessitate additional efforts and care to avoid the pitfalls encountered in the past.

Indeed, numerous standards have been created over the years for public-key encryption (and hybrid public-key encryption), including ANSI X9.63 (ECIES) [8], ANSI X9.44 (RSA-KEM) [6], IEEE P1363a [44], ISO/IEC 18033-2 [90], and SECG SEC 1 [88], and no less than four RFCs for PKCS [51–54]. Martínez et al. [33] provide a thorough comparison of the elliptic-curve public-key encryption standards, highlighting that the differences between them prevented ECIES from being fully interoperable. The lack of clear PKE standard has further led to inconsistent support across libraries; e.g., NaCL and BouncyCastle implement their own versions of hybrid encryption.

(Hybrid) Public-Key Encryption. In 2022, Hybrid Public Key Encryption (HPKE) was published in RFC 9180 [10]. HPKE aims at addressing interoperability issues with ECIES. It has been designed to be generic, with simplicity and modularity in mind. It offers a "base" mode which only encrypts data, and "authenticate" and "psk" modes which authenticate the sender and encrypt data. HPKE has seen immediate adoption by Internet protocols such as TLS Encrypted Client Hello [82], Oblivious DNS-over-HTTPS (RFC 9230 [61]), Message Layer Security[9], and Privacy Preserving Measurement[10]. Since its ciphersuites consist of specifying a KEM, a Key Derivation Function (KDF), and an AEAD, HPKE naturally supports the addition of new ciphersuites in the future [10, Sec. 9.2]. At ICMC 2022, Anastassova et al. [7] presented the first implementation of a post-quantum HPKE (PQ-HPKE) using Kyber as KEM[11], and a combination of Kyber and DHKEM [10] in "PQ-hybrid" mode. While they conclude that the performance is acceptable (especially for larger messages), they also emphasize that Kyber does not allow to use HPKE in "authenticated" mode since it does not provide a direct API for authenticated encapsulation and decapsulation. As such, there is no known construction of post-quantum HPKE resisting key impersonation attacks. Similar discussions were held on the CFRG mailing list[12], further emphasizing the need of authenticated KEM in protocols, such as the Certificate Management Protocol (CMP) [70].

To address some of these open issues with quantum-safe PKE, we propose the following research investigation and standardization takeaways:

Takeway 11. Standardize an HPKE variant that provides post-quantum security in the near future, and addresses the security proof gaps with PQ-hybrid HPKE identified in [7, Sec. IV.C].

Takeway 12. Research and standardize post-quantum authenticated KEMs to enable the migration of protocols requiring such a primitive.

Key Wrapping. While the KEM-DEM paradigm above (or HPKE) enable us to construct an IND-CCA secure public key encryption, the encryptor does not fully control the value of the shared key for the data-encapsulation mechanism. In some applications, this is not desirable. For example, when sending the same message to many recipients, a natural approach is to encrypt the message with a fresh AES key, and then encrypt the AES key to each recipient. Henceforth, the data to encrypt with the KEM-DEM (or HPKE) would be the fresh AES key. While any secure authenticated encryption scheme can be used to encrypt the fresh key, there exist specialized symmetric key-wrapping algorithms that are more compact like those defined in NIST SP 800-38F, IETF RFC 3394, RFC 5297, RFC 5649. Some of these symmetric key wrapping algorithms have been combined with public key encryption in RFC 6637 [50] and deployed by major vendors[13,14] . In many other deployments, the fresh AES key is directly

---

[9] https://datatracker.ietf.org/wg/mls/about/.

[10] https://datatracker.ietf.org/wg/ppm/about/.

[11] They also instantiated the KEM using SIKE [48], which subsequently suffered fatal attacks [16,66] and should no longer be used [47], so we do not discuss this further.

[12] https://mailarchive.ietf.org/arch/msg/cfrg/zTnaLhO5N7ipvPyJ8lmV7Iic9RU/.

[13] https://opensource.apple.com/source/Security/Security-59754.80.3/keychain/SecureObjectSync/SOSECWrapUnwrap.c.

[14] https://cloud.google.com/kms/docs/key-wrapping.

encrypted (using padding) using the PKE scheme, in particular using RSA-OAEP (as in AWS KMS[15] , AWS CloudHSM[16] , or Apple[17]).

It is clear there is a need for a standard to wrap data using a KEM public key. It is worth asking ourselves whether the few bytes that were gained by using key wrapping (rather than an AEAD) would be as impactful when using a post-quantum primitive for which the ciphertext is at least an order of magnitude larger than the expected gain (Table 1). A potential avenue (which requires proper evaluation) may be to use symmetric key wrapping as the data encapsulation mechanism in HPKE. Thus, we propose the following research investigation and standardization takeaway:

Takeway 13. Research and standardize a public-key wrapping method, either as a direct application of a (post-quantum) HPKE, or as a specialized construction.

4 Password-Authenticated Key Exchange

Asymmetric Password Authenticated Key Exchange (PAKE) protocols allow password authentication and mutually authenticated key exchange without disclosing passwords to servers. The most widely deployed PKI-free asymmetric PAKE is the Secure Remote Password (SRP) protocol [43, 45, 102]. SRP continues, as of today, to be the default asymmetric PAKE in many settings such as authentication in applications (e.g., AWS Cognito , keychains[18], mail authentication[19]).

In 2019, the IETF Crypto Forum Research Group held a PAKE selection process, with the goal of recommending a symmetric and an asymmetric PAKE for usage in IETF protocols. It respectively selected CPace [1] and OPAQUE [15] in 2020. Although those state-of-the-art PAKEs now feature proofs in the Universal Composability model and good performance, they rely on primitives which fail to provide quantum resistance. OPAQUE was designed with modularity in mind by combining an oblivious pseudorandom function (OPRF [20]) and an authenticated key exchange. [15, Appendix B] explicitly mentions that a post-quantum AKE can be used in OPAQUE (further strengthening Takeway 12), but a fully-fledged post-quantum OPAQUE would also necessitate the OPRF to be quantum-resistant. Unfortunately, state-of-the-art post-quantum OPRFs are orders of magnitude away from being practical (Sect. 5). Few papers have looked at constructing post-quantum PAKEs directly [32].

---

[15] https://docs.aws.amazon.com/kms/latest/developerguide/importing-keys-get-public-key-and-token.html.

[16] https://docs.aws.amazon.com/cloudhsm/latest/userguide/key_mgmt_util-wrapKey.html.

[17] https://support.apple.com/guide/security/how-imessage-sends-and-receives-messages-sec70e68c949/1/web/1.

[18] https://blog.1password.com/developers-how-we-use-srp-and-you-can-too/.

[19] https://proton.me/blog/encrypted-email-authentication.

During the PAKE selection process, the notion of a PAKE being "quantum annoying" was proposed[20], and this property was later formalized and proved to hold for CPace [27]. Informally, a scheme is said to be quantum annoying if being able to solve discrete logarithms does not immediately provide the ability to compromise a system but rather only allows to eliminate a single possible password guess. In the absence of a post-quantum PAKE, such a property becomes very appealing as considerable quantum resources would be needed to compromise a single well-constructed password. While CPace can serve as a quantum-annoying balanced PAKE where possible, we propose the following research investigation and standardization takeaway:

Takeway 14. Research and standardize a post-quantum PAKE (and authenticated KEM; Takeway 12).

5   OPRF, Privacy Pass, and Blind Signatures

Besides OPAQUE, (verifiable) OPRFs are used to construct anonymous tokens [21,26,62], a form of lightweight anonymous credentials used as a trust signal by major vendors[21,22,23] . These anonymous tokens aim at providing a private-key alternative to blind signatures, and are being developed and standardized in the IETF Privacy Pass working group[24].

As mentioned in Sect. 4, there exists no efficient post-quantum OPRF to date. Boneh et al. proposed two constructions based on isogenies in [14]. The first one was based on SIDH and is therefore insecure [16,47,66], and was recently improved by Basso in [12]. The second was based on CSIDH (a relatively novel hardness assumption) and had communication cost around 500 kB per evaluation (no computation cost was provided). Albrecht et al. proposed a lattice-based construction [5] which is "*practically instantiable [but] far less efficient [than its classical counterpart]*". They suggested that one may want to "*accept, for now, that VOPRFs are less appealing building blocks in a post-quantum world*" and to propose post-quantum alternatives on a per application basis instead. To address this gap, we propose the following research takeaway:

Takeway 15. Construct an efficient post-quantum OPRF for use in anonymous authentication schemes or propose post-quantum anonymous credential primitives using general-purpose zero-knowledge proofs.

---

[20] https://mailarchive.ietf.org/arch/msg/cfrg/dtf91cmavpzT47U3AVxrVGNB5UM/.
[21] https://support.cloudflare.com/hc/en-us/articles/115001992652-Using-Privacy-Pass-with-Cloudflare.
[22] https://blog.cloudflare.com/eliminating-captchas-on-iphones-and-macs-using-new-standard/.
[23] https://web.dev/trust-tokens/.
[24] https://datatracker.ietf.org/wg/privacypass/about/.

The past two years have also seen a significant interest renewal for blind signatures, including constructions [17,18,22,36–38,58,59], attacks [13], specification [23], and deployments by major vendors (See footnote 22)[25]. State-of-the-art post-quantum blind signatures were initially proposed in 2010 by Rückert [85], and the latest state-of-the-art protocols [2,22,65] yield signatures of the order of 50 kB, i.e., two orders of magnitude larger than an RSA-based blind signature as defined in [23]. Recent deployments and standardization of RSA-based blind signatures motivates the following research takeaway:

Takeway 16. Construct efficient quantum-safe blind signatures for privacy-preserving and authentication use-cases.

6   Conclusion

In this paper, we proposed 16 research and standardization open questions posed by the upcoming post-quantum migration. We emphasized the impact of post-quantum authentication in transport protocols: the size increase may exacerbate amplification attacks and congestion and requires new research and standards. Additionally, we pointed out the need of going beyond KEM standardization as done by NIST: many protocols would benefit from an authenticated KEM, as the generic construction of public-key encryption from KEM does not capture the versatility of public-key encryption use-cases today. Finally, we briefly discussed the state of the art for post-quantum password-authenticated key exchange and anonymous authentication to motivate future research.

Beyond what is discussed above, we invite the reader to consider standards and protocols which would benefit from increased public attention. One example is SSH. Although SSH carries huge amounts of proprietary data today, the IETF working group responsible for it has concluded. The harvest-now-decrypt-later concern is an important one, so that the IETF TLS working group embarked on a journey of updating TLS with new quantum-safe hybrid key exchanges. There is no SSH group to introduce post-quantum algorithms to SSH, and although there have been some initial efforts to address this [57], it will not be addressed by the PQUIP working group. Other than SSH, there are important cryptographic standards that will need to embark on a post-quantum journey as well. These include Trusted Platform Modules (ISO/IEC 11889), UEFI Secure Boot, OASIS Key Management Interoperability Protocol (KMIP) and PKCS#11 and more.

Finally, one should always ponder the impact of a post-quantum transition in proper context. Investigations so far [11,56,63,91,92] have been considering the time-to-first-byte at the $90–95^{th}$-percentile as an indication of overall impact for post-quantum connections. The tail-ends of the $90–95^{th}$-percentile may be overestimating this impact. At the time of this writing, web clients perform $\approx$13 connections per page to fetch $\approx$2 MB of total data [40] on average. Connections at the tail-ends of the $90–95^{th}$-percentile that suffer significantly with 10–20 kB of additional data are already suffering with $\approx$150 kB per connection.

---

[25] https://one.google.com/about/vpn/howitworks.

Henceforth, even though one should aim for fairness of impact for upcoming changes, we stress that the post-quantum transition should avoid rendering poor connections with low time-to-last-byte much poorer than before.

References

1. Abdalla, M., Haase, B., Hesse, J.: CPace, a balanced composable PAKE. Technical report, Internet Research Task Force (2022). https://datatracker.ietf.org/doc/draft-irtf-cfrg-cpace/
2. Agrawal, S., Kirshanova, E., Stehle, D., Yadav, A.: Can round-optimal lattice-based blind signatures be practical? Cryptology ePrint Archive, Report 2021/1565 (2021). https://ia.cr/2021/1565
3. Aguilar Melchor, C., et al.: HQC. Technical report, National Institute of Standards and Technology (2022). https://csrc.nist.gov/Projects/post-quantum-cryptography/round-4-submissions
4. Albrecht, M.R., et al.: Classic McEliece. Technical report, National Institute of Standards and Technology (2022). https://csrc.nist.gov/projects/post-quantum-cryptography/round-4-submissions
5. Albrecht, M.R., Davidson, A., Deo, A., Smart, N.P.: Round-optimal verifiable oblivious pseudorandom functions from ideal lattices. In: Garay, J.A. (ed.) PKC 2021. LNCS, vol. 12711, pp. 261–289. Springer, Cham (2021). https://doi.org/10.1007/978-3-030-75248-4_10
6. American National Standards Institute Inc: ANSI X9.44-2007 key establishment using integer factorization cryptography (2007). https://webstore.ansi.org/standards/ascx9/ansix9442007r2017
7. Anastasova, M., Kampanakis, P., Massimo, J.: PQ-HPKE: post-quantum hybrid public key encryption. In: International Cryptographic Module Conference 2022 (2022). https://ia.cr/2022/414
8. American National Standards Institute (ANSI) X9.F1 subcommittee. ANSI X9.63 Public key cryptography for the Financial Services Industry: Elliptic curve key agreement and key transport schemes, 5 July 1998. working draft version 2.0
9. Aragon, N., et al.: BIKE. Technical report, National Institute of Standards and Technology (2022). https://csrc.nist.gov/Projects/post-quantum-cryptography/round-4-submissions
10. Barnes, R., Bhargavan, K., Lipp, B., Wood, C.A.: Hybrid public key encryption. RFC, Internet Engineering Task Force (2022). https://www.rfc-editor.org/rfc/rfc9180
11. Bas Westerbaan, C.: Sizing Up Post-Quantum Signatures, November 2021. https://blog.cloudflare.com/sizing-up-post-quantum-signatures/
12. Basso, A.: A post-quantum round-optimal oblivious PRF from isogenies. Cryptology ePrint Archive, Paper 2023/225 (2023). https://eprint.iacr.org/2023/225
13. Benhamouda, F., Lepoint, T., Loss, J., Orrù, M., Raykova, M.: On the (in)security of ROS. In: Canteaut, A., Standaert, F.-X. (eds.) EUROCRYPT 2021. LNCS, vol. 12696, pp. 33–53. Springer, Cham (2021). https://doi.org/10.1007/978-3-030-77870-5_2
14. Boneh, D., Kogan, D., Woo, K.: Oblivious pseudorandom functions from isogenies. In: Moriai, S., Wang, H. (eds.) ASIACRYPT 2020. LNCS, vol. 12492, pp. 520–550. Springer, Cham (2020). https://doi.org/10.1007/978-3-030-64834-3_18

15. Bourdrez, D., Krawczyk, D.H., Lewi, K., Wood, C.A.: The OPAQUE asymmetric PAKE protocol. Technical report, Internet Research Task Force (2022). https://datatracker.ietf.org/doc/draft-irtf-cfrg-opaque/

16. Castryck, W., Decru, T.: An efficient key recovery attack on SIDH (preliminary version). Cryptology ePrint Archive, Report 2022/975 (2022). https://ia.cr/2022/975

17. Chairattana-Apirom, R., Hanzlik, L., Loss, J., Lysyanskaya, A., Wagner, B.: PI-cut-choo and friends: compact blind signatures via parallel instance cut-and-choose and more. In: Dodis, Y., Shrimpton, T. (eds.) CRYPTO 2022, Part III. LNCS, vol. 13509, pp. 3–31. Springer, Heidelberg, Germany, Santa Barbara, CA, USA, 15–18 August 2022. https://doi.org/10.1007/978-3-031-15982-4_1

18. Chairattana-Apirom, R., Lysyanskaya, A.: Compact cut-and-choose: boosting the security of blind signature schemes, compactly. Cryptology ePrint Archive, Report 2022/003 (2022). https://ia.cr/2022/003

19. Chu, J., Dukkipati, N., Cheng, Y., Mathis, M.: Increasing TCP's Initial Window. RFC 6928, April 2013. https://www.rfc-editor.org/info/rfc6928

20. Davidson, A., Faz-Hernandez, A., Sullivan, N., Wood, C.A.: Oblivious pseudorandom functions (OPRFs) using prime-order groups. Technical report, Internet Research Task Force (2022). https://datatracker.ietf.org/doc/draft-irtf-cfrg-voprf/

21. Davidson, A., Goldberg, I., Sullivan, N., Tankersley, G., Valsorda, F.: Privacy pass: bypassing internet challenges anonymously. PoPETs **2018**(3), 164–180 (2018). https://doi.org/10.1515/popets-2018-0026

22. del Pino, R., Katsumata, S.: A new framework for more efficient round-optimal lattice-based (partially) blind signature via trapdoor sampling. In: Dodis, Y., Shrimpton, T. (eds.) CRYPTO 2022, Part II. LNCS, vol. 13508, pp. 306–336. Springer, Heidelberg, Germany, Santa Barbara, CA, USA, 15–18 August 2022. https://doi.org/10.1007/978-3-031-15979-4_11

23. Denis, F., Jacobs, F., Wood, C.A.: RSA blind signatures. Technical report, Internet Research Task Force (2022). https://datatracker.ietf.org/doc/draft-irtf-cfrg-rsa-blind-signatures/

24. Dent, A.W.: A designer's guide to KEMs. In: Paterson, K.G. (ed.) Cryptography and Coding 2003. LNCS, vol. 2898, pp. 133–151. Springer, Heidelberg (2003). https://doi.org/10.1007/978-3-540-40974-8_12

25. Dukkipati, N., et al.: An argument for increasing TCP's initial congestion window. SIGCOMM Comput. Commun. Rev. **40**(3), 26–33 (2010). https://doi.org/10.1145/1823844.1823848

26. Durak, F.B., Vaudenay, S., Chase, M.: Anonymous tokens with hidden metadata bit from algebraic macs. Cryptology ePrint Archive, Paper 2022/1622 (2022). https://ia.cr/2022/1622

27. Eaton, E., Stebila, D.: The quantum annoying property of password-authenticated key exchange protocols. In: Cheon, J.H., Tillich, J.-P. (eds.) PQCrypto 2021 2021. LNCS, vol. 12841, pp. 154–173. Springer, Cham (2021). https://doi.org/10.1007/978-3-030-81293-5_9

28. ETSI: ETSI TC Cyber Working Group for Quantum-Safe Cryptography (2017). https://portal.etsi.org/TBSiteMap/CYBER/CYBERQSCToR.aspx. Accessed 25 July 2019

29. Fregly, A., Harvey, J., Jr., B.S.K., Sheth, S.: Merkle tree ladder mode: reducing the size impact of NIST PQC signature algorithms in practice. Cryptology ePrint Archive, Paper 2022/1730 (2022). https://ia.cr/2022/1730

30. Fujisaki, E., Okamoto, T.: Secure integration of asymmetric and symmetric encryption schemes. In: Wiener, M. (ed.) CRYPTO 1999. LNCS, vol. 1666, pp. 537–554. Springer, Heidelberg (1999). https://doi.org/10.1007/3-540-48405-1_34

31. Fujisaki, E., Okamoto, T.: Secure integration of asymmetric and symmetric encryption schemes. J. Cryptol. **26**(1), 80–101 (2011). https://doi.org/10.1007/s00145-011-9114-1

32. Gao, X., Ding, J., Liu, J., Li, L.: Post-quantum secure remote password protocol from RLWE problem. Cryptology ePrint Archive, Report 2017/1196 (2017). https://ia.cr/2017/1196

33. Gayoso Martínez, V., Hernández Á lvarez, F., Hernández Encinas, L., Sánchez Á vila, C.: A comparison of the standardized versions of ECIES. In: 2010 Sixth International Conference on Information Assurance and Security, pp. 1–4 (2010). https://doi.org/10.1109/ISIAS.2010.5604194

34. Ghedini, A., Vasiliev, V.: TLS Certificate Compression. RFC 8879, December 2020. https://doi.org/10.17487/RFC8879, https://www.rfc-editor.org/info/rfc8879

35. Goertzen, J., Stebila, D.: Post-quantum signatures in DNSSEC via request-based fragmentation. CoRR abs/2211.14196 (2022). https://doi.org/10.48550/arXiv.2211.14196

36. Hanzlik, L., Loss, J., Wagner, B.: Rai-choo! Evolving blind signatures to the next level. Cryptology ePrint Archive, Report 2022/1350 (2022). https://ia.cr/2022/1350

37. Hauck, E., Kiltz, E., Loss, J.: A modular treatment of blind signatures from identification schemes. In: Ishai, Y., Rijmen, V. (eds.) EUROCRYPT 2019. LNCS, vol. 11478, pp. 345–375. Springer, Cham (2019). https://doi.org/10.1007/978-3-030-17659-4_12

38. Hauck, E., Kiltz, E., Loss, J., Nguyen, N.K.: Lattice-based blind signatures, revisited. In: Micciancio, D., Ristenpart, T. (eds.) CRYPTO 2020. LNCS, vol. 12171, pp. 500–529. Springer, Cham (2020). https://doi.org/10.1007/978-3-030-56880-1_18

39. Housley, R.: Use of the HSS/LMS Hash-Based Signature Algorithm in the Cryptographic Message Syntax (CMS). RFC 8708, February 2020. https://www.rfc-editor.org/info/rfc8708

40. http archive: Report: State of the Web. http://httparchive.org/trends.php

41. Huelsing, A., Butin, D., Gazdag, S.L., Rijneveld, J., Mohaisen, A.: XMSS: eXtended Merkle Signature Scheme. RFC 8391, May 2018. https://rfc-editor.org/rfc/rfc8391

42. Hulsing, A.,et al.: SPHINCS+. Technical report, National Institute of Standards and Technology (2022). https://csrc.nist.gov/Projects/post-quantum-cryptography/selected-algorithms-2022

43. IEEE draft standard P1363.2. Password-based public key cryptography, May 2004. draft Version 15. http://grouper.ieee.org/groups/1363/passwdPK

44. IEEE P1363a Committee. IEEE P1363a / D9 – standard specifications for public key cryptography: Additional techniques, June 2001. draft Version 9. http://grouper.ieee.org/groups/1363/index.html/

45. ISO: Information technology - security techniques - key management - part 4: Mechanisms based on weak secrets. ISO/IEC, International Organization for Standardization (2017). https://www.iso.org/standard/67933.html

46. Iyengar, J., Swett, I.: QUIC Loss Detection and Congestion Control. RFC 9002, May 2021. https://www.rfc-editor.org/info/rfc9002

47. Jao, D., et al.: SIKE. Technical report, National Institute of Standards and Technology (2022). https://csrc.nist.gov/Projects/post-quantum-cryptography/round-4-submissions

48. Jao, D., et al.: SIKE. Technical report, National Institute of Standards and Technology (2020). https://csrc.nist.gov/projects/post-quantum-cryptography/round-3-submissions

49. Jaques, S.: Landscape of quantum computing in 2022 (2022). https://sam-jaques.appspot.com/quantum_landscape_2022

50. Jivsov, A.: Elliptic curve cryptography (ECC) in OpenPGP. RFC, Internet Engineering Task Force (2016). https://www.rfc-editor.org/rfc/rfc6637

51. Jonsson, J., Kaliski, B.: Public-key cryptography standards (PKCS) #1: RSA cryptography specifications version 2.1. RFC, Internet Engineering Task Force (2003). https://www.rfc-editor.org/rfc/rfc3447

52. K. Moriarty, E., Kaliski, B., Jonsson, J., Rusch, A.: PKCS #1: RSA cryptography specifications version 2.2. RFC, Internet Engineering Task Force (2012). https://www.rfc-editor.org/rfc/rfc8017

53. Kaliski, B.: PKCS #1: RSA encryption version 1.5. RFC, Internet Engineering Task Force (1998). https://www.rfc-editor.org/rfc/rfc2313

54. Kaliski, B., Jonsson, J.: PKCS #1: RSA cryptography specifications version 2.0. RFC, Internet Engineering Task Force (1998). https://www.rfc-editor.org/rfc/rfc2437

55. Kampanakis, P., Kallitsis, M.: Faster post-quantum TLS handshakes without intermediate CA certificates. In: Dolev, S., Katz, J., Meisels, A. (eds.) Cyber Security, Cryptology, and Machine Learning. CSCML 2022. LNCS, vol. 13301, pp. 337–355. Springer, Cham (2022). https://doi.org/10.1007/978-3-031-07689-3_25

56. Kampanakis, P., Sikeridis, D.: Two PQ signature use-cases: Non-issues, challenges and potential solutions. Cryptology ePrint Archive, Report 2019/1276 (2019). https://ia.cr/2019/1276

57. Kampanakis, P., Stebila, D., Hansen, T.: Post-quantum Hybrid Key Exchange in SSH. Internet-Draft draft-kampanakis-curdle-ssh-pq-ke-00, Internet Engineering Task Force, November 2022. work in Progress. https://datatracker.ietf.org/doc/draft-kampanakis-curdle-ssh-pq-ke/00/

58. Kastner, J., Loss, J., Xu, J.: The abe-okamoto partially blind signature scheme revisited. Cryptology ePrint Archive, Report 2022/1232 (2022). https://ia.cr/2022/1232

59. Katz, J., Loss, J., Rosenberg, M.: Boosting the security of blind signature schemes. In: Tibouchi, M., Wang, H. (eds.) ASIACRYPT 2021. LNCS, vol. 13093, pp. 468–492. Springer, Cham (2021). https://doi.org/10.1007/978-3-030-92068-5_16

60. Kaufman, C., Hoffman, P.E., Nir, Y., Eronen, P., Kivinen, T.: Internet Key Exchange Protocol Version 2 (IKEv2). RFC 7296, October 2014. https://www.rfc-editor.org/info/rfc7296

61. Kinnear, E., McManus, P., Pauly, T., Verma, T., Wood, C.A.: Oblivious DNS over HTTPS. RFC, Internet Engineering Task Force (2022). https://www.rfc-editor.org/rfc/rfc9230

62. Kreuter, B., Lepoint, T., Orrù, M., Raykova, M.: Anonymous tokens with private metadata bit. In: Micciancio, D., Ristenpart, T. (eds.) CRYPTO 2020. LNCS, vol. 12170, pp. 308–336. Springer, Cham (2020). https://doi.org/10.1007/978-3-030-56784-2_11

63. Kris Kwiatkowski, L.V.: The TLS Post-Quantum Experiment, October 2020. https://blog.cloudflare.com/the-tls-post-quantum-experiment/

64. Lyubashevsky, V., et al.: CRYSTALS-DILITHIUM. Technical report, National Institute of Standards and Technology (2022). https://csrc.nist.gov/Projects/post-quantum-cryptography/selected-algorithms-2022
65. Lyubashevsky, V., Nguyen, N.K., Plancon, M.: Efficient lattice-based blind signatures via gaussian one-time signatures. Cryptology ePrint Archive, Report 2022/006 (2022). https://ia.cr/2022/006
66. Maino, L., Martindale, C.: An attack on SIDH with arbitrary starting curve. Cryptology ePrint Archive, Report 2022/1026 (2022). https://ia.cr/2022/1026
67. Majkowski, M.: Reflections on reflection (attacks), May 2017. https://blog.cloudflare.com/reflections-on-reflections/
68. Massimo, J., Kampanakis, P., Turner, S., Westerbaan, B.: Internet X.509 Public Key Infrastructure: Algorithm Identifiers for Dilithium. Internet-Draft draft-ietf-lamps-dilithium-certificates-00, Internet Engineering Task Force, September 2022. work in Progress. https://datatracker.ietf.org/doc/draft-ietf-lamps-dilithium-certificates/00/
69. McGrew, D., Curcio, M., Fluhrer, S.: Leighton-Micali Hash-Based Signatures. RFC 8554, April 2019. https://rfc-editor.org/rfc/rfc8554
70. Mononen, T., Kause, T., Farrell, S., Adams, D.C.: Internet X.509 public key infrastructure certificate management protocol (CMP). RFC, Internet Engineering Task Force (2005). https://www.rfc-editor.org/rfc/rfc4210
71. Müller, M., de Jong, J., van Heesch, M., Overeinder, B., van Rijswijk-Deij, R.: Retrofitting post-quantum cryptography in internet protocols: a case study of DNSSEC. SIGCOMM Comput. Commun. Rev. **50**(4), 49–57 (2020). https://doi.org/10.1145/3431832.3431838
72. Nawrocki, M., Tehrani, P.F., Hiesgen, R., Mücke, J., Schmidt, T.C., Wählisch, M.: On the interplay between TLS certificates and QUIC performance. In: Proceedings of the 18th International Conference on emerging Networking EXperiments and Technologies. ACM, November 2022. https://doi.org/10.1145/3555050.3569123
73. NIST: NIST PQ project, February 2022. https://csrc.nist.gov/projects/post-quantum-cryptography
74. Paquin, C., Stebila, D., Tamvada, G.: Benchmarking post-quantum cryptography in TLS. In: Ding, J., Tillich, J.-P. (eds.) PQCrypto 2020. LNCS, vol. 12100, pp. 72–91. Springer, Cham (2020). https://doi.org/10.1007/978-3-030-44223-1_5
75. Partridge, D.C., Allman, M., Floyd, S.: Increasing TCP's Initial Window. RFC 3390, November 2002. https://www.rfc-editor.org/info/rfc3390
76. Paxson, D.V., Allman, M., Stevens, W.R.: TCP Congestion Control. RFC 2581, April 1999. https://www.rfc-editor.org/info/rfc2581
77. Planet, C.: Initcwnd settings of major CDN providers, February 2017. https://www.cdnplanet.com/blog/initcwnd-settings-major-cdn-providers/
78. Prest, T., et al.: FALCON. Technical report, National Institute of Standards and Technology (2022). https://csrc.nist.gov/Projects/post-quantum-cryptography/selected-algorithms-2022
79. Prince, M.: The DDoS That Almost Broke the Internet, May 2017. https://blog.cloudflare.com/the-ddos-that-almost-broke-the-internet/
80. Rescorla, E.: The Transport Layer Security (TLS) Protocol Version 1.3. RFC 8446, August 2018. https://rfc-editor.org/rfc/rfc8446
81. Rescorla, E., Modadugu, N.: Datagram Transport Layer Security Version 1.2. RFC 6347, January 2012. https://www.rfc-editor.org/info/rfc6347

82. Rescorla, E., Oku, K., Sullivan, N., Wood, C.A.: TLS encrypted client hello. Technical report, Internet Engineering Task Force (2022). https://datatracker. ietf.org/doc/draft-ietf-tls-esni/

83. Rescorla, E., Tschofenig, H., Modadugu, N.: The Datagram Transport Layer Security (DTLS) Protocol Version 1.3. RFC 9147, April 2022. https://www.rfc-editor. org/info/rfc9147

84. Rossow, C.: Amplification hell: revisiting network protocols for ddos abuse, January 2014. https://doi.org/10.14722/ndss.2014.23233

85. Rückert, M.: Lattice-based blind signatures. In: Abe, M. (ed.) ASIACRYPT 2010. LNCS, vol. 6477, pp. 413–430. Springer, Heidelberg (2010). https://doi.org/10. 1007/978-3-642-17373-8_24

86. Rüth, J., Bormann, C., Hohlfeld, O.: Large-scale scanning of TCP's initial window. In: Proceedings of the 2017 Internet Measurement Conference, pp. 304–310. IMC 2017, Association for Computing Machinery, New York, NY, USA (2017). https://doi.org/10.1145/3131365.3131370

87. Schwabe, P., et al.: CRYSTALS-KYBER. Technical report, National Institute of Standards and Technology (2022). https://csrc.nist.gov/Projects/post-quantum-cryptography/selected-algorithms-2022

88. Certicom research, standards for efficient cryptography group (SECG) – sec 1: Elliptic curve cryptography, 20 September 2000. version 1.0. http://www.secg. org/secg_docs.htm

89. Shoup, V.: A proposal for an ISO standard for public key encryption. Cryptology ePrint Archive, Report 2001/112 (2001). https://ia.cr/2001/112

90. Shoup, V.: ISO 18033-2: an emerging standard for public-key encryption, December 2004. final Committee Draft. https://shoup.net/iso/std6.pdf

91. Sikeridis, D., Kampanakis, P., Devetsikiotis, M.: Assessing the overhead of post-quantum cryptography in TLS 1.3 and SSH. In: Proceedings of the 16th International Conference on Emerging Networking EXperiments and Technologies, pp. 149–156. CoNEXT 2020, Association for Computing Machinery, New York, NY, USA (2020). https://doi.org/10.1145/3386367.3431305

92. Sikeridis, D., Kampanakis, P., Devetsikiotis, M.: Post-quantum authentication in TLS 1.3: a performance study. In: 27th Annual Network and Distributed System Security Symposium, NDSS 2020, San Diego, California, USA, 23–26 February 2020. The Internet Society (2020). https://www.ndss-symposium.org/ndss-paper/post-quantum-authentication-in-tls-1-3-a-performance-study/

93. Smyslov, V.: Intermediate Exchange in the Internet Key Exchange Protocol Version 2 (IKEv2). RFC 9242, May 2022. https://www.rfc-editor.org/info/rfc9242

94. Stebila, D., Fluhrer, S., Gueron, S.: Hybrid key exchange in TLS 1.3. Internet-Draft draft-ietf-tls-hybrid-design-04, Internet Engineering Task Force, January 2022. work in Progress. https://datatracker.ietf.org/doc/html/draft-ietf-tls-hybrid-design-04

95. Stebila, D., Fluhrer, S., Gueron, S.: Hybrid key exchange in TLS 1.3. Internet-Draft draft-ietf-tls-hybrid-design-05, Internet Engineering Task Force, August 2022. work in Progress. https://datatracker.ietf.org/doc/draft-ietf-tls-hybrid-design/05/

96. Stevens, W.R.: TCP Slow Start, Congestion Avoidance, Fast Retransmit, and Fast Recovery Algorithms. RFC 2001, January 1997. https://www.rfc-editor.org/info/ rfc2001

97. Thomson, M., Kampanakis, P., Bytheway, C., Westerbaan, B.: Suppressing CA Certificates in TLS 1.3. Internet-Draft draft-kampanakis-tls-scas-latest-02, Inter-

net Engineering Task Force, July 2022. work in Progress. https://datatracker.ietf.org/doc/draft-kampanakis-tls-scas-latest/02/

98. Thomson, M., Turner, S.: Using TLS to Secure QUIC. RFC 9001, May 2021. https://www.rfc-editor.org/info/rfc9001

99. Tjhai, C., et al.: Multiple key exchanges in IKEv2. Internet-Draft draft-ietf-ipsecme-ikev2-multiple-ke-04, Internet Engineering Task Force, September 2021. work in Progress. https://datatracker.ietf.org/doc/html/draft-ietf-ipsecme-ikev2-multiple-ke-04

100. Tjhai, C., et al.: Multiple key exchanges in IKEv2. Internet-Draft draft-ietf-ipsecme-ikev2-multiple-ke-12, Internet Engineering Task Force, December 2022. work in Progress. https://datatracker.ietf.org/doc/draft-ietf-ipsecme-ikev2-multiple-ke/12/

101. Touch, D.J.D.: Automating the Initial Window in TCP. Internet-Draft draft-touch-tcpm-automatic-iw-03, Internet Engineering Task Force, July 2012. work in Progress. https://datatracker.ietf.org/doc/draft-touch-tcpm-automatic-iw/03/

102. Wu, T.: The SRP authentication and key exchange system. RFC, Internet Engineering Task Force (2000). https://www.rfc-editor.org/rfc/rfc2945

On Reducing Underutilization of Security Standards by Deriving Actionable Rules: An Application to IoT

Md. Wasiuddin Pathan Shuvo[1]([✉]) [ID], Md. Nazmul Hoq[1] [ID],
Suryadipta Majumdar[1] [ID], and Paria Shirani[2] [ID]

[1] Concordia University, Montreal, Canada
wpshuvo57@gmail.com, {mdnazmul.hoq,suryadipta.majumdar}@concordia.ca
[2] University of Ottawa, Ottawa, Canada
pshirani@uottawa.ca

Abstract. Even though there exist a number of security guidelines and recommendations from various worldwide standardization authorities (e.g., NIST, ISO, ENISA), it is evident from many of the recent attacks that these standards are not strictly followed in the implementation of real-world products. Furthermore, most security applications (e.g., monitoring and auditing) do not consider those standards as the basis of their security check. Therefore, regardless of continuous efforts in publishing security standards, they are still under-utilized in practice. Such under-utilization might be caused by the fact that existing security standards are intended more for high-level recommendations than for being readily adopted to automated security applications on the system-level data. Bridging this gap between high-level recommendations and low-level system implementations becomes extremely difficult, as a fully automated solution might suffer from high inaccuracy, whereas a fully manual approach might require tedious efforts. Therefore, in this paper, we aim for a more practical solution by proposing a partially automated approach, where it automates the tedious tasks (e.g., summarizing long standard documents and extracting device specifications) and relies on manual efforts from security experts to avoid mistakes in finalizing security rules. We apply our solution to IoT by implementing it with IoT-specific standards (NISTIR 8228) and smart home networks. We further demonstrate the actionability of our derived rules in three major applications: security auditing, Intrusion Detection systems (IDS), and secure application development.

1 Introduction

Recent cyber-attacks are typically caused by various safety and security threats that result from implementation flaws and insecure default configurations [2, 15, 21, 38, 42, 45, 53]. For instance, the Mirai botnet infecting millions of devices and conducting massive DDoS attacks on major services, e.g., Amazon, GitHub, and Netflix, mainly resulted from not following the best practices (e.g., latest

© The Author(s), under exclusive license to Springer Nature Switzerland AG 2023
F. Günther and J. Hesse (Eds.): SSR 2023, LNCS 13895, pp. 103–128, 2023.
https://doi.org/10.1007/978-3-031-30731-7_5

versions of libraries and protocols, no weak passwords, etc.) [5]. Due to similar issues in implementing the best practices, several other recent attacks also led to severe security and safety consequences, such as unauthorized access to smart homes [21], injecting fake voice commands to smart home devices and hubs [49], and health hazards to infants in a smart home [14]. As a result, the accountability and transparency of those devices and their operations often become questionable [2]. This might be due to the fact that most security solutions (e.g., [12–14]) are not using standards as a basis for their security evaluation.

Several works (e.g., [4,9–11,14,16,25,34,54,57]) are addressing different security issues such as intrusion detection, device fingerprinting, application monitoring, and access control. However, none of those works focus on developing a generic approach to automatically define actionable security rules for verifying different system and device security. Moreover, none of them choose existing security standards as the basis of their security evaluation, which as a result, endangers billions of devices and systems against many severe security threats (e.g., Mirai [5]).

One of the main reasons behind this under-utilization might be due to the high-level nature of most of those security standards (e.g., NIST IR 8228 [8], ENISA [17], OWASP [40]) which renders additional overhead to adopt them in different security applications that typically operate on system-level data. Interpreting high-level recommendations and deriving actionable security rules for low-level system implementations becomes infeasible using any extreme solutions, i.e., a fully automated solution (which is less accurate) and a fully manual approach (which is tedious and error-prone). This problem is further illustrated using a motivating example in Sect. 2.4.

In this paper, we propose a partially automated approach (which appears to be more practical) to derive actionable security rules from various security standards and show its application to IoT. More specifically, first, we conduct a study on major security standards such as [8,13,17,18,23,40]. Second, we extract IoT device-specific information from product specifications, API documentation, and configuration files to build a knowledge base. Third, we leverage Natural Language Processing (NLP) techniques for summarizing and a fine-tuned Named Entity Recognition (NER) model to extract key recommendations from those security controls. Fourth, we instantiate each recommendation as a security rule, expressed in formal language, on various IoT systems by collecting IoT log data, API, and configuration files. Due to the criticality of security applications, our derived security rules are preferred to be examined by a security expert to assure their correctness. Finally, our derived rules are applied to various security applications, such as security auditing, IDS, and secure application development.

The main contributions of this paper are as follows.

- As per our knowledge, this is the first effort to derive actionable security rules from IoT security standards. This actionability of derived rules is demonstrated by integrating our approach in a smart home ecosystem and applying those rules to various security applications, i.e., security auditing, intrusion detection systems (IDS), and secure application development.

– Our experimental results further show the effectiveness of our solution in reducing the manual efforts (e.g., 50% effort reduction on average) and adaptability of our derived rules for security auditing (where 5,000 smart home devices can be audited within ten seconds).

The paper is organized as follows. Section 2 describes the preliminaries and challenges. Section 3 details our methodology. Section 4 provides the application to different security mechanisms, and Sect. 5 presents the experimental results. Section 6 discusses different aspects of our approach. Section 7 reviews related works and compares them with our approach. Section 8 concludes the paper by providing future research directions.

2 Preliminaries

To keep our discussion more concrete, the rest of the paper will be on the scope of IoT standards and smart home networks. In the following, we provide backgrounds on common terminologies in security standards, review major IoT standards, and illustrate our motivating example.

2.1 Background on Security Standards

Security Standards describe the best practices from several security documents, organizations, and publications. A security standard is designed as a framework for an organization requiring stringent security measures. Each security standard contains several *security controls*, which describe the protection capabilities for particular security objectives of an organization and reflect the protection needs of organizational stakeholders. *Security expectations* are the expected outcomes from a security control to ensure the secure operation of a system.

2.2 Review of Major IoT Security Standards

To identify unique challenges in deriving actionable security rules, we review several major IoT security standards (as summarized in Table 1).

NISTIR 8228 [8]. It is an internal report published by the National Institute of Standards and Technology (NIST), a federal agency of the US government. The goal of this report is to assist users in better understanding and managing the cybersecurity and privacy risks associated with individual IoT devices across their life cycles. Particularly, this 44-page report outlines three high-level risk mitigation goals for the security of IoT devices, and each risk mitigation goal is further divided into several risk mitigation areas. Moreover, NISTIR 8228 has listed 25 expectations along with 49 challenges to achieve those expectations and their mapping with the NIST SP 800-53r5 [37] for mitigating security and privacy risks in IoT systems.

Table 1. Summary of different IoT security standards

Security Standard	Purpose	Targeted to	Scope	# pages
NISTIR 8228 [8]	Security and privacy risk management	Users	All kinds of IoT Devices	44
NISTIR 8259 [18]	Building secure IoT device	Manufacturers	All kinds of IoT Devices	36
ENISA [17]	Recommendation for baseline security	Users and manufacturers	All kinds of IoT Devices	103
ETSI EN 303 645 [23]	Consumer IoT security	Manufacturers	All kinds of IoT Devices	34
OWASP [40]	Secure building and usage of IoT	Manufacturer, developers and consumers	All kinds of IoT Devices	12
UK Govt [13]	Improve the security of consumer IoT	Manufacturers, developers and service providers	Smart homes and smart wearables	24

NISTIR 8259 [18]. It is also an internal report from NIST, which is intended for IoT device manufacturers to assist them to improve the security of their IoT products. This 36-page report describes six cybersecurity activities which are broken down into 65 questions that a device manufacturer should consider to secure their IoT devices. During the pre-market phase, the manufacturer's decisions and actions are primarily influenced by the first four of those six activities, whereas the remaining two activities are primarily for the post-market phase of an IoT device. Each activity's questions are open-ended and allow for speculation, which may cause the manufacturers to make a perplexing choice that is unsuitable for use as actionable rules.

ENISA Baseline Security Recommendation for IoT [17]. The purpose of this report is to develop baseline cybersecurity recommendations for both users and IoT manufacturers, with a special focus on critical infrastructures. This report covers many domains of IoT (e.g., smart homes, smart cities, smart grids, etc.), and it is intended for IoT software developers, manufacturers, information security experts, security solution architects, etc. There are 83 security measures outlined, divided into 11 security domains that cover every IoT ecosystem horizontally, in this 103-page report. However, all of these security measures can not be used as actionable security rules as they are insufficiently specific.

ETSI EN 303 645 - V2.1.1 [23]. ETSI EN 303 645 establishes a security baseline while covering all consumer IoT devices. Although the target audience of this article is primarily manufacturers of various IoT devices, it also aims to assist IoT users. This 34-page document has 67 provisions with examples divided into 13 high-level recommendations and refers to multiple external documents for further technical details. With a focus on technical controls, the ETSI document has specific guidelines, but technical details are insufficient to be used for actionable security rules [7].

OWASP IoT Security Guidance [40]. The OWASP Internet of Things Project has released the OWASP IoT top ten lists of IoT vulnerabilities in an effort to help manufacturers, developers, and consumers better understand IoT security risks and take appropriate mitigation measures. The specialty of this project is its simplicity, where they avoid separating guidelines for different stakeholders. That is why it is the shortest security guideline, with only 12 pages, among the security standards that we reviewed. This report lists the top 10 recommendations to secure IoT devices without providing detailed or specific steps on how to follow those recommendations in real-world product development.

Code of Practice by the UK Government [13]. This security guideline is developed by the UK Department for Digital, Culture, Media, and Sport in conjunction with the National Cyber Security Centre and follows engagement with industry, consumer associations, and academia. Its goal is to provide guidelines to all organizations involved in developing, manufacturing, and retailing consumer IoT products on achieving a secure-by-design approach. It lists 13 high-level security outcomes that are to be reached by following the recommendations in this 24-page report. In spite of those outcomes, this guideline gives stakeholders the liberty to apply each guideline on their own terms instead of providing concrete ways to do so [7].

2.3 Challenges in Deriving Actionable Rules from Standards

There are several challenges in deriving actionable rules from security standards.

- Firstly, most existing security standards are provided at a high-level without any clear mapping between those recommendations with the actual design and implementation of IoT products available in the market. Thus, it becomes almost infeasible to use them to conduct security applications (that require more low-level granular security rules).
- Secondly, those standards significantly differ from each other in terms of scope, objective, and level of descriptions. Therefore, interpreting the security recommendations from each standard for deriving rules becomes non-trivial.
- Thirdly, among those standards, there are conflicting recommendations. As a result, a systematic analysis of those high-level recommendations is required to interpret them and resolve their conflicts before deriving actionable rules.
- Fourthly, the knowledge and expertise required from a target audience of these security standards is not explicitly specified, and the guidelines are not crafted as actionable for the target audience [7].
- Lastly, security standards contain too many different types of interrelated guidance on a single subject [52], which are frequently cross-referenced to dozens of other security documents. This can make the recommendations challenging to follow and fully utilize at times.

We will address these challenges in Sect. 3.

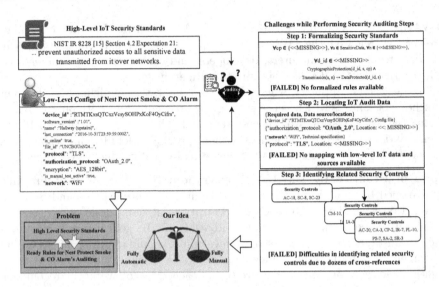

Fig. 1. Motivating example depicting major challenges in converting high-level security standards to actionable security rules for security auditing of low-level IoT system implementation

2.4 Motivating Example

A motivating example is shown in Fig. 1 where an IoT security standard (NISTIR 8228) is directly used to perform security auditing (but failed, as explained later) of a smart home device (Nest Protect Smoke and CO Alarm [36]). Particularly, the left side of the figure shows typical inputs to an auditing tool: a "high-level" recommendation from NISTIR 8228 (top) and "low-level" configurations from a Nest Protect Smoke and CO Alarm (middle). The right side depicts the challenges encountered while performing different security auditing steps (Steps 1–3). On the bottom left, we briefly illustrate the problem and our idea to solve it.

Specifically, this example depicts a scenario where an auditor aims at auditing a Nest Protect Smoke and CO Alarm device against the Expectation 21 in Sect. 4.2 of NISTIR 8228 [8]. The expectation states: *"a device can prevent unauthorized access to all sensitive data transmitted from it over networks"*. On the other hand, configurations from a Nest Protect Smoke and CO Alarm include information about device_id, software_version, protocol, network, etc. While performing auditing using these inputs, an auditor encounters several challenges, as follows. (i) During Step 1 (for formalizing security standards), the allowed list of cryptographic protection (cp) methods, networks (n), and device IDs (d_id) are missing from the Expectation 21 description in NISTIR 8228. During Step 2 (for locating audit data), the auditor cannot easily find the source of authorization_protocol and protocol in a Nest Protect Smoke and CO Alarm, even if she can locate others (e.g., device_id, network) from its configuration files or technical specifications. During Step 3 (for identifying related security controls), the auditor might struggle to link between various controls, such as the AC-18 control refers to nine other controls: CA-9, CM-7, IA-2, IA-3, etc. Therefore, very likely, most of those auditing steps might fail, if not all.

The main problem is to address those challenges and allow interpreting high-level security standards and defining ready rules for auditing Nest Protect Smoke and CO Alarm. To that end, both fully automated and fully manual solutions might also fail the auditing process because full automation might change the semantics of the original recommendations, and relying only on manual effort would be time-consuming and error-prone. Therefore, our idea is to balance those two extreme approaches and find a practical solution to derive actionable rules for IoT devices by proposing a semi-automated approach. In the following, we elaborate on our proposed approach.

3 Methodology

This section first provides an overview and then details our methodology.

3.1 Overview

The overview of the proposed methodology is shown in Fig. 2.

The inputs to our system are originated from security standards (e.g., their description) and logs and configurations from a target system (e.g., IoT, clouds, networks). Our approach is divided into two primary phases: (i) *building a knowledge base*, and (ii) *defining actionable security rules*. More specifically, during the first phase (elaborated in Sect. 3.2), we map various security standard recommendations with their controls in NIST SP 800-53r5 [37] and annotate those mappings (Step 1.1). Then, we collect various IoT device-specific information to construct *structural knowledge* base (e.g., their sensors and actuators) and *functional knowledge* base (e.g., their network interfaces) (Step 1.2). During the second phase (elaborated in Sect. 3.3), we summarize the security controls, extract values from different summarized controls, and derive security rules for that control, which will be inspected by an expert (Step 2.1). Afterwards, we instantiate the derived security rules with device-specific information stored in the structural and functional knowledge bases and interpret them in a formal language (Step 2.2). In the figure, for both phases, we indicate if a step is fully automated (A), semi-automated (SA), or manual (M); their rationale is detailed in Sect. 3.5. Finally, we demonstrate the applicability of our approach in security applications such as security auditing (in Sect. 4). The details of each phase are described as follows.

3.2 Knowledge Base Creation

The *knowledge base* is created for both security standards and devices as follows.

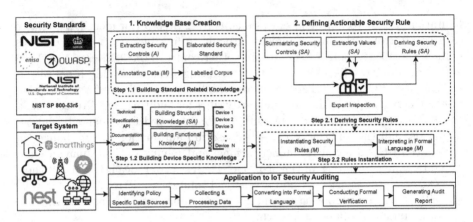

Fig. 2. An overview of our methodology (where (A): fully automated step, (SA): semi-automated step, and (M): manual step)

Building Standard Related Knowledge. The goal of creating a knowledge base of security standards is to centralize all IoT security standards and their corresponding security controls (which provide preventive measures to mitigate a particular security issue in a system) from NIST SP 800-53r5 [37] (which defines security controls for IT in general) to be used for actionable rule derivation. There are application-specific recommendations, such as those found in NISTIR 8228, which provide security advice for IoT devices, and general security implementation guidelines in NIST 800-53r5, which are application agnostic. In our knowledge base, we simply merge them to provide more insight on how to implement an application-specific security recommendation using generic security implementation guidelines. Note that security control contains multiple sub-controls, each with a name and discussion, which either add functionality or specificity to a base control or increase the strength of a base control by further clarifying the technicalities. Figure 3 demonstrates the development and arrangement of our elaborated security standard from the referred security controls. To this end, we first extract security expectations and their mappings to security controls specified in each expectation, and then we extract corresponding security controls from NIST SP 800-53r5 to complete the mappings and build the elaborated security standards organized by variables, expectations, controls, sub-controls, and discussions. Afterwards, to further understand a control, we extract values and attributes from each security control. To that end, we first manually annotate the security control values based on the answers to the following three questions: (i) *Do the values accomplish a particular task?* (ii) *Are the procedures to complete this task known?* (iii) *Is it possible to implement a control technically?* After value annotation, we consider security sub-controls as our attributes and accordingly annotate them. Second, we train a Named Entity Recognition (NER) [12] model with annotated security controls and extract both values and attributes by utilizing the learned model.

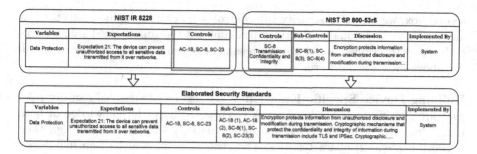

Fig. 3. Development and Arrangement of Elaborated Security Standards

Example 1. The `Expectation` 21 from NISTIR 8228 refers to the security controls `SC-8`, `SC-23`, and `AC-18` in NIST SP 800-53r5. We first extract these three security controls and their sub-controls with their discussions from NIST SP 800-53r5. Then, we create our elaborated security standards, which are arranged by variables, controls, sub-controls, and their discussions. In Fig. 4, the first box contains the variable highlighted in red along with the `Expectation` 21. In the

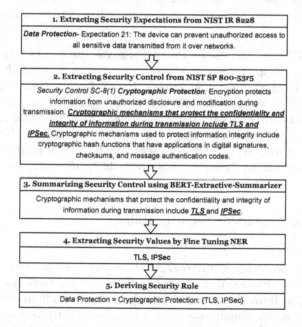

Fig. 4. An illustration of automatically derived security rules. The `Expectation` 21 from NISTIR 8228 is shown in the first box, then the security sub-control is displayed in the second box, and the summarised form of it is presented in red. The red-underlined terms in the third box's summary of the security sub-control represent values that were retrieved using the NER model displayed in the fourth box. The final box displays our automatically derived security rule.

second box, we annotate security sub-control (e.g., cryptographic protection) as an attribute. Additionally, the third box contains the summarized security control, where the values in red are the results of our annotation after meeting all the above-mentioned criteria.

Building Device Specific Knowledge. To instantiate derived security rules that are specific to IoT devices, it is essential to have the knowledge of both their *structural* (e.g., their sensors and actuators) and *functional* (e.g., their network behaviour) characteristics. The *structural knowledge* of an IoT device includes different capabilities of its sensors and actuators, which are derived from the manufacture design specifications of different IoT devices. For this purpose, we leverage the approach proposed by Dolan et al. [15] as follows. First, we gather all the technical information that is provided on a device's website. Second, we extract that information from the device's API documentation that describes API calls to change system states. Third, we gather essential information from IoT device configuration files, which are publicly accessible and include all essential device characteristics [15]. The *functional knowledge* of an IoT device includes its network behaviors that can be captured through manufacturer usage descriptor (MUD) (i.e., a framework by IETF for formally describing the network behaviour [27]) profiles using MUDGEE [20]. MUD provides the list of all the protocols and ports that are used by IoT devices to communicate over the network.

Example 2. Given the Nest Protect Smoke and CO Alarm Sensor obtained from Nest Protect technical specs [36] and API documentation [35], obtained structural knowledge is: "*Software version: 4.0*; *Device Unique Identifier:* `peyiJNoOIldT2YlIVtYaGQ`; *is_online:* `true`; *Read Permission:* `Enabled/Disabled`; *last_connection:* `2016-10-31T23:59:59.000Z`; *is_online:* `true`; *battery_health:* `ok`; *co_alarm_state:* `ok`; *smoke_alarm_state:* `ok`; *is_manual_test_active:* `true`". The corresponding functional knowledge obtained by using MUDGEE is: "*IP Protocols: TCP, UDP, HOPOPT, IPv6-ICMP*; *and Ports: 443, 11095, 53, 67*".

3.3   Defining Actionable Security Rules

We describe how we define actionable rules in the following.

Summarizing Security Controls. As there are many security controls and sub-controls with detailed descriptions of their security recommendations, we summarize them from the standard knowledge base (built in Sect. 3.2) utilizing BERT-Extractive-Summarizer [33], which is a BERT-based summarizing package. BERT is the state-of-the-art word embedding technique that is bi-directionally trained and can have a deeper sense of language context. BERT's extractive summarizing approach evaluates each sentence's comprehension and significance to the text and then delivers the most crucial segments. Thus, in this work, we opt for the extractive summarization technique instead of abstractive summarization, which changes the semantics of the recommendations due to newly generated words and phrases. BERT is used by a python-based REST-ful service for text embedding, and for summary selection, KMeans clustering is used to identify sentences closest to the centroid [33]. Text summarization is still an ongoing topic in NLP research to achieve a competitive accuracy to that of a human [55]. Due to this factor, our generated summaries need to be reviewed by experts to ensure their correctness.

Extracting Values. Before deriving security rules, we extract attributes and values from the security controls. We use Named Entity Recognition (NER), an NLP approach, to extract values from the security sub-control's discussion. As we only need to extract two types of entities from the security controls, we annotate our values and attributes as described in Sect. 3.2 in order to use them as training data to fine-tune a Hugging Face model (e.g., BERT-base-NER [12]). After fine-tuning the model, we utilize it to extract values from the summarized security controls and sub-control's discussion, and for attributes, we extract the security sub-controls. In Example 3, we explain the value and attribute extraction process.

Deriving Security Rules. After extracting security values and attributes from security controls, we generate our security rules. Our security rules are initially generated automatically by utilizing the variables along with attributes and values, and then we express them in formal language. More specifically, we pull the variable names which are stored in the elaborated security standards, then we acquire the attributes and values from the previous step and put all these data into the format of our rule. The format of our derived security rule is as follows: $variable_1 = \{attribute_1 : \{values_1, values_2, ..., values_n\}, attribute_2 : \{values_1, values_2, ..., values_n\}, ...\}$. Below using an example, we show how we define our security rules with the obtained values and attributes.

Example 3. The summarization process for the `Expectation 21` and security control `SC-8(1)` is shown in Fig. 4. The first two boxes contain `Expectation 21` and its related security sub-control, respectively, and the red highlighted texts indicate the summarized security sub-control. We extract the low-level security values, which are `TLS` and `IPSec` and attribute (e.g., `Cryptographic protection`) highlighted in red. The last box shows our low-level security rule: "*Data Protection = { Cryptographic protection: {TLS, IPSec}}*".

3.4   Instantiating to Actionable Rules

This section instantiates our derived security rules for IoT device-specific information and formalizes them into first-order logic for security applications. Specifically, *instantiation* is the process of making derived security rules specific to IoT devices so that a rule can be efficiently verified from the available IoT device data (e.g., logs, console output, etc.). However, it is insufficient to rely only on the automatically derived security rules because the security controls' values and attributes do not encompass all possible values in the context of IoT devices. To maintain accuracy, our system requires expert intervention after automatically extracting values from security controls. A specialist will eliminate undesirable or irrelevant values and determine whether any missing values should be added to our knowledge base, as illustrated at the beginning of Example 4. We then instantiate security rules to customize them for a particular IoT device, since security rules produced from IoT security standards are generally applicable to all sorts of IoT devices. We leverage our knowledge base from Sect. 3.2 to instantiate our derived security rules. After instantiating the security rules, we translate them into first-order logic because formal verification methods are more useful and effective than manual inspection for automated reasoning [30,31]. Table 2 shows an excerpt of our derived actionable rules.

Example 4. Device's sensitive data during transmission over Network: {`WiFi`, `BLE`, `LTE`, `NFC`, `PLC`, `RFID`, `Z-Wave`, `Zigbee`} should be cryptographically protected using Cryptographic mechanism: {`TLS`, `IPSec`, `AMQP`, `CoAP`, `DDS`, `MQTT`}. Suppose an example of an instantiated security rule for Nest Protect Smoke and CO Alarm Sensor is: *"Nest Protect Smoke and CO Alarm Sensor device's (device_id: `peyiJNoOIldT2YlIVtYaGQ`) smoke_alarm_state during transmission over Network: `WiFi` should be cryptographically protected using Cryptographic mechanism: `TLS`; should use protocol: `TCP` and port numbers: {443, 11095, 53, 67}"*. Leveraging our proposed method, we formalize this rule as follows.

Rule 1:

$$\forall cp \in \{TLS, IPSec, AMQP, CoAP, DDS, MQTT\},$$
$$\forall s \in SensitiveData, \forall n \in \{WiFi, BLE, LTE, NFC,$$
$$PLC, RFID, Z-Wave, Zigbee\}, \forall d\_id \in DeviceID$$
$$CryptographicProtection(d\_id, s, cp) \wedge$$
$$transmission(s, n) \implies DataProtected(d\_id, s)$$

3.5   Rationale Behind Our Semi-automated Approach

Table 3 shows the objective of different steps of our approach, as well as our explanation as to why each of the steps is either manual, semi-automated, or fully automated. Specifically, the first column lists all the steps of our approach, second column indicates how those steps are performed (i.e., automatic, semi-automatic, or manual), third column describes each step's objective, and fourth column states the rationale behind using the stated approach of those steps.

4   Applications

This section shows how our actionable rules can be applied to different security mechanisms (e.g., security auditing, IDS, and secure application development).

Table 2. An excerpt of derived and instantiated security rules using our approach

Sub-Controls	Summaries	Derived Rules	Instantiated Rules
SC-8(1)	Cryptographic mechanisms that protect the confidentiality of information during transmission include TLS and IPSec	Data Protection1 = Cryptographic protection: {TLS, IPSec}	Device's sensitive data during transmission over Network: {WiFi, BLE, LTE, NFC, PLC, RFID, Z-Wave, Zigbee} should be cryptographically protected using Cryptographic mechanism: {TLS, IPSec, AMQP, CoAP, DDS, MQTT}
SC-8(3)	Message externals include message headers and routing information should be cryptographically protected	Data Protection2 = Cryptographic protection for message externals: {headers information, routing information}	Device's network packet's Message headers and routing information: {Version, Traffic Class, Flow Label, Payload Length, Next Header, Hop Limit, Source Address, Destination address} should be protected using Cryptographic mechanism: {TLS, IPSec}
SC-8(4)	Communication patterns (e.g., frequency, periods, predictability amount) should be concealed or randomized by encrypting the links and transmitting in continuous, fixed, or random patterns	Data Protection3 = Randomized communication pattern: {frequency, periods, predictability, amount}	Device's Communication patterns: {frequency, periods, predictability, amount} should be randomized or concealed by Cryptographic mechanism: {TLS, IPSec}
SC-23(1)	Invalidate session identifiers upon user logout or other session termination	Data Protection4 = Invalidating session identifiers at logout: Enabled	Device's Session identifiers: {''CD723LGeXlf-01:34''} should be invalidated upon user_state: {logout or session termination}
AC-18(3)	Wireless networking should be disabled when not used	Data Protection5 = Disable wireless networking: Enabled	Device's Network: {WiFi, BLE, LTE, NFC, PLC, RFID, ZWave, Zigbee} should be disabled when not used

4.1 Application to IoT Security Auditing

Identifying, Collecting, and Processing Rule-Specific Audit Data. To validate security compliance for each security rule, it is essential to determine the relevant IoT data sources, collect them, and prepare them for the specific audit tools (e.g., formal methods). Logs, configuration files, and databases are the primary sources of audit data in IoT devices, and IoT hub or IoT cloud server stores these data. Different data types and sources, such as device-related data, connectivity-related data, user-related data, and application-related data, are identified based on the security rules [28]. After identifying relevant data sources, we gather data and process them in a structured manner so that they can be converted into formal language. It is crucial to transform the data into a consistent format because different data sources store the data in different formats. Finally, audit data and security rules are converted to formal language for verification. In this work, we particularly use constraint satisfaction problem (CSP), which is also used in other auditing solutions (e.g., [30–32]). To that

Table 3. Different steps of our approach, their objectives, and rationales

Steps	Approach	Objective	Rationale
Step 1.1.1 *Extracting Security Controls*	Automatic	To centralize all IoT security standards and their corresponding security controls in a single document so that it can be efficiently used by our toolchain later	Since it extracts security controls based on the mappings and it is error-free, extracting security controls from NIST SP 800-53r5 does not necessitate any expert review
Step 1.1.2 *Annotating Data*	Manual	To fine-tune the NER model so that it can extract security values from security controls	As there are no trained NER models available to extract security values, we had to annotate the security values manually to fine-tune the NER model
Step 1.2.1 *Building Structural Knowledge*	Semi-automatic	To instantiate derived security rules that are specific to IoT devices by using the structural knowledge of IoT devices.	We leverage the approach in [15] to automatically extract device specifications, configs, and API documentation, while all additional device-specific data is manually verified to assure its completeness
Step 1.2.2 *Building Functional Knowledge*	Automatic	To instantiate derived security rules using the functional knowledge such as the network behavior of IoT devices.	We utilize MUDGEE [20], which automatically delivers the IoT network port and protocol number without manual inspection
Step 2.1.1 *Summarizing Security Controls*	Semi-automatic	To extract the most crucial information from lengthy security controls, which are otherwise tedious and time-consuming tasks.	After automatically generating the summary using the BERT-Extractive-Summarizer, we need expert assessment to ensure the semantics and validity of the summaries
Step 2.1.2 *Extracting Values*	Semi-automatic	To automatically extract security values from security controls which can be used in the security rules.	We have a fine-tuned NER model to extract security values from security controls, but expert inspection is vital to ensure that the model does not exclude any required values or extract extraneous information
Step 2.1.3 *Deriving Security Rules*	Semi-automatic	To help security experts to utilize the actionable security rules in different security applications	We derive actionable security rules after extracting values and using our knowledge base; however, expert evaluation is crucial to preserve the accuracy of the generated rules because security controls do not include all of the potential security values or attributes in the context of IoT
Step 2.2.1 *Instantiating Security Rules*	Manual	To make the derived security rules specific to IoT devices so that a rule can be efficiently verified from the available IoT device data	Security rules are manually instantiated with IoT device-specific information stored in our knowledge since there is no mapping between security rules and IoT device-specific data, ensuring that only a particular device-specific information is included in the instantiated rule
Step 2.2.2 *Interpreting in Formal Language*	Manual	To enable formal verification tools to carry out security verification	Instantiated security rules are converted manually to formal language as there are no readily available tools to convert the natural language to mathematical expressions

end, each data group is represented as tuples, and the code is append with the relationships for security rules (discussed in Sect. 3.4). Listing 1 shows the tuples in our Sugar [50] code.

Conducting Formal Verification. For verification, we utilize formal verification techniques, e.g., Boolean satisfiability problem (SAT) solver. Specifically, we leverage an SAT-based tool, namely, Sugar [50], to perform the verification process and interpret the verification results. Afterward, Sugar verifies all the constraints, and then we can interpret if any security rule is breached. Lastly, an audit report is generated after getting results from a formal verification tool. The Sugar tool evaluates "true" or "false" based on the result of a security rule breach. A security expert can investigate further to determine the root cause of a breach only after discovering it in an auditing process, eliminating the need for them to manually go through all the irrelevant information of IoT devices for security breaches.

Example 5. The CSP code to audit the data protection using the rule presented in Listing 1.1. Each domain and variable is first declared (Lines 2–5). Then, the set of involved relations, namely, *CryptProtection* and *Transmission* are defined and populated with their supporting tuples (Lines 7–8), where the support is generated from simulated data by utilizing the Amazon IoT simulator [3]. Then, the data protection at transmission is declared as a predicate, denoted by *DataProtectionTransmission*, over these relations (Lines 10–11). Finally, the predicate should be instantiated (Line 19) to be able to be verified. The UNSAT result on Sugar means that all constraints are not satisfied, and hence, there is no violation of the rule. Note that the predicate will be unfolded internally by Sugar for all possible values of the variables, which allows verifying each instance of the problem among possible values of device ID, cryptographic mechanism, and network types. We evaluate this auditing step in Sect. 5.

Listing 1.1. Sugar source code for verifying Rule 1

```
1  // Declaration
2  (domain DeviceID 0 5000) (domain CryptoMech 1 6)
3  (domain NetType 11 20)(domain SensitiveData 21 40)
4  (int D DeviceID) (int CR CryptoMech)
5  (int N NetType) (int S SensitiveData)

6  // Relations Declarations and Audit Data as their Support
7  (relation CryptProtection 3 (supports ((2471 13 4) (2798
        29 2) (861 9 4) ))
8  (relation Transmission 2 (supports ((12 9) (29 10) (9 1) )
        )

9  // Security property: DataProtectionTransmission
10 (predicate (DataProtectionTransmission D S CR N) (and (
       CryptProtection D S CR) (Transmission S N) (not (
       DataProtection D S)) ))
11 (DataProtectionTransmission D S CR N)
```

4.2 Other Applications

Snort IDS. Snort [47], a potent open-source intrusion detection system (IDS) and intrusion prevention system (IPS), finds potentially malicious activities by employing a rule-based language that integrates anomaly, protocol, and signature inspection techniques. Our low-level security rules obtained from security standards can be easily translated into snort rules. To convert our low-level security rules into Snort rules, first, we need to know the format of Snort rules and the required data for the rules. Snort IDS/IPS rules consist of two parts, *rule header* and *rule option*. The *rule header* contains the following fields: `action`, `protocol`, `source address`, `source port`, `direction`, `destination address`, and `destination port`. The *rule option* of Snort is divided into a keyword and an argument, defined inside parentheses and separated by a semicolon. In this work, we obtain protocol and port numbers from our low-level security rules. In the same manner, our security rules can be utilized by other IDS systems, such as Suricata[1], Zeek[2], OSSEC[3], etc.

Example 6. Below is a low-level rule instantiated for Nest Protect Smoke and CO Alarm device, which ensures encrypted data transmission, and then we convert it into a Snort rule. Our derived security rule is: *"Nest Protect Smoke and CO Alarm Sensor device's (device_id: `peyiJNoOIldT2YlIVtYaGQ`) `smoke_alarm_state` during transmission over Network: WiFi should be cryptographically protected using Cryptographic mechanism: TLS; should use protocol: TCP and port numbers: {443, 11095, 53, 67}"*. The corresponding Snort rule is: *"`alert tcp any any <> $HOME_NET ![443, 11095, 53, 67]` (msg: \Unencrypted Traffic"; sid:1000005)"*. If this snort rule matches the network traffic data - which actually means the fields of TCP packet (source address, source port, destination address, and destination port) match with the rule (`any, any, IP address of $HOME_NET`, *port numbers other than 443, 11095, 53, or 67*), respectively, then an alert is generated that outputs the message *"Unencrypted Traffic"* with the signature ID `1000005`.

Secure Application Development. As most IoT application developers are not security experts, they might need concrete guidelines and recommendations to develop secure applications and interfaces following existing security standards and best practices. Our security rules provide IoT manufacturers and developers with actionable guidelines which can be followed to implement them in actual IoT systems, as demonstrated through the following example.

Example 7. We utilize the used port numbers (443, 11095, 53, and 67) from IoT device-specific data (in Example 2) to communicate with servers, while the high-level security standard is ambiguous about which port to use. A code snippet is presented in Listing 1.2 and shows the port numbers (Line 4) used by SmartThings SmartApp [46] to listen to the server (Line 6).

---

[1] https://suricata.io/.
[2] https://zeek.org/.
[3] https://www.ossec.net/.

Listing 1.2. Port numbers derived from our security rules used by Smart-Things SmartApp

```
1 const SmartApp = require('@smartthings/smartapp');
2 const express = require('express');
3 const server = express();
4 const PORT = [443, 11095, 53, 67];

5 /* Start listening at your defined PORT */
6 server.listen(PORT, () => console.log('Server is up
      and running on port ${PORT}'));
```

Similar to these applications, our actionable security rules might further be applied to other security mechanisms, such as access control, monitoring, risk assessment, etc., to cover various security aspects of IoT.

5 Implementation and Experiments

This section describes the details of our implementation and experiments.

5.1 Implementation

We describe the implementation of the automated steps of our approach as follows. To build knowledge of security standards, we develop a Python script that extracts the security expectations from NISTIR 8228 and the referenced NIST SP 800-53r5 security controls from control catalog (provided by NIST), and store them in a CSV file with attributes such as variables, expectations, controls, sub-controls, and their discussions. To build device-specific knowledge, network data such as port numbers and protocols are extracted by leveraging MUDGEE [20], which creates MUD [27] profiles of IoT devices by monitoring network traces and technical specifications of different IoT devices are extracted by leveraging the approach from [15]. For the summarization of security controls, we use BERT-Extractive-Summarizer [33]. Then, annotation of security controls is performed using NER Annotator [6]. To extract values from security controls, we fine-tune a Hugging Face transformer-based named entity recognition model called Bert-base-uncased [12]. Lastly, for verification, we use the Boolean satisfaction (SAT) solver tool, namely, Sugar V2.2.1 [50].

5.2 Experiments

Experimental Setting. We run our experiment on a workstation with an Intel(R) Core(TM) i7-10700 2.90GHz CPU and 16 GB of physical memory. To generate our dataset, we utilize NISTIR 8228 [8] and NIST SP 800-53r5 [37] and Amazon IoT device simulator platform [3] with 5,000 IoT devices and their logs, configuration files, and network data. Figure 5a illustrates the count of technical and non-technical security controls for each expectation of NISTIR 8228. We

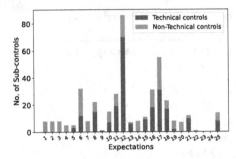 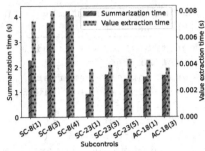

(a) Count of security controls for each expectation from NISTIR 8228 [8]

(b) Time required for summarizing and value extraction by our approach

Fig. 5. Count of security controls and efficiency of summarization and extraction

Table 4. Performance evaluation of value extraction

	Precision	Recall	F1-Score
Values	0.82	0.98	0.89
Attributes	0.97	0.94	0.95
Average	0.87	0.97	0.91

convert them into the input format, Constraint Satisfaction Problem (CSP), of Sugar [50]. We average the results after 200 iterations of each experiment.

Evaluation of Summarization and Value Extraction. In the first set of experiments, we measure the time required for summarizing each security control's discussion and value extraction step as well as the accuracy of our value extraction using precision, recall, and F1-score. Figure 5b shows that the time required for summarizing varies from less than one second to just over four seconds, because some security sub-controls are rather lengthy over others, and summarising them requires more time. However, since the summarization procedure is performed only once, overheads are tolerable for auditing such big settings. This figure also demonstrates that extracting values from the discussion of summarized security sub-controls takes only a fraction of a second, which is very time efficient compared to the summarization process. As shown in Table 4, the precision scores for values and attributes are 82% and 97%, respectively. For recall, scores of values and attributes are 98% and 94%, respectively. Values and attributes have an F1-score of 89% and 95%, respectively.

Evaluation of Derived Security Rules. Our second set of experiments is to evaluate the effectiveness of our derived security rules by examining their execution time, memory usage, and CPU usage, along with the measurement of the reduction in manual effort.

Our approach aims at reducing the manual effort required by an expert for deriving actionable security rules. Figure 6 demonstrates the amount of reduction in manual effort for summarizing and deriving actionable security rules, where we compare a fully manual approach with ours for this measurement using four similarity metrics (e.g., Cosine similarity [1], Jaro-Winkler similarity [24], Sorensen similarity [48], and Jaccard similarity metrics [26]). Based on the similarity between summarized sub-controls and derived security rules, we measure the reduction in manual effort by security experts. In other words, a security expert needs to exert less work when the summaries and derived security rules are more similar or closely resemble manually summarized and derived security rules. Figure 6a shows how our summarization tool reduced the amount of work required to summarise eight security sub-controls, with Cosine and Jaro-Winkler similarity scores averaging the highest percentages of 57% and 65%, respectively, among these four. The Sorensen similarity score is then anywhere between 50% and 37%, with Jaccard's score being the lowest. Next, Fig. 6b shows the effort reduced in deriving a security rule, with Cosine and Jaro-Winkler similarity scores again averaging the highest percentages of 50% and 52%, respectively, among these four. The Sorensen similarity score is then anywhere between 45% and 30%, with Jaccard's score being the lowest again. Overall it reduces around 50% of manual effort, and for security experts, this represents a significant decrease in manual work and time-consuming activities. The main purpose of this set of experiments is to show the resemblance of our derived rules with manually summarized sub-controls. For this purpose, we use popular similarity metrics and compare their results. We assume that those scores (i.e., calculating resemblance between two outputs) might give a hint on the reduced manual effort that these derived rules can bring. However, we acknowledge that a user survey will be needed to more accurately evaluate the usability of our approach (as further discussed in Sect. 6).

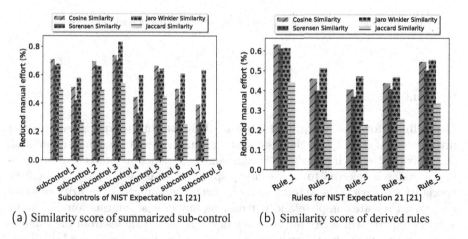

(a) Similarity score of summarized sub-control   (b) Similarity score of derived rules

Fig. 6. Manual effort reduction for summarizing and deriving rules

We then evaluate the efficiency of our derived security rules in terms of time, CPU, and memory utilization. In Fig. 7a, we observe that overall it takes less than ten seconds for 5,000 IoT devices to validate each of the five rules derived from Expectation 21. As the number of devices grows, the required time to validate each rule also increases, but after 1,500 devices, a significant reduction in increase is observed, which again increases after 4,000 devices. Given the number of devices, ten seconds is a very realistic amount of time to perform auditing. Figure 7b shows the CPU usage by varying the number of devices. With a range of between 20% and 25%, CPU utilization increases almost linearly for all five security rules. Since there are 5,000 IoT devices, and each one generates a unique set of data, the CPU usage for auditing is reasonable. Note that we only utilize a single PC for our experiments; the cost would be significantly lower if we could run Sugar for verification on multiple VMs. Our final experiment (Figs. 7c) measures the memory usage of our auditing solution. All of the five rules show a similar trend as CPU consumption. At its peak, it requires around 43 MB of memory, and overall, it requires less than 41 MB. It is noteworthy that rule 1 uses more resources because there are more tuples and, therefore, more data to validate.

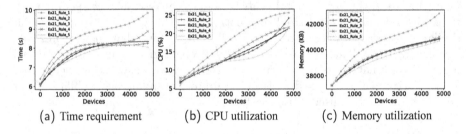

(a) Time requirement   (b) CPU utilization   (c) Memory utilization

Fig. 7. Efficiency results of our auditing step for 5,000 smart home devices.

6   Discussion

Guidelines for the Required Manual Effort. Our approach requires the involvement of security specialists in order to function to its maximum potential. An individual with in-depth knowledge and experience in protecting information systems is referred to as a security specialist or expert. Firstly, a security specialist will review the automatically generated summaries of security controls to ensure they are complete and not missing any crucial information. Secondly, security experts will verify the accuracy of the retrieved values from the summarized security controls. Following these actions, low-level security rules will be created using the retrieved values and any additional potential values relevant to the IoT. Lastly, a security expert must carefully consider each possible value of a security rule that will be applied during security auditing. The formalization of the low-level security rule into first-order logic will result in CSP code for the Sugar tool. Our derived actionable security rules can be converted into any formal language based on the requirement of the security tools and can be used for various security purposes.

Covering Other Security Standards. In this paper, we consider the IoT security standard from NIST IR 8228 and utilize its mapping to NIST SP 800-53r5 to derive actionable security rules. However, there are many other security standards from different federal and non-federal organizations available for IoT systems which can be easily incorporated with our methodology by getting their mapping to NIST SP 800-53r5. To that end, European Union Agency for Cybersecurity (ENISA) Baseline Security Recommendations for IoT in the context of Critical Information Infrastructures [17] provides a mapping with NIST SP 800-53r5 in their security standard. Additionally, OWASP is working on a project to provide a mapping of the OWASP IoT Top 10 2018 to various industry policies and publications [39]. Once available, those mappings can be utilized to cover other security standards using our approach.

Validating the Usability of Our Solution. To further validate the usability of our approach, we plan to carry out a user survey in the future. This study might provide feedback on the effectiveness (e.g., possible increasing efforts due to any incorrectness or mistake in our derived rules) and usability of our tool; The results and feedback of this study can be considered in the following version of our proposed approach. Specifically, to analyze the usability of our derived security rules, we will develop multiple scenarios where participants can experience our tool in contrast to a fully manual approach as well as a semi-guided approach to derive rules followed by a questionnaire with a variety of closed-ended (e.g., multiple choice and Likert scale) and open-ended (e.g., strength, weakness, and suggestions) questions. Our target group for this survey will be security researchers and industry practitioners (leveraging our existing collaborations) as potential users of such tools.

Feedback to Standardization Authorities. As our solution aims at mapping high-level security standard specifications to low-level system implementations, it might be able to identify existing issues (e.g., missing concrete or related information to realize a security recommendation) in a standard specification. Additionally, interpreting the final and intermediate outcomes of our solution might provide insights into further clarifying the recommendations in current security standards. We intend to provide such feedback to the standardization authorities that might be useful to design future standards in a clearer and more useful manner.

7   Related Works

This section reviews existing IoT security works and compares them with ours. We first review rule-based IoT security solutions. Fung et al. [19] introduce a user-defined rule-sharing model for the IoT environment and track the reputation of rules based on the feedback of different rules adopted by users without the need for central facilities. PFIREWALL [11] generates data minimization rules to control data flow by filtering communication between devices and platforms of IoT systems to reduce data leakage. IoTSAFE [14] performs static analysis and dynamic testing to identify run-time physical interactions in the IoT environment to enforce security rules. Soteria [9] verifies the safety and security rules of IoT platforms by performing static code analysis in IoT applications. On the other hand, IoTGuard [10] is a dynamic safety and security rule enforcement system by code instrumentation. Nespoli et al. [34] detect vulnerabilities in IoT and dynamically adapt to surrounding devices and services based on rules. Dome et al. [16] utilize the Random-Forest model to convert behavioral patterns into rules, build a threat prediction model, and monitor rule violations. Majumdar et al. [31] [32] conduct security auditing leveraging formal techniques in cloud platforms. Madi et al. [30] also carried out security auditing on a cloud platform by proposing an auditing framework for OpenStack. Most of the above-mentioned works develop their own rules, whereas our goal is to utilize existing security standards.

Another line of research focuses on access control, monitoring, and intrusion detection of IoT systems. ContexIoT [25] is a context-based permission system to provide contextual integrity for different IoT platforms. SmartAuth [51] uses static analysis to collect security-related data from IoT apps to design authorization procedures to address over-privileged issues in IoT systems. HoMonit [57] utilizes side-channel techniques to monitor the encrypted traffic of IoT systems. IoTArgos [54] is a multi-layer security monitoring system that uses machine learning techniques to find intrusions and anomalies in IoT platforms. Anthi et al. [4] develop a multi-layer intrusion detection system. In contrast, our work provides actionable security rules which can be utilized in various security applications.

We also review the association rule mining works. P. Lou et al. [29] obtain association rules on multi-source logs based on the Adaptive Miner algorithm to provide critical information for cyber intrusion detection and assist non-experts in conducting security problem investigations in cloud computing platforms. Ozawa et al. [41] use association rule mining to discover regularities in darknet data. Husak et al. [22] use sequential rule mining to analyze intrusion detection alerts and to predict security events for creating a predictive blacklist. Safara et al. [43] use an association rule mining algorithm to extract appropriate features from raw data and then use the features for detecting anomalies in communication networks. Xu et al. [56] propose an Attribute-based access control (ABAC) policy mining algorithm. Sanders et al. [44] use the rule mining approach to analyze systems' audit logs for automatically generating ABAC policies. Unlike them, this work derives actionable security rules from IoT standards.

Comparative Study. Table 5 summarizes a comparative study of existing works. The first two columns enlist existing works and their methods, respectively. The next two columns compare the coverage, such as the supported environment (IoT, cloud) and main objectives (auditing, intrusion detection).

Table 5. Comparing existing solutions with ours. (•), (○), (-), and (NA) mean supported, partially supported, not supported, and not applicable, respectively.

Proposals	Methods	Coverage		Features						
		Environment	Objective	Knowledge base	First Order Logic	Automatic Rule Derivation	Expressiveness	Automatic System	Run time Enforcement	Using Security Standards
ContextIoT [25]	Custom Algorithm	IoT	Access Control	NA	-	-	NA	•	•	-
Soteria [9]	Static Analysis	IoT	Intrusion Detection	-	-	-	NA	•	•	-
IoTGuard [10]	Dynamic Analysis	IoT	Intrusion Detection	-	-	-	NA	•	•	-
Majumdar et al. [31]	Formal Method	Cloud	Auditing	-	•	-	•	•	-	•
Madi et al. [30]	Formal Method	Cloud	Auditing	-	•	-	•	NA	-	○
Majumdar et al. [32]	Formal Method	Cloud	Auditing	-	•	-	•	NA	•	•
Homonit [57]	Custom Algorithm	IoT	Monitoring System	NA	-	-	-	-	-	-
IoTSafe [14]	Static and Dynamic	IoT	Intrusion Detection	NA	-	-	-	•	•	-
PFIREWALL [11]	Custom Algorithm	IoT	Access Control	NA	-	•	-	•	•	-
This Work	Formal Method	IoT	Auditing, Secure development, etc.	•	•	•	•	•	•	•

The remaining columns compare these works based on different features, i.e., knowledge-base, first-order logic, automatic rule derivation, expressiveness, automatic system, run-time enforcement, and utilization of security standards. In summary, our work mainly differs from other works as follows. Firstly, we only propose an approach to derive actionable security rules from existing IoT security standards. Secondly, we build a knowledge base for both IoT standards and IoT devices that can be utilized in other related research. Finally, our derived security rules can be used directly for various security applications.

8 Conclusion

This paper proposed an approach to derive actionable security rules from high-level security standards. Additionally, we collected device-specific data to instantiate derived security rules and conducted verification leveraging formal tools for IoT devices. Our experiment results showed the effectiveness of our derived rules in security auditing. Moreover, our derived actionable security rules can be utilized in other security applications. In the following steps, we envision being able to automate device-specific data collection, which is collected manually now. Our future work will incorporate more security standards into our methodology and automate the majority of the stages involved in the derivation of actionable security rules, requiring the least amount of work from security specialists. Additionally, in our future work, we intend to conduct a user study to evaluate the usability of our solution from the feedback of real-world security practitioners.

Acknowledgments. The authors thank the anonymous reviewers and our shepherd, Christopher Wood, for their valuable comments. This material is based upon work supported by the Natural Sciences and Engineering Research Council of Canada and Department of National Defence Canada under the Discovery Grants RGPIN-2021-04106 and DGDND-2021-04106.

References

1. Alake, R.: Understanding cosine similarity and its application (2021). https://towardsdatascience.com/understanding-cosine-similarity-and-its-application-fd42f585296a

2. Alrawi, O., Lever, C., Antonakakis, M., Monrose, F.: SoK: security evaluation of home-based IoT deployments. In: IEEE SP. IEEE (2019)

3. Amazon IoT device simulator. https://aws.amazon.com/solutions/implementations/iot-device-simulator/

4. Anthi, E., Williams, L., Słowińska, M., Theodorakopoulos, G., Burnap, P.: A supervised intrusion detection system for smart home IoT devices. IEEE Internet Things J. **6**(5), 9042–9053 (2019)

5. Antonakakis, M., et al.: Understanding the Mirai botnet. In: USENIX Security (2017)

6. Arunmozhi: Annotation tool for NER. NER annotator (2022). https://tecoholic.github.io/ner-annotator/

7. Bellman, C., van Oorschot, P.C.: Systematic analysis and comparison of security advice as datasets. Comput. Secur. **124**, 102989 (2023)

8. Boeckl, K., et al.: Considerations for managing Internet of Things (IoT) cybersecurity and privacy risks. US Department of Commerce, National Institute of Standards and Technology (2019)

9. Celik, Z.B., McDaniel, P., Tan, G.: Soteria: automated IoT safety and security analysis. In: USENIX ATC, pp. 147–158 (2018)

10. Celik, Z.B., Tan, G., McDaniel, P.D.: IoTGuard: dynamic enforcement of security and safety policy in commodity IoT. In: NDSS (2019)

11. Chi, H., Zeng, Q., Du, X., Luo, L.: PFIREWALL: semantics-aware customizable data flow control for smart home privacy protection. arXiv preprint arXiv:2101.10522 (2021)

12. Devlin, J., Chang, M., Lee, K., Toutanova, K.: BERT: pre-training of deep bidirectional transformers for language understanding. CoRR abs/1810.04805 (2018). https://arxiv.org/abs/1810.04805

13. Department for Digital, Culture, MS: The UK government. code of practice for consumer IoT security (2019). https://www.gov.uk/government/publications/code-of-practice-for-consumer-iot-security

14. Ding, W., Hu, H., Cheng, L.: IOTSAFE: enforcing safety and security policy with real IoT physical interaction discovery. In: NDSS (2021)

15. Dolan, A., Ray, I., Majumdar, S.: Proactively extracting IoT device capabilities: an application to smart homes. In: Singhal, A., Vaidya, J. (eds.) DBSec 2020. LNCS, vol. 12122, pp. 42–63. Springer, Cham (2020). https://doi.org/10.1007/978-3-030-49669-2_3

16. Domb, M., Bonchek-Dokow, E., Leshem, G.: Lightweight adaptive random-forest for IoT rule generation and execution. J. Inf. Secur. Appl. **34**, 218–224 (2017)

17. ENISA, E: Baseline security recommendations for IoT in the context of critical information infrastructures. European Union Agency for Cybersecurity Heraklion, Greece (2017)

18. Fagan, M., Megas, K., Scarfone, K., Smith, M.: Recommendations for IoT device manufacturers: foundational activities and core device cybersecurity capability baseline (2nd draft). Technical report, National Institute of Standards and Technology (2020)

19. Fung, C.J., McCormick, B.: An effective policy sharing mechanism for smart home networks. In: IEEE CNSM. IEEE (2020)

20. Hamza, A., Gharakheili, H.H., Sivaraman, V.: Combining MUD policies with SDN for IoT intrusion detection. In: IoT S&P (2018)

21. Ho, G., Leung, D., Mishra, P., Hosseini, A., Song, D., Wagner, D.: Smart locks: lessons for securing commodity internet of things devices. In: ACM ASIACCS, pp. 461–472 (2016)

22. Husák, M., Bajtoš, T., Kašpar, J., Bou-Harb, E., Čeleda, P.: Predictive cyber situational awareness and personalized blacklisting: a sequential rule mining approach. ACM Trans. Manag. Inf. Syst. (TMIS) **11**(4), 1–16 (2020)
23. ETS Institute: En 303 645 - v2.1.1 - cyber; cyber security for consumer internet of things: baseline requirements (2020). https://www.etsi.org/deliver/etsi_en/303600_303699/303645/02.01.01_60/en_303645v020101p.pdf
24. Jaro-winkler distance (2022). https://en.wikipedia.org/wiki/Jaro-Winkler_distance
25. Jia, Y.J., et al.: ContexIoT: Towards providing contextual integrity to appified IoT platforms. In: NDSS (2017)
26. Karabiber, F.: Jaccard similarity. https://www.learndatasci.com/glossary/jaccard-similarity/
27. Lear, E., Droms, R., Romascanu, D.: Manufacturer usage description specification. Technical report, Internet Engineering Task Force (2019)
28. Li, S., Choo, K.K.R., Sun, Q., Buchanan, W.J., Cao, J.: IoT forensics: Amazon echo as a use case. IEEE Internet Things J. **6**(4), 6487–6497 (2019)
29. Lou, P., Lu, G., Jiang, X., Xiao, Z., Hu, J., Yan, J.: Cyber intrusion detection through association rule mining on multi-source logs. Appl. Intell. **51**(6), 4043–4057 (2021)
30. Madi, T., Majumdar, S., Wang, Y., Jarraya, Y., Pourzandi, M., Wang, L.: Auditing security compliance of the virtualized infrastructure in the cloud: application to OpenStack. In: ACM CODASPY (2016)
31. Majumdar, S., et al.: Security compliance auditing of identity and access management in the cloud: application to OpenStack. In: IEEE CloudCom. IEEE (2015)
32. Majumdar, S., et al.: User-level runtime security auditing for the cloud. IEEE Trans. Inf. Forensics Secur. **13**(5), 1185–1199 (2017)
33. Miller, D.: Leveraging BERT for extractive text summarization on lectures. arXiv preprint arXiv:1906.04165 (2019)
34. Nespoli, P., Díaz-López, D., Mármol, F.G.: Cyberprotection in IoT environments: a dynamic rule-based solution to defend smart devices. J. Inf. Secur. Appl. **60**, 102878 (2021)
35. Nest API reference. https://developers.nest.com/documentation/api-reference
36. Nest protect and CO alarm. https://store.google.com/product/nest_protect_2nd_gen_specs?hl=en-US
37. NIST: Security and privacy controls for information systems and organizations. https://nvlpubs.nist.gov/nistpubs/SpecialPublications/NIST.SP.800-53r5.pdf
38. Notra, S., Siddiqi, M., Gharakheili, H.H., Sivaraman, V., Boreli, R.: An experimental study of security and privacy risks with emerging household appliances. In: IEEE CNS. IEEE (2014)
39. OWASP: OWASP IoT top 10 2018 mapping project. https://github.com/scriptingxss/OWASP-IoT-Top-10-2018-Mapping
40. OWASP: OWASP top 10 Internet of Things 2018 (2018). https://owasp.org/www-pdf-archive/OWASP-IoT-Top-10-2018-final.pdf
41. Ozawa, S., Ban, T., Hashimoto, N., Nakazato, J., Shimamura, J.: A study of IoT malware activities using association rule learning for darknet sensor data. Int. J. Inf. Secur. **19**(1), 83–92 (2020)
42. Ronen, E., Shamir, A.: Extended functionality attacks on IoT devices: the case of smart lights. In: IEEE EuroS&P. IEEE (2016)
43. Safara, F., Souri, A., Serrizadeh, M.: Improved intrusion detection method for communication networks using association rule mining and artificial neural networks. IET Commun. **14**(7), 1192–1197 (2020)

44. Sanders, M.W., Yue, C.: Mining least privilege attribute based access control policies. In: ACSAC (2019)

45. Sivaraman, V., Chan, D., Earl, D., Boreli, R.: Smart-phones attacking smart-homes. In: ACM WiSec (2016)

46. SmartThingsCommunity: SmartThings   SmartApp   Node.js   SDK. https://github.com/SmartThingsCommunity/smartapp-sdk-nodejs/blob/ 2fb4f4612e946a11b223531ca60557869d4abe49/README.md

47. Snort. https://www.snort.org/

48. Sorensen-dice coefficient (2022). https://en.wikipedia.org/wiki/Sorensen-Dice_ coefficient

49. Sugawara, T., Cyr, B., Rampazzi, S., Genkin, D., Fu, K.: Light commands: laser-based audio injection attacks on voice-controllable systems. In: USENIX Security (2020)

50. Tamura, N., Taga, A., Kitagawa, S., Banbara, M.: Compiling finite linear CSP into SAT. Constraints 14(2), 254–272 (2009)

51. Tian, Y., et al.: SmartAuth: user-centered authorization for the internet of things. In: USENIX Security (2017)

52. Verry, J.: Should I use NIST 8228 or NIST 8259 for IoT design or IoT testing? (2020). https://www.pivotpointsecurity.com/should-i-use-nist-8228-or-nist-8259-for-iot-design-or-iot-testing/

53. Vervier, P.-A., Shen, Y.: Before toasters rise up: a view into the emerging IoT threat landscape. In: Bailey, M., Holz, T., Stamatogiannakis, M., Ioannidis, S. (eds.) RAID 2018. LNCS, vol. 11050, pp. 556–576. Springer, Cham (2018). https:// doi.org/10.1007/978-3-030-00470-5_26

54. Wan, Y., Xu, K., Xue, G., Wang, F.: IoTArgos: a multi-layer security monitoring system for internet-of-things in smart homes. In: IEEE INFOCOM. IEEE (2020)

55. Widyassari, A.P., et al.: Review of automatic text summarization techniques & methods. J. King Saud Univ.-Comput. Inf. Sci. (2020)

56. Xu, Z., Stoller, S.D.: Mining attribute-based access control policies. IEEE Trans. Dependable Secure Comput. 12(5), 533–545 (2014)

57. Zhang, W., Meng, Y., Liu, Y., Zhang, X., Zhang, Y., Zhu, H.: HoMonit: monitoring smart home apps from encrypted traffic. In: ACM CCS (2018)

SoK: Anonymous Credentials

Saqib A. Kakvi[(✉)] , Keith M. Martin , Colin Putman,
and Elizabeth A. Quaglia

Royal Holloway, University of London, Egham, UK
{kakvi,Keith.Martin,Colin.Putman.2017,Elizabeth.Quaglia}@rhul.ac.uk

Abstract. Anonymous credentials are a powerful tool for making assertions about identity while maintaining privacy and have been the subject of study for many years. The interest in anonymous credentials has intensified in recent years as the Internet and Web have become more and more interwoven into the fabric of our daily lives, causing large scale concerns about privacy. In particular, users are now wanting to reduce the amount of personal information they share in order to gain access to services. Since their introduction by Chaum (Comm. ACM 1985) there have been a plethora of results attempting to instantiate them with the first fully anonymous scheme being realised by Camenish and Lysyanskaya (EUROCRYPT 2001). Since this breakthrough result, there have been several newer schemes that have been proposed that not only improve on the Camenish-Lysyanskaya scheme but also introduce new features. In fact there have been a large variety of extensions proposed that have led to a seemingly incomparable landscape of schemes. In this paper, we review the many properties of anonymous credential systems, and systematically categorise and compare the approaches in the literature. Our analysis allows us to highlight gaps, open questions and directions for future research in the space of anonymous credentials.

Keywords: Anonymous Credentials · Revocable Credentials · Group Signature · Zero Knowledge · Ring Signatures · Structure Preserving Signatures · Updatable Credentials

1 Introduction

As the world becomes more and more digitally connected, protecting one's data and preserving as much privacy as possible has become of paramount importance. In particular, the upward trend of services requiring users to provide large, often superfluous, amounts of *Personally Identifiable Information (PII)* for access is of great concern. While the problem of PII being inaccurate, shared or sold without informed consent can be minimised with legal instruments such as the General Data Protection Regulation, the potential theft or misuse of such information once it has been collected is still an issue. Users must often provide PII to prove that they meet the criteria to access certain services, e.g., that they have reached the age of majority. Ideally we would like to be able to prove that we meet these

© The Author(s), under exclusive license to Springer Nature Switzerland AG 2023
F. Günther and J. Hesse (Eds.): SSR 2023, LNCS 13895, pp. 129–151, 2023.
https://doi.org/10.1007/978-3-031-30731-7_6

criteria without revealing any further information. Even when no PII is provided, the ability to link a user's activities from one session to the next often allows for extensive profiles to be built up over time. The primary solution to address both of these problems is to use *anonymous credentials*.

Anonymous credentials are a class of cryptographic tools, first proposed by Chaum in 1985 [38], that allows users to prove their identity, membership in a group or indeed any other arbitrary attribute without revealing their personal information. Anonymous credentials are a type of data structure with associated protocols, similar in nature to a PKI certificate but with additional, privacy-focused security properties. They are well-suited to use in identity management systems, particularly in realising self-sovereign identity, as well as in access control and provision of online services in a privacy-friendly way. These systems are designed to protect the privacy of individuals while still allowing them to authenticate themselves and access certain resources or services. Anonymous credentials have a wide range of applications, including enabling users to access online services without revealing their identity [34], building privacy into electronic ID cards [28], managing health information [77], traffic communication [49], and smart energy grids [69], enabling e-voting systems [47], and providing privacy-preserving access control in cloud computing environments [5].

Anonymous credentials have predominantly been a matter of academic study for many decades, however they have also started to find their way into practice [3,14,34,63], in particular there are now commercial implementations of anonymous credentials, for instance in Microsoft's uProve [22,76] and in IBM's idemix [34,59]. While anonymous credentials themselves have not as of yet been standardised, there have been standards based on related primitives, namely group signatures by ISO [60,61], Direct Anonymous Attestation (DAA) protocols by the TCG [84] and verifiable credentials, of which anonymous credentials can be seen as a special case, by the W3C [82]. These primitives are closely related to, and indeed share many of the same goals with, anonymous credentials, but they are not strictly speaking anonymous credentials.

Since the publication in 2001 of the first fully anonymous credential scheme by Camenish and Lysyanskaya [30] there have been numerous constructions of anonymous credentials in various settings. Not only have there been many schemes using zero-knowledge as in [30], but there have also been several of the so-called "self-blinding" schemes, starting from the proposal of Verheul [88]. In addition to new credential schemes based on these paradigms, there have also been a wide range of extensions proposing interesting new properties. This has led to several seemingly incomparable schemes, all of which fall under the umbrella of anonymous credentials.

In this paper, we address this issue of incomparability by providing a comprehensive overview of anonymous credential schemes, creating a full taxonomy of their properties. To this end, we will explore all the known properties and, where relevant, show how they relate to one another. Once we have this, we will take all extant anonymous credentials and split them by their construction paradigm and show which properties they achieve. This will enable us to directly compare the most recent anonymous credential schemes, which was lacking until now. We will also give an overview of the *asymptotic* efficiency of the schemes.

1.1 Our Contribution

We begin our study by providing an overview of anonymous credentials and discuss both fundamental and advanced properties. After this we explore the different approaches to achieving anonymous credentials and highlight some key results. We continue with a discussion of various aspects that are relevant to the practical deployment of anonymous credentials. We conclude with a systematic categorization of the state-of-the-art approaches to achieving anonymous credentials and compare them in terms of the advanced properties they achieve, the assumptions on which their security relies, and their efficiency. In particular, our results provide insights into gaps in the literature and directions for future work.

2 Definition of Anonymous Credentials

Anonymous credentials have been defined numerous times in the literature, including past efforts to produce unified frameworks or languages for describing them [9,27,33], though different authors do not always agree on which properties are considered necessary. In this section we provide a definition that is stripped down to only the core functions of an anonymous credential system, which forms our basis for deciding which schemes are or are not considered to be anonymous credentials. We then present an overview of the many additional properties that exist in the literature as optional, often desirable extensions.

Similarly to digital certificates and W3C verifiable credentials, an anonymous credential is a data structure that encapsulates some information pertaining to its holder as well as a signature on that information by another entity. This data structure is designed to operate in a specific environment of actors and protocols referred to as an *anonymous credential system*, which defines how credentials are generated and used, and the security goals they are expected to achieve.

The most basic model for an anonymous credential system defines three types of entities: provers, issuers, and verifiers. These entities behave as follows:

- *Provers* are the credential holders, and most often identified with the users of the system. A prover has one or more items of data, called *attributes*, pertaining to themself which they wish to have certified by an issuer so that they can be attested to verifiers. Provers are assumed to be concerned with their own privacy, and so they do not want to disclose any more information than necessary in a particular transaction, or to be tracked from one transaction to the next.
- *Issuers* are entities that sign and issue credentials for provers. A given system may have one or many issuers, and an issuer may also be responsible for initialising the system. Issuers interact with provers to issue credentials, but

are not trusted by the provers; they are generally not expected to interact directly with verifiers, but their public keys are made known, and it is assumed that verifiers trust issuers not to issue inappropriate or erroneous credentials. Similarly to certificate authorities, an issuer that loses the verifiers' trust ceases to be able to issue credentials that will be accepted.

- *Verifiers*, sometimes called service providers, are entities that have legitimate reason to want to know one or more of a prover's attributes, such as for access control or enriching a service. Provers interact with verifiers to disclose their attributes, but do not trust verifiers not to try to infer undisclosed information. Verifiers, meanwhile, want to be assured that provers cannot fabricate attributes in order to bypass the verifier's checks.

Participants in the system are not limited to occupying only one of these roles; for example, a verifier might also issue its own credentials for later access control, or a peer-to-peer environment may have provers mutually verifying each other. More advanced systems may also involve one or more *trusted third parties (TTPs)* for purposes such as initialisation, credential revocation, and arbitrating conditional disclosure of attributes [27], but this is not universal in the literature, and some systems specifically avoid the use of TTPs [85, 86].

To achieve the necessary interactions between these participants, an anonymous credential system must also include certain functions available to those participants:

- Issue($nym,attr,auth,isk$) → ($attr,\sigma$): An issuer calls this function, inputting a pseudonym by which a prover has identified itself, a representation of the (possibly empty) attribute set the prover wants certified, the outcome of some external authentication check (which may include actions ranging from verifying a pre-existing credential to authenticating face-to-face), and the issuer's secret key, to generate a signature on the attributes suitable for use in a credential and return it to the prover.
- Receive($attr,\sigma,usk$) → ($cred$): A prover, on receiving credential information from an issuer, calls this function to perform any prover-side processing needed to transform the credential into a usable form.
- Prove($cred,attr,usk$) → (ϕ,ipk): A prover calls this function, inputting a credential, any attribute information to be disclosed, and the prover's own secret information, to generate a proof token ϕ which (in conjunction with the issuer's public key ipk) attests that the information $attr$ is contained in the credential $cred$ in such a way as to convince a verifier.
- Verify(ϕ,ipk) → $\{0,1\}$: A verifier calls this function to test whether a proof token ϕ correctly verifies under the issuer's public key ipk.

These functions can be paired up into Issue/Receive and Prove/Verify protocols, the former being run between a prover and an issuer to generate a credential, and the latter being run between a prover and a verifier to disclose information from a credential. These protocols may be interactive, but non-interactivity is considered very desirable to minimise rounds of communication. It is also worth noting that the proof token ϕ does not necessarily include any direct representation of the credential itself, and is typically the output of a zero-knowledge proof.

No entity in this basic system is fully trusted, and there are two main threats to consider. Firstly, a malicious prover may attempt to run a successful Prove/Verify protocol using a credential that is invalid, was never issued, or contains data different to that which the prover is claiming. We will refer to this as credential fraud. Secondly, a malicious issuer, verifier, eavesdropper, or coalition may attempt to identify a prover from a protocol transcript, in particular by connecting that transcript to a previous interaction by the same prover. We refer to this as linking or tracking.

Therefore, the basic properties an anonymous credential system must achieve are as follows:

- **Correctness:** A Prove/Verify protocol will succeed if the input is a valid credential resulting from an Issue/Receive protocol previously run between the prover and an issuer known to the verifier, and containing any information claimed by the prover.
- **Unforgeability:** A prover cannot feasibly run a successful Prove/Verify protocol without a valid, unaltered credential that was issued by the claimed issuer and does contain any claimed information. This property includes collusion resistance, meaning that two or more provers cannot combine their credentials to produce a proof that no one prover could have created alone. A successful protocol can therefore convince the verifier that the prover does hold a valid credential from a known issuer.
- **Issuer Unlinkability:** A witness to a valid Prove/Verify protocol transcript should have negligible advantage in determining which Issue/Receive protocol run generated the prover's credential, except for any advantage gained from attributes disclosed by the prover, even if the prover and verifier collude.
- **Multi-show Unlinkability:** A witness to multiple Prove/Verify protocol runs linked to the same issuer should have negligible advantage in determining which, if any, protocol runs involved the same credential, except for any advantage gained from attributes disclosed by the prover(s), even if the issuer and verifier collude.

Of these, multi-show unlinkability is the most significant, as it distinguishes anonymous credentials from more general verifiable credentials and from other primitives such as blind signatures. It is also the most complex to achieve, and in Sect. 3 we categorise anonymous credentials primarily on whether they address this challenge using zero-knowledge proofs or malleable, randomisable signatures.

While this model is broad enough to encompass the anonymous credential literature and identifies the most defining characteristic of anonymous credentials, even the first construction of an anonymous credential scheme offered many more features on top of these core functions [30]. For the remainder of this section, we will give an overview of the wide range of features and properties that have been proposed and built for anonymous credentials, and in some cases we highlight details that arise from combining these properties.

2.1   Credential Attributes

An attribute is the term for any data item pertaining to an individual, whether it is an atom or an expression involving one or more atoms. In real-world terms, attributes may include PII such as a person's age or address, or the expression "age > 18", and non-PII such as membership in a group or club. Every credential can be considered to encode at least one attribute, since ownership of a credential is itself a Boolean attribute, which in typical use cases will be predicated on another, more meaningful attribute. Most anonymous credential schemes, however, are designed to encode multiple attributes explicitly. Such credentials are also referred to as attribute-based credentials (ABCs).

Selective Disclosure. Because anonymous credentials are traditionally motivated by the goal of allowing minimal disclosure of information, credentials that encode multiple attributes almost always provide the feature of selective disclosure, allowing provers to disclose any subset (including the empty subset) of their credential attributes during the Prove/Verify protocol, while keeping the undisclosed attributes concealed.

Blind Attributes. It is also common for some attributes to be encoded in such a way that the issuer can sign the credential without learning the values of those attributes. This is particularly important in credential schemes that encode the prover's secret key as an attribute for the purpose of proving ownership of the credential [30]. It can also be used to include attributes from pre-existing credentials without revealing the values of those attributes to the issuer [27].

2.2   Delegatable Credentials

Proposed by Chase and Lysyanskaya [35], delegatable credentials allow a credential owner to issue a credential derived from their own to another party, in such a way that a verifier can still link the delegated credential back to the original (root) issuer. Delegatable credentials closely resemble certificate chains in a classic PKI, but differ in that the identities of the intermediate entities on the chain are obfuscated, revealing only the root issuer and the number of times the credential was delegated. They are useful if an issuer wishes to act through branch offices or other intermediaries, or if a user might want to share some of their privileges or authorise a third party to act on their behalf.

There is no clear standard set for how attributes should function in delegatable credentials. Early constructions of delegatable credentials allowed attributes to be added to a credential, but did not hide the attributes on the delegation chain [10]. Blömer and Bobolz [17] propose a model in which a delegator can only delegate subsets of the attributes in the delegator's own credential.

2.3 Issuer-Hiding Credentials

A recent development from delegatable credentials, issuer-hiding credentials replace the issuer's public key in the Prove function with a proof that the credential's signature is valid under one of a set of public keys, corresponding to the list of issuers the verifier is known to trust. This conceals the specific identity of the credential issuer, similarly to how the identities of delegators are concealed by delegatable credentials, and thereby avoids linking the credential back to a single root of trust. Issuer-hiding has been realised by Bobolz et al. [19] with a zero-knowledge proof scheme, and by Connolly et al. [42] with a self-blindable scheme.

2.4 Updatable Credentials

Proposed by Blömer et al. in 2019 [18], an updatable credential scheme is one that provides some additional functions for a prover interacting with an issuer that allow the attributes on that prover's credential to be changed in specific, pre-determined ways after they have been issued. Crucially, the issuer does not learn the values of the attributes it is involved in updating, only the relationship between the new value and the old value. The authors propose that this idea can be used to develop anonymous incentive systems such as retailer reward point systems.

2.5 Issuer/Verifier Combination

While the standard assumption in anonymous credential systems is that issuers and verifiers can and will be distinct entities in the system, there are many use cases in which the two roles are combined. In 2014, Chase et al. [36] proposed keyed-verification anonymous credentials (KVACs), which use MACs instead of digital signatures as their underlying primitive; this requires that the issuer and verifier share a secret key, but the use of symmetric rather than asymmetric cryptography results in a significantly more efficient scheme. KVACs have recently been implemented as part of the Signal messenger platform [37].

3 Categorizing Anonymous Credentials

Even before considering the other features provided, credential schemes can be broadly categorised based on how they achieve their core properties and how they are used. In particular, they can be divided into credentials that operate using zero-knowledge proofs and credentials that are re-randomised (blinded) by the prover between showings. Group signatures represent an alternative tool for anonymous credentials, which may be based on either zero-knowledge or self-blindable credentials, and there exist schemes lacking multi-show unlinkability that are adjacent to the field of anonymous credentials and are worth considering as the closest alternative in many environments. We discuss these approaches in detail next.

3.1   Zero-knowledge Credentials

The first fully realised anonymous credential scheme was published in 2001 by Camenisch and Lysyanskaya [30], establishing both the model of zero-knowledge credentials and the idea that an attribute-based credential scheme can be constructed from a group signature scheme, a commitment scheme, and (zero-knowledge) protocols to generate and prove knowledge of signatures on committed values and to prove the equality of two commitments, a combination of elements that came to be known as CL-signatures [12]. The original Camenisch-Lysyanskaya credentials remain one of the best-known and most successful credential schemes, being incorporated into numerous later works including the *idemix* [34] and Hyperledger libraries, the Direct Anonymous Attestation (DAA) scheme [34] adopted by the Trusted Computing Group for remotely authenticating trusted computing modules, and the IRMA Project [4,90] prototyping an ABC ecosystem suitable for general, everyday public use.

A common feature of the Camenisch-Lysyanskaya branch of zero-knowledge credentials is that they are based on the RSA public-key encryption algorithm and the factorisation hard problem. In contrast, most credential schemes developed to date are based on Diffie-Hellman-hard bilinear groups, enabling similar security with much shorter key sizes. The CL-signature method was subsequently used to construct numerous credential schemes, first in 2004 by Camenisch and Lysyanskaya [32] on bilinear map-based group signatures, and notably in 2009 onwards to generate ABCs from attribute-based signatures [63,81,92]. Kaaniche et al's scheme *PCS* [63] in particular can be seen as a culmination of this branch, as it is the latest and has been implemented as part of the EU-funded TeSLA project. The fact that attribute-based functionality is a part of the underlying signature scheme allows for very streamlined issuing protocols compared with other credential schemes, as well as constant-cost selective disclosure proofs.

Another notable development came in 2007 when Belenkiy et al. [11] designed a credential scheme using Groth-Sahai non-interactive zero-knowledge (NIZK) proofs. Though more cumbersome than interactive proofs, NIZKs allow the proof to be computed in advance to streamline the Prove/Verify transaction itself, and have remained a popular option for subsequent anonymous credentials as a result.

Delegatable credentials were first shown to be feasible in 2006 by Chase and Lysyanskaya [35], and were realised with storage requirements linear in the credential chain length in 2009 by Belenkiy et al. [10], and with non-interactive protocols by Fuchsbauer in 2011 [50]. Other examples include work by Acar and Nguyen [1] and by Camenisch et al. [25]. However, it was not until a 2018 publication by Blömer and Bobolz [17] that delegators' attributes were fully concealed and a notion of restricting the attributes a credential holder is able to issue when delegating was formalised.

3.2   Self-blindable Credentials

As an alternative to zero-knowledge credentials, self-blindable credentials were also proposed in 2001, by Verheul [88]. Based on the Weil pairing, Verheul's self-blindable construction achieved multi-show unlinkability by allowing the credential itself to be randomised between showings, effectively making the credential function as its own zero-knowledge proof. However, Verheul's credentials lacked attribute support and were not proven secure.

In 2014, Hanser and Slamanig [51,56] extended structure-preserving signatures, in which the message and signature are composed of elements of the same group, to produce SPS on equivalence classes (SPS-EQ). This primitive defines an equivalence relation on the message and signature spaces such that a message-signature pair can be efficiently randomised to another equivalent (and valid) pair, but a trapdoor function is needed to recognise that the two pairs are equivalent. SPS-EQ can therefore function as a self-blindable credential, and the authors paired their prototype with a compatible randomisable set commitment to support attributes with selective disclosure.

Multiple authors have extended SPS-EQ to create delegatable self-blindable credentials [7,43,44]. Dubbed mercurial signatures by Crites and Lysyanskaya, these schemes add randomisation of key pairs to SPS-EQ, allowing a credential holder to delegate their credential by signing the recipient's public key as a new mercurial signature, which is added to the credential chain. However, mercurial signatures do not currently support attributes, and existing constructions suffer from a severe anonymity weakness, though a new construction by Connolly et al. [42] solves that weakness if keys are not maliciously generated.

Hoepman et al. [57] have examined several broken self-blindable schemes and designed a criterion that can indicate when a deterministic self-blindable scheme is vulnerable, and subsequently designed their own self-blindable scheme [78] based on a more well-established assumption than SPS-EQ.

3.3   Group Signatures

First proposed in 1991 by Chaum and Van Heyst [39], group signatures allow the creation of a curated group of users, the members of which are able to sign digital signatures on behalf of the group in such a way that verifiers cannot directly determine which group member produced the signature. Group signatures and anonymous credentials are often directly compared or used to construct one another [30,32,81,92]. There is some debate over whether group signatures are a form of anonymous credential, but they are at least closely analogous, with the key distinction being that the Prove and Verify functions take the form of a signature scheme, making them not only non-interactive but asynchronous. Group signatures also traditionally place the issuer in a trusted position and allow it to "open" a signature to reveal which member produced it, but some later schemes have eschewed this practice [68,72].

The first group signature scheme to be considered practical came in 2000, developed by Ateniese et al. [6], improving on previous schemes by altering the protocol with which new users join a group, using efficient proofs of knowledge of discrete logarithms instead of the much more cumbersome proofs of knowledge of RSA factorisations. In 2004, Camenisch and Lysyanskaya [32] and Boneh et al. [20] independently developed group signatures based on bilinear maps, eliminating the RSA assumptions entirely.

Classic group signatures only capture anonymous credentials that lack attributes with selective disclosure, but in 2007, Dalia Khader [64] developed the first attribute-based signature scheme, allowing granular management of the attributes associated with the group by providing different verification keys for different attribute combinations. Maji et al. [72] and Li and Kim [68] also constructed attribute-based signatures, based on mesh signatures and ring signatures respectively, both of which can be seen as relaxation of group signatures. Ring signatures [79] allow users to sign as a member of an ad hoc group, where mesh signatures [21] allow for more expressive relations. Both primitives lack the opening/tracing functions provided by group signatures.

Shahandashti et al. [81] propose a system dubbed Threshold Attribute-Based Signatures, or t-ABS. This system allows signatures to pass verification if they are signed using any subset of at least a threshold size, as defined by the verifier, taken from a set of desired attributes. Two key points about this system are that the user is not required to know a verifier's exact authorisation requirements when signing, and the verifier does not learn exactly which attributes the user attested, only that they were sufficient to pass the verifier's requirements. This provides the system with greater degrees of both flexibility and privacy compared to earlier signature schemes. The same paper also described how to convert this class of signature schemes into anonymous credentials.

3.4 Schemes Without Unlinkability

An alternative form of privacy-preserving certification can be found by removing the property of multi-show unlinkability. While not technically anonymous credentials, such schemes are often suited to similar use cases. The most prominent example is Microsoft's U-Prove scheme based on the work of Brands [22], which closely resembles an anonymous credential but is suitable only for pseudonymous use cases, and is often used as a baseline when analysing the efficiency of anonymous credentials. Other, more lightweight schemes of this type such as Nymble [62] and Privacy Pass [46] mitigate their lack of multi-show unlinkability by creating multiple mutually-unlinkable tokens each time they are issued.

3.5 Post-Quantum Anonymous Credentials

With the increasing likelihood of quantum computers being developed and deployed, it has been of great interest to develop cryptographic schemes that remain secure in the presence of a quantum computer, termed "post-quantum cryptography". While this is a highly active area of research and we have several candidates for a large number of cryptographic primitives, there are to the best of our knowledge no post-quantum anonymous credentials scheme. To this statement we add the caveat that there are post-quantum version of related primitives, e.g., group signatures based on lattices [53] and codes [2], as well as post-quantum primitives required for some generic constructions, e.g., lattice-based signatures [48] and Zero-Knowledge Proofs [80] and code-based blind-signatures [16].

4 Anonymous Credentials in Practice

Despite fully realised anonymous credentials having existed for more than twenty years, their adoption in real-world contexts is still extremely rare. While this is likely due to a combination of factors, there are several well-recognised challenges that separate theoretical credential designs from practical real-world implementations. In this section, we examine the key challenges that practical anonymous credential systems must address in addition to the main credential properties, and some of the solutions the existing literature offers.

4.1 Efficiency

The most consistent challenge addressed in the literature is that of efficiency. Most credential schemes incur high computation costs in order to achieve their core unlinkability properties. The overall efficiency of anonymous credentials has steadily increased over their history, as a result of improvements in zero-knowledge proofs, more streamlined protocols, and the development of self-blindable credentials with less reliance on complex zero-knowledge proofs.

In this paper, we analyse trends in the efficiency of the extant anonymous credential schemes, by considering in particular the size of the credential, and the computational costs of the Prove and Verify procedures. A full-blown comparison is however very challenging due to the lack of comparable reference implementations (although there has been some work in that area [13]), but also due to the nature of the schemes. The main issue stems from the large number of metrics that need to be considered. These different metrics are often traded off against each other in a non-trivial manner, for example by shifting the burden of computation from one participant to another, and some schemes allow a flexible allocation of this burden depending on which participants are most limited. . Thus, we see that the true run-times of anonymous credential schemes are highly multidimensional. Nevertheless, some comparisons are still possible, as we shall see in Sect. 5.

4.2 Credential Revocation

An important and practical component of traditional certificate infrastructure is the ability to revoke a certificate and render it invalid if it is no longer secure, for example because of leaked key material or misuse of privileges. This is no less important for anonymous credential systems, but it is significantly more challenging to achieve when credentials are designed to be untraceable from one use to the next.

The naïve solution is generating a new signing key and re-issuing all non-revoked credentials whenever a revocation occurs, which achieves zero latency but incurs a massive overhead linear in the number of valid credentials in the system. Lapon et al. [66] discuss strategies to support credential revocation, identifying six categories of revocation approach with varying strengths and weaknesses; we will briefly analyse these, and give an overview of the development of each category.

Pseudonyms. The first of the six categories, pseudonymous access, is a straightforward case of attaching a consistent alias to each credential, which can then be used to register which credentials have been revoked. However, this clearly sacrifices multi-show unlinkability, and so exclusively using this approach negates the advantage of using anonymous credentials over linkable alternatives such as U-Prove [76].

Limited Lifespan. Another option is to encode an expiry date in each credential with a short lifespan requiring regular renewal of valid credentials. As a sole mechanism for credential revocation, this is similar to the naïve solution, but permits a trade-off between revocation latency and overhead costs incurred by frequent renewal. Regardless, this is one of the least scalable options.

Expiry dates are an important component for practical credentials in their own right, and have most often been encoded as one or more required attributes since the original Camenisch-Lysyanskaya credentials [30]. For zero-knowledge credentials, this typically requires using a somewhat cumbersome range proof to show that the expiry date is in the future without revealing the date itself, since the expiry date can otherwise become linkable information. However, credentials that are capable of supporting a large number of attributes can instead encode every date within the valid period, allowing the prover to use selective disclosure to show only the current date whenever the credential is used. For self-blindable credentials, encoding expiry dates remains an open problem.

Verifiable Encryption. This method, which also dates back to Camenisch and Lysyanskaya's original scheme [30], involves attaching a unique identifier to each credential; verifiers can then require on a per-showing basis that the prover use verifiable encryption, which is a special form of encryption that allows us to prove some properties about the underlying plaintext. The provers uses this to share an obfuscated copy of their identifier alongside their showing. The identifier can be decrypted by a TTP, which the verifier can query to find out whether that identifier has been revoked, without learning the identifier itself. However, this approach incurs a significant overhead on the prover when it is invoked, and places a bottleneck on the process through the need to interact with the TTP, which is itself put in a very privileged position by its ability to decrypt the identifiers it is sent [66].

Signature Lists. The fourth approach emerged to circumvent the need for a TTP, with work such as that of Tsang et al. [85,87] and Brands et al. [23]. This approach is based on the provision of a public list of (typically obfuscated) revoked credential identifiers rather than a TTP curating the list privately. This list enables the prover to show directly that their credential is not on the list with a zero-knowledge proof, while hiding their credential identifier with a one-way function instead of a reversible encryption algorithm.

This approach is likewise expensive for the prover, owing to the complexity of non-membership proofs. Nakanishi et al. [74] address this by ordering the revocation list and deriving a signature from each pair of adjacent entries, allowing the prover to show that their identifier would be between two adjacent entries if it were on the list. However, this requires revealing revoked identifiers fully so that the list can be ordered, which is usually considered undesirable outside traditional, traceable group signatures. Lapon et al. [66] also describe using an allow list instead of a revocation list, changing the non-membership proof to a more efficient membership proof, but this incurs much higher administrative costs as the list must be updated with every new credential.

Accumulators. Dynamic accumulators were first suggested as a tool for storing revocation lists by Camenisch and Lysyanskaya in 2002 [31]. This primitive allows a large set of integer values to be compressed into a single value, with each member of the set having an associated witness that can be used in conjunction with the accumulator value to prove its membership in the set without access to the full set. There exist suitable accumulator constructions based both on RSA [31,52,67,70] and on bilinear maps [29,45,75], as well as other primitives such as hash trees [24].

Accumulators have more efficient proving and verifying protocols than signature lists, and reduce the communication cost of publishing the list, but their primary drawback is the need for provers to update their witness values regularly with update information sent by the entity (usually an issuer) managing the accumulator. They also typically require that revoked credentials have their identifiers revealed, in the same way as ordered signature lists, though Tsang et al. [86] proposed a per-verifier accumulator scheme that uses single-use revocation tokens instead.

Accumulators with non-membership proofs were later developed, leading to universal accumulators [45,67] which guarantee that every possible element has either a membership or a non-membership proof. These allow for accumulators containing ban lists rather than valid credential lists, removing the need to update witnesses whenever a new credential is issued at the expense of more complex proofs of non-revocation. More recently, Baldimtsi et al. [8] published a new method of constructing accumulators which enabled them to design a secure accumulator that does not require witness updates when an element is added, thereby achieving the reduction in update frequency while still using cheaper membership proofs.

Verifier-Local Revocation. Verifier-local revocation (VLR) refers to revocation systems in which each credential is associated with a revocation token which can be used during verification to test whether a prover is the owner of that token, without learning anything else if the test is negative. A TTP with access to the revocation tokens can then publish those of revoked credentials or send them directly to each verifier, enabling the verifiers to perform revocation checks locally. Notably, this method imposes almost no overhead on provers, though it incurs significant computation costs on verifiers as well as requiring regular communication between verifiers and the TTP.

VLR has been widely used with group signatures [20,40,41,91], which it is particularly suited for as revocation checks are not inherently time-specific, unlike with signature lists and accumulators which rely on zero-knowledge proofs tied to the current state of changeable published information. VLR has also been used for synchronous credential applications, particularly those for which provers are expected to be using constrained devices such as smart cards [54,71].

A VLR system can only maintain multi-show unlinkability if provers do not reveal the same revocation token twice. This can be ensured either by obfuscating the tokens with one-way functions or verifiable encryption, or by dividing time into fixed-length epochs within which provers limit their own credential use, with new revocation tokens derived for each epoch [26,58,71,89]. The latter approach is useful for providing backward unlinkability, preventing a credential revocation from retroactively breaking the anonymity of all the past uses of that credential, but in most cases it is reliant on access to a trusted time source for the prover.

In addition to backward unlinkability, VLR schemes often aim to provide exculpability, a property whereby a prover can disavow a signature it did not sign, which is important for supporting non-repudiation for group signatures [83,91]. Selfless anonymity, a weakening of anonymity properties that allows provers to retrieve their own identities [15], expiry of group signature keys [41], and probabilistic revocation that can occasionally result in false rejections [65] have also been used to improve the efficiency of VLR.

4.3   Non-transferability

One of the most difficult and rarely-addressed practical challenges is that of preventing users from sharing credentials with each other. While anonymous credentials do include collusion resistance preventing attributes from multiple credentials from being pooled, this does not address the possibility of one user giving access to their credential to another.

This problem was recognised by Camenisch and Lysyanskaya [30] in their seminal paper, but they could offer no mechanism to prevent it. Instead, they proposed discouraging the practice either by ensuring the secrets used to show ownership of a credential are shared between all credentials belonging to the same user, or requiring that they use a secret tied to some valuable out-of-band asset such as a bank account.

Another proposal exists as part of the IRMA project [55], and entails using an enrolment procedure for new provers to bind the device storing their credentials

strongly to their identity. While this does not wholly prevent credential sharing, it does discourage it in a similar fashion to Camenisch and Lysyanskaya's
proposal, and could make detection easier as well. However, it relies on IRMA's
establishment of a dedicated credential wallet for each user.

5 Comparative Analysis

Table 1 summarises and compares the major functionality of a range of particularly notable anonymous credentials. The schemes shown all either implement
significant new features, have developed real-world implementations, or otherwise represent the state of the art in a particular taxonomic branch of credentials. Also indicated is whether each scheme is based on a zero-knowledge (ZK) or
self-blindable (SB) paradigm. As the U-Prove protocol does not have multi-show
linkability, we do not assign it a category.

Even restricted to these state-of-the-art schemes, the table shows that zero-
knowledge credentials are more numerous than self-blindable credentials. This
can be attributed to the fact that with the exception of Verheul's initial proposal,
self-blindable credentials are all more recent. This has the additional effect that
some of the major features have only been realised in zero-knowledge based
credentials. Furthermore, there are currently no real-world implementations of
self-blindable schemes, also most likely due to the fact that they are much more
recent than zero-knowledge based credentials.

The majority of the schemes considered achieve selective disclosure, but this
is unsurprising as this generally considered one of the fundamental features.
What is more interesting to note is that half of the self-blindable schemes are
delegatable, compared to only two zero-knowledge schemes. Beyond this, all
schemes achieve at most two of the features we have considered, mostly selective
disclosure and one advanced feature.

It is noteworthy that none of the schemes explicitly support more than one
advanced feature (although Connolly et al. [42] indicate that supporting delegation should be only a small additional step for CLP22).

The only properties that cannot be simultaneously achieved are issuer-hiding
and issuer/verifier combination as the issuer/verifier will be able to recognise
their own credentials. Beyond, there is no obvious reason why other properties could not be combined, but it may be that some turn out to be mutually
exclusive, which is one clear path for further investigation.

Efficiency Considerations. In Table 1 we also provide a comparison of hardness
assumptions used by the various schemes, and detail the credential size and the
complexity of the Prove and Verify procedures. Firstly, we note that while there
is some variety in assumptions (for the interested reader, the detailed definitions
can be found in the relevant papers), none of the considered schemes is post-
quantum secure, as we have discussed in Sect. 3.5. In terms of efficiency, we note
that while some schemes provide constant-size credentials, most grow linearly in
the number of attributes/delegations, and the Prove and Verify procedures often
involved quite a large number of pairings.

Unfortunately, as previously discussed, full efficiency metrics for the schemes we discuss are difficult to present in a concise way, owing both to the number of different metrics and scaling factors to consider and to the variety of formats in which they are presented in the source papers.

In our analysis the trends we see are although *idemix* is still the most prominently implemented anonymous credential scheme, the use of bilinear maps in most other schemes allows for greater efficiency and smaller key sizes [32]. Self-blindable credentials are also generally more lightweight than zero-knowledge credentials despite their relative infancy [77,78]. Delegatable credentials come at an efficiency cost with the requirement to transmit information on the delegation chain in most cases [10,73], resulting in bandwidth costs at least linear in the number of delegations [73]. KVACs [36,37] enjoy some of the greatest efficiency benefits of all, but are only applicable in certain use cases as discussed in Sect. 2. In general, further development of the more recent schemes is likely to result in much more efficient and versatile credential implementations than those that currently exist.

Table 1. A comparison of the properties achieved by the state-of-the-art anonymous credential schemes. A ✓ indicates the property is achieved, a • indicates the property is not achieved and a ✗ indicates this property cannot be achieved. The hardness assumptions are formalized in the relevant papers. In the size/complexity columns, $\mathbb{G}$ denotes a group element, $\mathbb{Z}_\star$ indicates an integer modulo $\star$, e an exponentiation, p a pairing, π is a proof of knowledge as required by the scheme of size $|\pi|$, π_p is the computational costs for the prover to generate an appropriate proof, π_v is computational cost to verify the proof, ℓ number of attributes or delegations, as applicable, C a commitment, and C_t indicates the time to compute C. Finally, − means we cannot evaluate the paper's contribution to performance, as the proposed scheme is either a generic construction or an add-on.

	Category	Assumptions	Selective disclosure	Delegatable	Issuer-hiding	Updatable	Issuer/Verifier Combo	Credential Size	Prove Complexity	Verify Complexity	Implemented
U-Prove [76]	-	DLog	✓	•	•	•	•	$(\ell+4)\mathbb{G} + (\ell+2)\mathbb{Z}_p$	$(\ell+5)e$	$(5\ell+6)e$	✓
idemix [34]	ZK	SRSA	✓	•	•	•	•	$3\mathbb{Z}_N + \pi$	$3e + \pi_p$	π_v	✓
CL04 [32]	ZK	LRSW, DDH	✓	•	•	•	•	$(2\ell+3)\mathbb{G}$	$(2\ell+3)e$	$(\ell+1)e + 3p$	
BCC+09 [10]	ZK	HSDH, CDH	•	✓	•	•	•	$\ell \cdot \pi$	$(2\ell \cdot |\pi|)e$	$(\ell \cdot |\pi|)p$	
PCS [63]	ZK	q-DHE, CDH	✓	•	•	•	•	$(\ell+5)\mathbb{G}$	$(2\ell+N+5)e$	$(2\ell+3)p$	✓
BB18 [17]	ZK	GGM	✓	✓	•	•	•	$(\ell+2)\mathbb{G} + \pi$	$(\ell+1)e + \pi_p$	π_v	
BEKRS21 [19]	ZK	NIZK + Sig	✓	•	✓	•	✗	-	-	-	-
BBDE19 [18]	ZK	Blind Sig	•	•	•	✓	•	-	-	-	-
CMZ14 [36]	ZK	DDH, q-SDH	✓	•	✗	•	✓	$(\ell+5)\mathbb{G} + \pi$	$(4\ell+4)e$	$(2\ell+2)e$	✓
CPZ20 [37]	ZK	DDH	✓	•	✗	•	✓	$(\ell+3)\mathbb{G} + \pi$	$(\ell+4)e$	ℓp	✓
Verheul [88]	SB	DDH	•	•	•	•	✗	-	-	-	-
RVH17 [78]	SB	whLRSW	✓	•	•	•	✗	$(\ell+4)\mathbb{G}$	$(2\ell+7)e$	$(3\ell+1)e + 4p$	
PO19 [77]	SB	DDH, SXDH	✓	✓	•	•	✗	$6\mathbb{G}+\ell\mathbb{Z}_p$	$(\ell+1)e$	$(\ell+2)e$	
CL20 [44]	SB	ABDDH+, GGM	•	✓	•	•	✗	-	-	-	
CLP22 [42]	SB	XKerMDH	✓	•	✓	•	✗	$32\,\mathbb{G} + 4\,\mathbb{Z}_p$	$19p$	$17p$	
BMMS22 [73]	SB	DDH, GGM	✓	✓	•	•	✗	$5\,\mathbb{G} + \ell \cdot C$	$\ell \cdot C_t + \pi_p$	π_v	

6   Conclusions

In this paper, we have given a broad overview of the state of the art in anonymous credentials, including a basic definition of the primitive, a categorisation of approaches taken to realise it, and an exploration of optional features and properties that have been proposed as extensions. In doing so, we have brought together several disparate lines of research and shown how they compare and relate to one another. We have also identified gaps and shortcomings in the current literature, which suggest directions for future research in the field. In particular it would be of great interest to know which combinations of properties can be achieved with which paradigms and indeed if any properties, or combinations thereof, preclude other properties.

This also leads to a potential road-map for future standardisation work. We believe that it would be of interest to have anonymous credentials be standardised, primarily to facilitate their deployment. Currently all systems that provide the functionalities of anonymous credentials rely on non-cryptographic mechanisms, e.g., OAuth. We believe that anonymous credentials would be a more robust solution.

Using our systematisation could provide a good basis for the start of a standard. Depending on the exact context and requirements, the standard could require a scheme to fulfil certain properties as listed above. Furthermore, we could have some requirements on the efficiency, such as when credentials must be used on restricted devices such as smart cards.

While we have addressed some significant trends in the efficiency of credential schemes, there remains space for a more in-depth analysis of credential efficiency, a complex endeavour outside the scope of this paper. We have also shown that several branches of credential development are still new and immature, but promise useful benefits if they are developed into a full implementation. In particular, self-blindable credentials are a fast-growing field with promising efficiency results, but still lack the full range of features available to more traditional zero-knowledge credentials.

Acknowledgements. We would like to thank the reviewers of SSR 2023 for their excellent insights and helpful comments. We would also like to thank Olivier Blazy for his invaluable inputs.

References

1. Acar, T., Nguyen, L.: Revocation for delegatable anonymous credentials. In: Catalano, D., Fazio, N., Gennaro, R., Nicolosi, A. (eds.) PKC 2011. LNCS, vol. 6571, pp. 423–440. Springer, Heidelberg (2011). https://doi.org/10.1007/978-3-642-19379-8_26

2. Alamélou, Q., Blazy, O., Cauchie, S., Gaborit, P.: A code-based group signature scheme. Des. Codes Cryptogr. 469–493 (2016). https://doi.org/10.1007/s10623-016-0276-6

3. Alpár, G., van den Broek, F., Hampiholi, B., Jacobs, B., Lueks, W., Ringers, S.: Irma: practical, decentralized and privacy-friendly identity management using smartphones. In: 10th Workshop on Hot Topics in Privacy Enhancing Technologies (HotPETs 2017) (2017)

4. Alpár, G., Jacobs, B.: Credential design in attribute-based identity management (2013)

5. Angin, P., et al.: An entity-centric approach for privacy and identity management in cloud computing. In: 2010 29th IEEE Symposium on Reliable Distributed Systems, pp. 177–183. IEEE (2010)

6. Ateniese, G., Camenisch, J., Joye, M., Tsudik, G.: A practical and provably secure coalition-resistant group signature scheme. In: Bellare, M. (ed.) CRYPTO 2000. LNCS, vol. 1880, pp. 255–270. Springer, Heidelberg (2000). https://doi.org/10.1007/3-540-44598-6_16

7. Backes, M., Hanzlik, L., Kluczniak, K., Schneider, J.: Signatures with flexible public key: introducing equivalence classes for public keys. In: Peyrin, T., Galbraith, S. (eds.) ASIACRYPT 2018. LNCS, vol. 11273, pp. 405–434. Springer, Cham (2018). https://doi.org/10.1007/978-3-030-03329-3_14

8. Baldimtsi, F., et al.: Accumulators with applications to anonymity-pre-serving revocation. In: 2017 IEEE European Symposium on Security and Privacy (EuroS&P), pp. 301–315. IEEE (2017)

9. Bangerter, E., Camenisch, J., Lysyanskaya, A.: A cryptographic framework for the controlled release of certified data. In: Christianson, B., Crispo, B., Malcolm, J.A., Roe, M. (eds.) Security Protocols 2004. LNCS, vol. 3957, pp. 20–42. Springer, Heidelberg (2006). https://doi.org/10.1007/11861386_4

10. Belenkiy, M., Camenisch, J., Chase, M., Kohlweiss, M., Lysyanskaya, A., Shacham, H.: Randomizable proofs and delegatable anonymous credentials. In: Halevi, S. (ed.) CRYPTO 2009. LNCS, vol. 5677, pp. 108–125. Springer, Heidelberg (2009). https://doi.org/10.1007/978-3-642-03356-8_7

11. Belenkiy, M., Chase, M., Kohlweiss, M., Lysyanskaya, A.: Non-interactive anonymous credentials. IACR Cryptol. ePrint Arch. **2007**, 384 (2007)

12. Belenkiy, M., Chase, M., Kohlweiss, M., Lysyanskaya, A.: P-signatures and non-interactive anonymous credentials. In: Canetti, R. (ed.) TCC 2008. LNCS, vol. 4948, pp. 356–374. Springer, Heidelberg (2008). https://doi.org/10.1007/978-3-540-78524-8_20

13. Bemmann, K., et al.: Fully-featured anonymous credentials with reputation system. In: Proceedings of the 13th International Conference on Availability, Reliability and Security. ARES 2018, Association for Computing Machinery, New York, NY, USA (2018). https://doi.org/10.1145/3230833.3234517

14. Bichsel, P., et al.: D2. 2 architecture for attribute-based credential technologies-final version. ABC4TRUST project deliverable (2014). https://abc4trust.eu/index.php/pub (2014)

15. Bichsel, P., Camenisch, J., Neven, G., Smart, N.P., Warinschi, B.: Get shorty via group signatures without encryption. In: Garay, J.A., De Prisco, R. (eds.) SCN 2010. LNCS, vol. 6280, pp. 381–398. Springer, Heidelberg (2010). https://doi.org/10.1007/978-3-642-15317-4_24

16. Blazy, O., Gaborit, P., Schrek, J., Sendrier, N.: A code-based blind signature. In: 2017 IEEE International Symposium on Information Theory, ISIT 2017, Aachen, Germany, 25–30 June 2017, pp. 2718–2722 (2017). https://doi.org/10.1109/ISIT.2017.8007023

17. Blömer, J., Bobolz, J.: Delegatable attribute-based anonymous credentials from dynamically malleable signatures. In: Preneel, B., Vercauteren, F. (eds.) ACNS 2018. LNCS, vol. 10892, pp. 221–239. Springer, Cham (2018). https://doi.org/10.1007/978-3-319-93387-0_12

18. Blömer, J., Bobolz, J., Diemert, D., Eidens, F.: Updatable anonymous credentials and applications to incentive systems. In: Proceedings of the 2019 ACM SIGSAC Conference on Computer and Communications Security, pp. 1671–1685 (2019)

19. Bobolz, J., Eidens, F., Krenn, S., Ramacher, S., Samelin, K.: Issuer-hiding attribute-based credentials. In: Conti, M., Stevens, M., Krenn, S. (eds.) CANS 2021. LNCS, vol. 13099, pp. 158–178. Springer, Cham (2021). https://doi.org/10.1007/978-3-030-92548-2_9

20. Boneh, D., Shacham, H.: Group signatures with verifier-local revocation. In: Proceedings of the 11th ACM Conference on Computer and Communications Security, pp. 168–177 (2004)
21. Boyen, X.: Mesh signatures. In: Naor, M. (ed.) EUROCRYPT 2007. LNCS, vol. 4515, pp. 210–227. Springer, Heidelberg (2007). https://doi.org/10.1007/978-3-540-72540-4_12
22. Brands, S.: Rethinking Public Key Infrastructures and Digital Certificates: Building in Privacy. MIT Press, Cambridge (2000)
23. Brands, S., Demuynck, L., De Decker, B.: A practical system for globally revoking the unlinkable pseudonyms of unknown users. In: Pieprzyk, J., Ghodosi, H., Dawson, E. (eds.) ACISP 2007. LNCS, vol. 4586, pp. 400–415. Springer, Heidelberg (2007). https://doi.org/10.1007/978-3-540-73458-1_29
24. Camacho, P., Hevia, A., Kiwi, M., Opazo, R.: Strong accumulators from collision-resistant hashing. In: Wu, T.-C., Lei, C.-L., Rijmen, V., Lee, D.-T. (eds.) ISC 2008. LNCS, vol. 5222, pp. 471–486. Springer, Heidelberg (2008). https://doi.org/10.1007/978-3-540-85886-7_32
25. Camenisch, J., Drijvers, M., Dubovitskaya, M.: Practical uc-secure delegatable credentials with attributes and their application to blockchain. In: Proceedings of the 2017 ACM SIGSAC Conference on Computer and Communications Security, pp. 683–699 (2017)
26. Camenisch, J., Drijvers, M., Hajny, J.: Scalable revocation scheme for anonymous credentials based on n-times unlinkable proofs. In: Proceedings of the 2016 ACM on Workshop on Privacy in the Electronic Society, pp. 123–133 (2016)
27. Camenisch, J., Dubovitskaya, M., Lehmann, A., Neven, G., Paquin, C., Preiss, F.-S.: Concepts and languages for privacy-preserving attribute-based authentication. In: Fischer-Hübner, S., de Leeuw, E., Mitchell, C. (eds.) IDMAN 2013. IAICT, vol. 396, pp. 34–52. Springer, Heidelberg (2013). https://doi.org/10.1007/978-3-642-37282-7_4
28. Camenisch, J., Groß, T.: Efficient attributes for anonymous credentials. In: Proceedings of the 15th ACM Conference on Computer and Communications Security, pp. 345–356 (2008)
29. Camenisch, J., Kohlweiss, M., Soriente, C.: An accumulator based on bilinear maps and efficient revocation for anonymous credentials. In: Jarecki, S., Tsudik, G. (eds.) PKC 2009. LNCS, vol. 5443, pp. 481–500. Springer, Heidelberg (2009). https://doi.org/10.1007/978-3-642-00468-1_27
30. Camenisch, J., Lysyanskaya, A.: An efficient system for non-transferable anonymous credentials with optional anonymity revocation. In: Pfitzmann, B. (ed.) EUROCRYPT 2001. LNCS, vol. 2045, pp. 93–118. Springer, Heidelberg (2001). https://doi.org/10.1007/3-540-44987-6_7
31. Camenisch, J., Lysyanskaya, A.: Dynamic accumulators and application to efficient revocation of anonymous credentials. In: Yung, M. (ed.) CRYPTO 2002. LNCS, vol. 2442, pp. 61–76. Springer, Heidelberg (2002). https://doi.org/10.1007/3-540-45708-9_5
32. Camenisch, J., Lysyanskaya, A.: Signature schemes and anonymous credentials from bilinear maps. In: Franklin, M. (ed.) CRYPTO 2004. LNCS, vol. 3152, pp. 56–72. Springer, Heidelberg (2004). https://doi.org/10.1007/978-3-540-28628-8_4
33. Camenisch, J., Sommer, D., Zimmermann, R.: A general certification framework with applications to privacy-enhancing certificate infrastructures. In: Fischer-Hübner, S., Rannenberg, K., Yngström, L., Lindskog, S. (eds.) SEC 2006. IIFIP, vol. 201, pp. 25–37. Springer, Boston, MA (2006). https://doi.org/10.1007/0-387-33406-8_3

34. Camenisch, J., Van Herreweghen, E.: Design and implementation of the idemix anonymous credential system. In: Proceedings of the 9th ACM Conference on Computer and Communications Security, pp. 21–30 (2002)
35. Chase, M., Lysyanskaya, A.: On signatures of knowledge. In: Dwork, C. (ed.) CRYPTO 2006. LNCS, vol. 4117, pp. 78–96. Springer, Heidelberg (2006). https://doi.org/10.1007/11818175_5
36. Chase, M., Meiklejohn, S., Zaverucha, G.: Algebraic macs and keyed-verification anonymous credentials. In: Proceedings of the 2014 ACM SIGSAC Conference on Computer and Communications Security, pp. 1205–1216 (2014)
37. Chase, M., Perrin, T., Zaverucha, G.: The signal private group system and anonymous credentials supporting efficient verifiable encryption. In: Proceedings of the 2020 ACM SIGSAC Conference on Computer and Communications Security, pp. 1445–1459 (2020)
38. Chaum, D.: Security without identification: transaction systems to make big brother obsolete. Commun. ACM **28**(10), 1030–1044 (1985). https://doi.org/10.1145/4372.4373
39. Chaum, D., van Heyst, E.: Group signatures. In: Davies, D.W. (eds.) Advances in Cryptology–EUROCRYPT 1991. EUROCRYPT 1991. LNCS, vol. 547, pp. 257–265. Springer, Berlin, Heidelberg (1991). https://doi.org/10.1007/3-540-46416-6_22
40. Chen, L., Li, J.: VLR group signatures with indisputable exculpability and efficient revocation. Int. J. Inf. Priv. Secur. Integr. 2 **1**(2–3), 129–159 (2010)
41. Chu, C.K., Liu, J.K., Huang, X., Zhou, J.: Verifier-local revocation group signatures with time-bound keys. In: Proceedings of the 7th ACM Symposium on Information, Computer and Communications Security, pp. 26–27 (2012)
42. Connolly, A., Lafourcade, P., Perez Kempner, O.: Improved constructions of anonymous credentials from structure-preserving signatures on equivalence classes. In: Hanaoka, G., Shikata, J., Watanabe, Y. (eds.) Public-Key Cryptography – PKC 2022. PKC 2022. LNCS, vol. 13177, pp. 409–438. Springer, Cham (2022). https://doi.org/10.1007/978-3-030-97121-2_15
43. Crites, E.C., Lysyanskaya, A.: Delegatable anonymous credentials from mercurial signatures. In: Matsui, M. (ed.) CT-RSA 2019. LNCS, vol. 11405, pp. 535–555. Springer, Cham (2019). https://doi.org/10.1007/978-3-030-12612-4_27
44. Crites, E.C., Lysyanskaya, A.: Mercurial signatures for variable-length messages. IACR Cryptol. ePrint Arch. **2020**, 979 (2020)
45. Damgård, I., Triandopoulos, N.: Supporting non-membership proofs with bilinear-map accumulators. IACR Cryptol. ePrint Arch. **2008**, 538 (2008)
46. Davidson, A., Goldberg, I., Sullivan, N., Tankersley, G., Valsorda, F.: Privacy pass: bypassing internet challenges anonymously. Proc. Priv. Enhanc. Technol. **2018**(3), 164–180 (2018)
47. Doesburg, J., Jacobs, B., Ringers, S.: Using IRMA for small scale digital elections (2020)
48. Ducas, L., Lepoint, T., Lyubashevsky, V., Schwabe, P., Seiler, G., Stehlé, D.: Crystals - dilithium: digital signatures from module lattices. IACR Cryptol. ePrint Arch. **2017**, 633 (2017)
49. Förster, D., Kargl, F., Löhr, H.: PUCA: a pseudonym scheme with user-controlled anonymity for vehicular ad-hoc networks (VANET). In: 2014 IEEE Vehicular Networking Conference (VNC), pp. 25–32. IEEE (2014)
50. Fuchsbauer, G.: Commuting signatures and verifiable encryption. In: Paterson, K.G. (ed.) EUROCRYPT 2011. LNCS, vol. 6632, pp. 224–245. Springer, Heidelberg (2011). https://doi.org/10.1007/978-3-642-20465-4_14

51. Fuchsbauer, G., Hanser, C., Slamanig, D.: Structure-preserving signatures on equivalence classes and constant-size anonymous credentials. J. Cryptol. **32**(2), 498–546 (2019)

52. Goodrich, M.T., Tamassia, R., Hasić, J.: An efficient dynamic and distributed cryptographic accumulator*. In: Chan, A.H., Gligor, V. (eds.) ISC 2002. LNCS, vol. 2433, pp. 372–388. Springer, Heidelberg (2002). https://doi.org/10.1007/3-540-45811-5_29

53. Gordon, S.D., Katz, J., Vaikuntanathan, V.: A group signature scheme from lattice assumptions. In: Abe, M. (ed.) ASIACRYPT 2010. LNCS, vol. 6477, pp. 395–412. Springer, Heidelberg (2010). https://doi.org/10.1007/978-3-642-17373-8_23

54. Hajny, J., Malina, L.: Anonymous credentials with practical revocation. In: 2012 IEEE First AESS European Conference on Satellite Telecommunications (ESTEL), pp. 1–6. IEEE (2012)

55. Hampiholi, B., Jacobs, B.: Trusted self-enrolment for attribute-based credentials on mobile phones. In: Proceedings of the IFIP Summer School 2015, Edinburgh, 16–21 August 2015 (2015)

56. Hanser, C., Slamanig, D.: Structure-preserving signatures on equivalence classes and their application to anonymous credentials. In: International Conference on the Theory and Application of Cryptology and Information Security. pp. 491–511. Springer (2014)

57. Hanser, C., Slamanig, D.: Structure-preserving signatures on equivalence classes and their application to anonymous credentials. In: Sarkar, P., Iwata, T. (eds.) ASIACRYPT 2014. LNCS, vol. 8873, pp. 491–511. Springer, Heidelberg (2014). https://doi.org/10.1007/978-3-662-45611-8_26

58. Hölzl, M., Roland, M., Mir, O., Mayrhofer, R.: Bridging the gap in privacy-preserving revocation: practical and scalable revocation of mobile eIDs. In: Proceedings of the 33rd Annual ACM Symposium on Applied Computing, pp. 1601–1609 (2018)

59. IBM: Iemix (2022). https://github.com/IBM/idemix

60. ISO: Information technology - security techniques - anonymous digital signatures - part 2: Mechanisms using a group public key. ISO 20008–2:2013, International Organization for Standardization, Geneva, Switzerland (2013). https://www.iso.org/standard/56916.html

61. ISO: Information technology - security techniques - anonymous entity authentication - part 2: Mechanisms using a group public key. ISO 20009–2:2013, International Organization for Standardization, Geneva, Switzerland (2013). https://www.iso.org/standard/56913.html

62. Johnson, P.C., Kapadia, A., Tsang, P.P., Smith, S.W.: Nymble: anonymous ip-address blocking. In: Borisov, N., Golle, P. (eds.) PET 2007. LNCS, vol. 4776, pp. 113–133. Springer, Heidelberg (2007). https://doi.org/10.1007/978-3-540-75551-7_8

63. Kaaniche, N., Laurent, M., Rocher, P.-O., Kiennert, C., Garcia-Alfaro, J.: $\mathcal{PCS}$, a privacy-preserving certification scheme. In: Garcia-Alfaro, J., Navarro-Arribas, G., Hartenstein, H., Herrera-Joancomartí, J. (eds.) ESORICS/DPM/CBT -2017. LNCS, vol. 10436, pp. 239–256. Springer, Cham (2017). https://doi.org/10.1007/978-3-319-67816-0_14

64. Khader, D.: Attribute based group signatures. IACR Cryptol. ePrint Arch. **2007**, 159 (2007)

65. Kumar, V., Li, H., Park, J.M., Bian, K., Yang, Y.: Group signatures with probabilistic revocation: a computationally-scalable approach for providing privacy-

preserving authentication. In: Proceedings of the 22nd ACM SIGSAC Conference on Computer and Communications Security, pp. 1334–1345 (2015)

66. Lapon, J., Kohlweiss, M., De Decker, B., Naessens, V.: Analysis of revocation strategies for anonymous idemix credentials. In: De Decker, B., Lapon, J., Naessens, V., Uhl, A. (eds.) CMS 2011. LNCS, vol. 7025, pp. 3–17. Springer, Heidelberg (2011). https://doi.org/10.1007/978-3-642-24712-5_1

67. Li, J., Li, N., Xue, R.: Universal accumulators with efficient nonmembership proofs. In: Katz, J., Yung, M. (eds.) ACNS 2007. LNCS, vol. 4521, pp. 253–269. Springer, Heidelberg (2007). https://doi.org/10.1007/978-3-540-72738-5_17

68. Li, J., Kim, K.: Attribute-based ring signatures. IACR Cryptol. ePrint Arch. **2008**, 394 (2008)

69. Lin, C., He, D., Zhang, H., Shao, L., Huang, X.: Privacy-enhancing decentralized anonymous credential in smart grids. Comput. Stand. Interfaces **75**, 103505 (2021)

70. Lipmaa, H.: Secure accumulators from Euclidean rings without trusted setup. In: Bao, F., Samarati, P., Zhou, J. (eds.) ACNS 2012. LNCS, vol. 7341, pp. 224–240. Springer, Heidelberg (2012). https://doi.org/10.1007/978-3-642-31284-7_14

71. Lueks, W., Alpár, G., Hoepman, J.H., Vullers, P.: Fast revocation of attribute-based credentials for both users and verifiers. In: Federrath, H., Gollmann, D. (eds.) SEC 2015. IAICT, vol. 455, pp. 463–478. Springer, Cham (2015). https://doi.org/10.1007/978-3-319-18467-8_31

72. Maji, H.K., Prabhakaran, M., Rosulek, M.: Attribute-based signatures: achieving attribute-privacy and collusion-resistance. IACR Cryptol. ePrint Arch. **2008**, 328 (2008)

73. Mir, O., Slamanig, D., Bauer, B., Mayrhofer, R.: Practical delegatable anonymous credentials from equivalence class signatures. Cryptology ePrint Archive (2022)

74. Nakanishi, T., Fujii, H., Hira, Y., Funabiki, N.: Revocable group signature schemes with constant costs for signing and verifying. In: Jarecki, S., Tsudik, G. (eds.) PKC 2009. LNCS, vol. 5443, pp. 463–480. Springer, Heidelberg (2009). https://doi.org/10.1007/978-3-642-00468-1_26

75. Nguyen, L.: Accumulators from bilinear pairings and applications. In: Menezes, A. (ed.) CT-RSA 2005. LNCS, vol. 3376, pp. 275–292. Springer, Heidelberg (2005). https://doi.org/10.1007/978-3-540-30574-3_19

76. Paquin, C., Zaverucha, G.: U-prove cryptographic specification v1. 1. Technical report, Microsoft Corporation (2011)

77. Pussewalage, H.S.G., Oleshchuk, V.A.: An anonymous delegatable attribute-based credential scheme for a collaborative e-health environment. ACM Trans. Internet Technol. (TOIT) **19**(3), 1–22 (2019)

78. Ringers, S., Verheul, E., Hoepman, J.-H.: An efficient self-blindable attribute-based credential scheme. In: Kiayias, A. (ed.) FC 2017. LNCS, vol. 10322, pp. 3–20. Springer, Cham (2017). https://doi.org/10.1007/978-3-319-70972-7_1

79. Rivest, R.L., Shamir, A., Tauman, Y.: How to leak a secret. In: Boyd, C. (ed.) ASIACRYPT 2001. LNCS, vol. 2248, pp. 552–565. Springer, Heidelberg (2001). https://doi.org/10.1007/3-540-45682-1_32

80. Rothblum, R.D., Sealfon, A., Sotiraki, K.: Toward non-interactive zero-knowledge proofs for NP from LWE. J. Cryptol. **34**(1), 1–35 (2021). https://doi.org/10.1007/s00145-020-09365-w

81. Shahandashti, S.F., Safavi-Naini, R.: Threshold attribute-based signatures and their application to anonymous credential systems. In: Preneel, B. (ed.) AFRICACRYPT 2009. LNCS, vol. 5580, pp. 198–216. Springer, Heidelberg (2009). https://doi.org/10.1007/978-3-642-02384-2_13

82. Sporny, M., Longley, D., Chadwick, D.: Verifiable credentials data model v1.1. Technical report, World Wide Web Consortium: Verifiable Credentials Working Group (2022). https://www.w3.org/TR/2022/REC-vc-data-model-20220303/
83. Sujing, Z., Dongdai, L.: A shorter group signature with verifier-location revocation and backward unlinkability. Technical report, Cryptology ePrint Archive: Report 2006/100 (2006)
84. TCG: Trusted platform module library part 1: Architecture. Technical report Revision 01.53, Trusted Computing Group (2019)
85. Tsang, P.P., Au, M.H., Kapadia, A., Smith, S.W.: Blacklistable anonymous credentials: blocking misbehaving users without TTPs. In: Proceedings of the 14th ACM Conference on Computer and Communications Security, pp. 72–81 (2007)
86. Tsang, P.P., Au, M.H., Kapadia, A., Smith, S.W.: PEREA: towards practical TTP-free revocation in anonymous authentication. In: Proceedings of the 15th ACM Conference on Computer and Communications Security, pp. 333–344 (2008)
87. Tsang, P.P., Au, M.H., Kapadia, A., Smith, S.W.: BLAC: revoking repeatedly misbehaving anonymous users without relying on TTPs. ACM Trans. Inf. Syst. Secur. (TISSEC) 13(4), 1–33 (2010)
88. Verheul, E.R.: Self-blindable credential certificates from the Weil pairing. In: Boyd, C. (ed.) ASIACRYPT 2001. LNCS, vol. 2248, pp. 533–551. Springer, Heidelberg (2001). https://doi.org/10.1007/3-540-45682-1_31
89. Verheul, E.R.: Practical backward unlinkable revocation in fido, German e-id, idemix and u-prove. IACR Cryptol. ePrint Arch. 2016, 217 (2016)
90. Vullers, P., Alpár, G.: Efficient selective disclosure on smart cards using idemix. In: Fischer-Hübner, S., de Leeuw, E., Mitchell, C. (eds.) IDMAN 2013. IAICT, vol. 396, pp. 53–67. Springer, Heidelberg (2013). https://doi.org/10.1007/978-3-642-37282-7_5
91. Zhang, J., Ma, L., Sun, R., Wang, Y.: More efficient VLR group signature satisfying exculpability. IEICE Trans. Fundam. Electron. Commun. Comput. Sci. 91(7), 1831–1835 (2008)
92. Zhang, Y., Feng, D.: Efficient attribute proofs in anonymous credential using attribute-based cryptography. In: Chim, T.W., Yuen, T.H. (eds.) ICICS 2012. LNCS, vol. 7618, pp. 408–415. Springer, Heidelberg (2012). https://doi.org/10.1007/978-3-642-34129-8_39

Author Index

© The Editor(s) (if applicable) and The Author(s), under exclusive license
to Springer Nature Switzerland AG 2023
F. Günther and J. Hesse (Eds.): SSR 2023, LNCS 13895, p. 153, 2023.
https://doi.org/10.1007/978-3-031-30731-7

Printed in the United States
by Baker & Taylor Publisher Services

Printed in the United States
by Baker & Taylor Publisher Services